Pocket Full of Dreams

Sweet Dreams!

Denise Law

Pocket Full of Dreams

Denise Linn

VVV

TRIPLE FIVE PUBLISHING
a division of Nacson and Sons Pty. Ltd.
Sydney • Australia
Seattle • USA

Pocket Full of Dreams

A Triple Five Publication
A Division of Nacson and Sons Pty. Ltd.
International Headquarters
Suite 204, George Street, Sydney
NSW 2000 Australia
Telephone (61-2)-281 2075

First Printing

ISBN 0-947266-00-3

Printed in Australia

Dedication

This book is dedicated to David,
the 'man of my dreams'

and to Meadow
my dream child.

ACKNOWLEDGEMENTS

Thank you Leon Nacson for having the dream that inspired this book. You are a profound visionary in every sense of the word, a wonderful friend.

Ann Sewell, it was your unwavering dedication that took this book to it's completion. Your willingness to consistently and undauntedly persevere will always be an inspiration to me. You brought this book to life.

To the computer mystic and Agent of Fortune, Karl Bettinger I give my sincere thanks.

Thanks Barb Kelly, you made creating this book so much fun. Who would think typing copy could be funny.

To Jane Bakken, as your long-awaited child grew within you, your gentle magic helped give birth to this book. Thank you.

Barabara Roper your quiet wisdom warmed many late nights.

To Alice Allen thank you for guiding us softly down the path of graciousness.

Lydia Christofides thank you for your remarkable insights.

Anne Sweet, your poems lightly carried us on dream wings of of the night.

Thanks to Cheryl Steinle for your steadfast dedication.

And a special thank you to Lydia Golden, and to the Last Shiatsu Class.

A special acknowledgement
Glynn Braddy, you have influenced my life tremendously.
Thank you!

POCKET FULL OF DREAMS

As I travel through this lifetime
swimming down the stream,
I pick up many baubles,
people, places, things.

The one thing I'll take with me
when it's time to leave the stream,
isn't any bauble, it's
my pocketful of dreams.

Karl Bettinger

INTENT

Each of us is on a quest...a journey through time and space. That quest has led you to this book and will continue to lead you to your own personal evolution. It is my intent in creating this book to generate a heart space in which you can delve more deeply, through your dreams, into that evolution and exquisite oneness with all things. The purpose of this book is not to show you the way, but rather to allow you to discover your own internal answers which will well up from the center of your being. It is for you to know that those answers are not found in anyone's teachings, but are woven within your feelings, within the pattern of your life, within your dreams and visions.

THE BEGINNING

Dreams are the mysterious language of the night. Each evening after the setting sun has beckoned the rising moon, a golden harvest is woven into our slumbering consciousness. Nocturnal visions from this enigmatic realm have been described as messages from the gods, and have helped shape the destiny of individuals as well as of entire nations. Since the dawn of time, dream weavers have slipped through the crack between two worlds to touch the outer reaches of inner space and reap the harvest of the night.

These secret messages from the mind can foretell your future and reveal your past. They can warn you of danger. They can contain creative inspiration or assist in melting the barriers in your waking life. Dreams can serve as a doorway to the mystic arena of the night for inner-dimensional travel and communication on the inner realms with loved ones. They can be a springboard for night healing, astral travel and soul searching.

But we have forgotten.

Dreams are now but relics of the human mind. We no longer can call upon the Muses of the Night by direct path.

In ancient times, when the cycles of nature and the cycles of man were closely intertwined, dreams of the past and dreams of the future, dreams of hunting and planting and those of war and peace all directed the course of the respective tribe or culture. Dreams were a natural outflow originating from a deep alignment with the forces of nature. In those twilight hours, Emissaries of Nighttime Wisdom were called upon to send forth inner truths. But we have forgotten. And in our sleep we are still.

It has become commonplace to consider sleeping as a time when we do nothing "productive." We acknowledge the reality of dreams; however, even if we recall our dreams, they are viewed as oddities or items of amusement. They are rarely considered valuable or imperative to our well-being as are the *real events* of the day.

When our children have nightmares, we comfort them with, "It's <u>only</u> a dream," casually tossing aside a most remarkable communication from the depths of their inner being. At best, dreams are treated as an inner "data processing" of the human computer mind.

But the time has come to remember. We are passing through a crucial period on our planet. It will become increasingly important to awaken the dreamer within each of us and listen to the oracle of the heart so that we may step lightly through the times ahead. A continual need exists for us to spin inwardly with our dream body, and to span that bridge across inner space enabling us to readily step with strength into the future. You will find that in the coming years, your dreams will become a much more potent source of information for you as the winds of change increase the need of the spirit world to give us guidance. It is time to remember our dreams so that we may awaken the deepest potential sleeping within each of us. It is time to remember so that we might contribute to the healing of others and the healing of our wounded planet.

My Dream Journey

My journey into the realm of dreams began one early summer afternoon over twenty years ago in the Midwestern United States. It was one of those glorious country afternoons. A golden summer haze had dusted the fields. Amber swirls of wheat and honey-colored tassels of ripe corn sailed by on either side of me as I joyously maneuvered my motor bike down back roads in our rural farming community. I was seventeen years old and I felt the carefree spirit of my youth. The warm wind playfully tousled my hair. Suddenly, the silken serenity of that summer day was shattered by the explosive reverberating force of a sniper's bullet. I was left for dead by an unknown assailant. In that one shattering instant, my life, and all that was familiar to me spun crazily and when settled, would never be the same again. A passing farmer summoned an ambulance. I'll never forget the incredible pain that ripped through me, the screaming sirens of the ambulance and the frantic cries of the doctors saying, "She's been shot!"

As I lay in the emergency room struggling with the searing pain racking my entire body, I was conscious of the pain subsiding and being enveloped by a quiet stillness...and then blackness...velvet-soft, gentle blackness. Was I dead? Where was I? I felt as if I had been encased in a black bubble. Then suddenly...the bubble burst and I was bathed in brilliant light. In fact, it was a most peculiar experience, I was the light. I was an all-pervading luminescent light. I became aware of an indescribable music that wafted through the universe. It sounded so sweet, so pure, ebbing and flowing like waves of liquid light. It was more exquisite than any symphony I had ever heard. An undulating harmony pervaded my luminous spirit until I became the music. It seemed in that moment I was made of only light and sound. There was nothing that was not me. I was only fluid light and sound. I had no sense of time...no past..no future. Everything just *was*.

Something about this place felt familiar. There was a deep and very real sense of familiarity. It was as if I had been there before. How can I possibly communicate to you what I felt? In each of us, at the very heart of our being, there resides an intuitive sense of a love that is as natural as breathing. This love goes beyond all boundaries, beyond form, like a vast unlimited ocean penetrating every cell and molecule of our being. There was a deep inner awareness of this kind of love.

3

It wasn't the type of love that you can fall "into" or "out of." There was no separation...no "me-ness" or "you-ness" in this love. It just was.

I felt as if I had come home. And then a voice as deep and ominous as an approaching storm declared, "You may not stay here. There is something that you still need to do." I recall shouting frantically, urgently, "Noooo!!" as I was pulled quickly back into my body.

I discovered in later years that my experience was very similar to what many individuals describe as a "near-death" experience. It has been documented as a common occurrence among persons who have been resuscitated or in some other way snatched from the brink of death, that they felt as if they were literally leaving their body. These individuals often recall seeing a bright light and feeling extraordinary peace. There is usually a vague sense of familiarity. Regardless of how one might define what happened to me, it changed my perception of reality forever.

My near-death experience was completely foreign to anything that I had experienced in my life until that time. I was the eldest of four children, and both my parents had spent time in the scientific community. My father was an engineer and my mother, who was of American Indian descent, had worked as a chemist. The only things that were real, I thought, were those that were tangible and able to be proved by the laws of science. Now, I struggled in finding a way to explain my near-death experience so that it could neatly fit into my belief system about the nature of reality. Instead, I found that slowly, everything in which I had believed began to disintegrate. In its place, a new understanding began to emerge. It seemed my life was to travel in an entirely new direction.

Following recovery from my injuries, my dreams began to take on a particular vividness and significance. In addition, I began to hear music that no one else could hear, and I was often aware of very loving spirit beings surrounding me. Somehow, my brush with death had allowed me to stumble into inner dimensions long forgotten. This was all very strange to someone like me with a very rational, linear approach to life.

Another astonishing revelation was the awareness that "I" was something separate from my body. "I" was not my body. As a result of the shooting, I had managed to lose my spleen, an adrenal gland, a kidney, part of my stomach, part of a lung, a portion of my intestine, part of my diaphragm and I now had a tube coming out of my heart. Yet, it didn't feel as if "I" had been diminished in any way by the injuries. My body was damaged, but "I" was not. Most people seem to know this, but to me it was a new and amazing realization. This realization began to assist me greatly in the healing journey of my body. I became extraordinarily healthy.

As time passed, I was finding the dreams I had were not always idyllic in nature. Somehow, when that nocturnal portal of perception opened for me, images that had been held back for so long surged forward en masse, and I was surfeited with extraordinary dreams of bright colors and intensity. Often the images were terrifying; others were profoundly soothing and reassuring. In my dreams I would occasionally catch a fleeting glimpse of that place to which I had traveled when I was thought to have died. I would clutch at these cloudy images only to find them vanishing like fine mist. I so longed to return, yet I wasn't willing to die to make that trip again.

During this time, there consistently appeared in my dreams a shadowy figure chasing me. I would often wake too terrified to return to sleep. This foreboding, formless creature of the night continued to haunt my dreams, doggedly trailing me through my next few years.

I began a career in journalism, and in the summer of '69, I was in Eastern Europe attending a journalism conference. At its culmination, I decided to camp on one of the numerous islands off the coast of Yugoslavia. I persuaded a very reluctant fisherman to take me to a particularly beautiful deserted island. As I lay in my sleeping bag that first night, I recall looking up at the silver pinpoints of light pasted on the ceiling of the night, and losing myself in the loneliness of the stars. God seemed so close, yet so very far away.

The next morning, the sun-dappled stillness was invaded by the sound of a plane flying low overhead...too low, I thought. Without warning, I was showered with a rain of bullets! Bullets were everywhere, ricocheting off the dirt and the trees! I dove for cover, crawling under the thick branches of some bushes for safety while the hail of bullets continued. And then, just as suddenly as it began, the shooting stopped. As I crept out from beneath the jagged branches, a black terror filled my soul.

Why was I being shot at? (Again!) It was as if I was being put on the brink of that dark chasm of death once more. Was I there to delve into a deeper understanding of self?

Within a short time, I was able to flag down a passing fisherman who, in broken English, explained that no one ever should have taken me to that island in the first place. It was out of bounds because it was sometimes used for aerial target practice.

In my dreams my shadowy pursuer increased his nightly rampage.

Another incident occurred that same year after I returned to the United States. The newspaper for which I worked sent me to cover anti-Vietnam war riots in the cities of Chicago, New York and Washington D.C. I recall being on the front line of a march in Washington D.C. when, without warning, policemen with gas masks and billy clubs exploded into the street from every direction, shooting tear gas and pepper gas into the front line of the march. This exceedingly painful and noxious gas feels as if it is tearing the skin away from your bones. Canisters of gas exploded at my feet. Added to the din were the screams of the crowd as it panicked. I watched as people both to the right and left of me, unable to match the force of the crowd, were swept under the stampeding feet of those desperately trying to flee from the gas.

6

As tumultuous as my daylight hours were, my nights were even more terrifying. My vigilant assailant of the night continued to hound me like a wolf tracking the scent of an impending kill. As if to hold at bay the tenacious grip of this midnight pursuer, I used my daylight hours to enhance my willingness to face "danger." To compensate for my fear, I would test my mettle with karate lessons and skydiving. At the same time, my working life concerned the violence associated with reporting riots and confrontations. I even found myself having to fend off the attack of a knife-wielding rapist.

One day, shortly after having fended off this knife attack, serendipity decreed that a book on Zen Buddhism would reach me. I began to read about the Zen experiences. I was impressed with the remarkable similarity between my near-death experience and the content of the book. It talked of the Great Light...the feeling of oneness with all things. It spoke of going beyond linear time. Perhaps, I mused, it was possible to reach that place once again without dying. I knew instinctively that it was time for a change in my life. The time had come for me to follow my own heart path, and to search for that vital perception I had once encountered at the age of 17.

Expecting to remain only a short while, I moved into a Zen monastery in the early seventies. My brief stay stretched into three years. During much of this time, I gazed at the wall for from four to sixteen hours a day, sitting in a full or half-lotus position. In a zendo it is easy to be distracted by pain or tiredness. So, as an act of compassion, with lightening accuracy, the Zen master would smite the shoulder of a Zen practitioner with a kyôsaku stick to ensure attentiveness in his discipline. A kyôsaku stick is similar to a flat baseball bat or a cricket wicket. The falling blow landing excruciatingly on my shoulder would reverberate off the Zen monastery walls. On the other hand, the Catch-22 of this practice was that if the Zen master deemed that I was doing really well, he would smack as hard as he could with the kyôsaku in order to encourage me.

Great visions would come to me and the Zen master would say, "Only illusions...go deeper." Great insights would come and

7

the Zen master would say, "Only illusions. Keep going. Go for the underlying reality...the true reality. See yourself as you really are." The Zen masters words echoed a future recurring theme in my life.

As life moved on in the Zen monastery, my dreams began to change. In one dream, a radiant three-dimensional, animated mandala appeared. A mandala is a graphic symbolic pattern divided into four separate sections, usually found within a circle or square, thought to represent the universe. When I inquired into this spontaneous appearance, I was told that Carl Jung (a Swiss psychologist), believed mandalas to be dream symbols that heralded wholeness. Jung indicated that the universal occurrence of the number four (four directions, a square with four sides, the number four or a mandala with four sides), promoted wholeness and self-integration.

While I was living in the zendo, I made a discovery concerning the nightly antagonist of my dreams. As I once again was chased relentlessly down a labyrinth of shadowy corridors, I stopped abruptly and was aware of thinking, "This is only a dream. I'm going to face whoever is chasing me." As I did so, my apocalyptic nemesis became a nebulous form slinking away into the shadows. Though the nightly appearances continued, as I would turn and face my pursuer each time it would disappear without revealing its face. (See chapter on "LUCID DREAMING.")

My Zen training enabled me to become aware that there were ways to heal my body from within.

It was during this time that I met a Hawaiian kahuna (shaman). who was a great healer. She allowed me to consciously glimpse the inner realms that I had been exploring randomly in my dreams. She agreed to train me only after she discovered my American Indian heritage. This wise woman opened the doors of my understanding so that I could see how Spirit resides in everything, and how one can call upon that Spirit for healing. I recall an occasion when I took her to Jackass Ginger, a tropical forest in Hawaii, so that she might present fruit to the

Menehune King. (Menehunes are the Hawaiian elves.) As I stood lingering at the forest's edge, I was struck with how incredulous it was that I was with someone who was indeed talking with *elves*. For the kahuna, the boundaries between the dream state and waking state were blurred, and one could step lightly between these two worlds.

During my training with the Kahuna, I begin to recognize an entirely new dimension of dreaming. I discovered that I could leave my body, walk around my cottage and even turn to look at my sleeping body. (See chapter on "ASTRAL TRAVEL.") The visitations of my nightly tormentor became less and less during this time. Even though the visits were not as terrifying, I still was never able to view the face. The lingering shadow continued to haunt me.

I wanted to understand as much as I could about my inner potential so I began to study with various teachers of ancient ways. Among those teachers who would touch me so deeply was a diminutive Japanese woman, Hawayo Takata. Upon our meeting, she announced that she had been waiting for me to contact her, and asked what had taken me so long. She was the world's foremost Reiki master, and she taught me to access the life force energy in such a fashion that it would surge down my arms in healing.

Another teacher, an eccentric shiatsu master, shared the wisdom of balancing the body through pressure points, those exquisite points of intergalactic synchronization.

As I began to explore further the healing realm, I was asked to teach healing through the University of Hawaii. Thus began my public healing practice.

An elusive waft of masculine serenity and strength began to drift into my dreams. Floating images of a tall shrouded man would emanate from the shadows of the midnight hours. Who was this pleasant intruder in my nightly meanderings? I made a list of the characteristics of this dream lover. It was a list of all I had ever wanted in a male lover and companion.

Two weeks after I made my list, I was attending a self-growth communication course. I found myself dissatisfied with the course. When I raised my hand to share this with the instructor, rather than deal with my questions, it was as though he thought what I really needed was something to keep me busy. His response was, "So, why don't you marry that guy sitting next to you?" Being in a rather irritated mood, I said to the tall, serene, bearded man next to me,"Will you marry me?" To my shock and utter amazement, he said,*"Yes* !"

I began to wilt as I realized I had just asked someone to marry me that I had never even dated. The instructor began to goad me as to when this momentous event would take place. Finally, I petulantly declared, "OK, I'll get married tomorrow." My logical, conscious mind thought, "This is completely absurd," but a gentle tugging welled up from deep within my subconscious mind...a gentle remembering. That vague benevolent phantom shape that had recently intruded my dreams in those moments began a metamorphosis into the man sitting next to me...the man who would become my husband, the man of my dreams.

As my healing profession expanded, I began to realize that I could take away someone's pain or disease by a very simple ancient process of taking the pain into my body. I felt the pain only for a moment and then it would be gone from my client. This was an exciting way to heal because seemingly everyone left "cured." I felt that this was a great service. What I didn't realize was that this particular kind of healing wasn't allowing each individual to get to the cause of his illness and that this kind of healing damaged my body. (See chapter on "DREAMS FOR HEALING")

One bright, San Francisco morning, I awoke to find that the tube into my heart had begun to separate, and hundreds of tiny blood clots were surging throughout my body. As my breathing became hesitant and my circulation began to shut down, I was startled to see someone, whom I did not know, enter our home. This man, whom I now lovingly refer to as the "little wizard," said with certainty, "You won't die." Within minutes, I began to feel my circulation improve and my breath deepen. This man, who stepped into my life at such a crucial time, was a trance medium who channeled a very powerful entity known as "Old Chinese" or Chung Fu.

This experience began a four-and-a-half-year training with this entity. Recently, studying with a spirit who is using someone else's body has become more common. Many well-known personalities now consult their "channel" for advice. Years ago, however, this was a peculiar phenomenon. Still, when I am faced with something that may be out of the range of my experience, my bottom line has always been, "Does it work?" The information that was being given by this spirit communication was valuable and practical. The trance medium would sit quietly in a chair, then he would abruptly slump over. When he sat up, his gestures and voice were those of an old Chinese man. Through him I was given very powerful ancient wisdoms regarding life's mysteries.

During this time, the most amazing thing happened regarding my dreams. The unprovoked tormentor of my twilight hours once again was chasing me! This time, when I turned to face this wanton menace of the night, I was determined to see the face. Shock!!! It was me! I realized it had always been me. It had never been anyone else. In that moment I embraced this lonely waif who had chased me for so long. I felt as if I were coming home. And, in my coming home, a child was conceived and born to David and me. The child that was never supposed to be, according to the medical profession, was conceived and born. A miracle to me, I had a healthy, easy home birth. Our daughter, Meadow, has since grown into a lovely child. Perhaps, being a mother has been the greatest "teacher" of all my paths of learning.

Before departing from this brief glimpse of my background, I want to mention a teacher who in my last years has brought me great joy. Dancing Feather of the Pueblo Indians connected me with my own American Indian heritage, and he has allowed me to seek even more deeply the quiet inner way. Through him, I have found that the most profound truths are the simple truths, and through his teaching the boundaries between my waking and sleeping lives are melting.

This book is a culmination of twenty years of self-exploration. Through many dramatic and often painful experiences, I have been beckoned to come closer to that dream conceived in the womb of knowledge. I have been nudged to understanding my own dreams more fully. Thank you for the honor in allowing me to participate in your life. May this book contribute to all your dreams coming true.

DREAM GATES

Come into my dream garden,
Across the bridge of sleep...

Experimenting,
*   I hung the moon*
*   on various*
branches of the pine

*   Hokushi*

WHAT SCIENTISTS SAY ABOUT DREAMS

Imagine a resplendent walled garden surrounded by many gates. As you enter the garden from the Eastern Gate, you view tall, lusty, golden-tasseled corn gently undulating in the warm breeze. Ripe, full pumpkins hang pregnant on the vines and giant tomatos heavy, eager to be picked, radiate their sweet fragrance. Ah, you ponder, this is surely a garden of abundant provisions for nourishment and sustenance.

Entering from the Southern Gate you look upon rich, black overturned soil. A warm pungent smell permeates the air. This garden is the fertile ground that seeds new beginnings, a place of regeneration and renewal.

The Western Gate swings open to reveal a magic carpet of dahlias, cosmos, sunflowers, daisies and marigolds. A fragrant symphony of flowered perfume titillates the senses and envelopes you with a warm blanket of spring. Oh, this is an exquisite flower garden...a cathedral of rare beauty.

The same garden...different gates.

Each gate offers a new and varied perception. Enter through these gates into your own garden of dreams.

Stepping through the well-worn garden gate of science, the verdant rows of new growth are neat and orderly, each carefully tended and numbered. Scientists believe that dreaming is an activity in which we all participate. Research indicates that <u>everyone</u> dreams. Even blind people dream. Children as young as eight months old dream. (It is assumed that very small infants dream, however, there is no way to confirm this hypothesis.) Individuals with an extremely low IQ have no fewer dreams than those possessing a high IQ. Dreaming is as natural a process as breathing. There is no way, with the exception of drug use or overindulgence in alcohol, that one can prevent it.

Though we can experience as few as three or as many as nine, generally we have an average of four to five dreams during a night. Even those who claim they don't dream, actually don't have difficulty dreaming. They only have difficulty remembering their dreams. In fact, each of us spends approximately 20 percent of our total sleep time dreaming. We dream on an average of 1 1/2 hours each night. This averages out to as much time dreaming during a lifetime as it takes to get an advanced university education. Yet, dreams are an area researchers really know very little about.

What researchers do know is that during the dream state, the heart rhythm speeds up or slows down for no accountable reason. The blood pressure climbs to new heights and dives unpredictably. The pulse becomes irregular and breathing is either haltingly uncertain or takes on a pattern of rapid panting. Metabolism increases, and the kidneys produce less but more concentrated urine. Spontaneous firing of brain cells are sometimes increased beyond normal waking levels. Blood flow to the brain increases 40 percent. Smaller muscles found in places such as the fingers tend to twitch while larger muscles go limp. One organ betrays this inner disquietude, however, more than any other organ. Penile or clitoral engorgement almost always accompanies the dream sleep. In conjunction

14

with this, it is interesting to note that neither wet dreams nor penile erections have ever been observed in dream laboratories. This suggests that with the smallest amount of effort, control of our sleeping states is possible.

REM Sleep

Dreams usually occur during REM sleep. It is called REM sleep in that there is rapid eye movement from side to side during the dream state, hence the initials, REM (rapid eye movement). REM sleep was discovered in the early 1950's. Until that time, most scientists even remotely interested in the sleep state agreed with the renowned Russian physiologist, Ivan Pavlov, who believed that the brain sort of "tuned down" during sleep. Then, Dr. Nathan Kleitman, a professor of physiology at the University of Chicago, considered the father of modern sleep research, requested that one of his graduate students, Eugene Aserinski, investigate the relationship between eye movement and sleep. Aserinski and Kleitman discovered that if they woke someone while his eyes were still moving rapidly from side to side, and inquired as to what was being experienced, the person would almost always respond by stating that he was in the middle of a dream. This discovery had amazing impact for the scientific community which could now commence the research and study of dream phenomena.

During REM sleep, vivid images in the brain issue commands to jump, run or kick. Movement of the eyes in various directions corresponds with the type of action being reported by the subject. This substantiates research indicating that the eye movements reflect the dreamer's attention to whatever is being seen in the dream. These action-oriented messages are countermanded by neurons in the brain stem which disconnect much of our muscular apparatus so that we are effectively paralyzed during this dream state. When this area of the brain stem has been damaged, people have been known to dramatically act out their dreams, even to the extent where one may need to be tied to a bed so as not to inflict damage upon himself or others.

REM states generally repeat in 90-minute cycles. A 90-minute cycle of non-REM sleep usually occurs when we first drift off to sleep. Our brain waves then commence to put on a remarkable display and the sleeper begins the first REM period of the night. The 90-minute pattern accounts for the difficulty an individual can have in going back to sleep when awakened during the night. In other words, he may not go back to sleep until one complete 90-minute sleep session has been missed. The average sleeper has four or five REM periods a night which occur every ninety minutes. These periods each begin with a very short REM period of ten minutes and end in the early morning with a dream period of 30 to 45 minutes. Some scientists say that dreaming refreshes the cortex (the outer layer of the brain) by clearing overloaded circuits. This means that dreams are considered an electrochemical process to clear away unusable data collected during the day.

Dreams and Twins

Recent experiments in France suggest that genetics play some role in the phenomena of dreaming. Research using identical twins, (those with the same genetic components) reflects an unusual similarity in REM patterns, one far greater than that existing between ordinary siblings. In fact, identical twins share the same timing and duration of the REM periods. These French scientists believe that the brain portion controlling the dream state is governed by heredity. They go on to note instances where twins have had the same dream on the same night. However, perceiving the same garden from the viewpoint of a different gate, a metaphysician would explain that twins dream the same dream because they are psychically connected. Current scientific investigation into clairvoyant and precognitive dreams proposes that the experiences and emotions of one's ancestors are encoded in the DNA and RNA through genetic coding.

Necessity of Dreams

Even if we do not recall our dreams, it is necessary to our emotional and physical balance to experience them. Deprived of our dreaming states, we have difficulty concentrating and become nervous and edgy. Without REM sleep, in some instances, there are psychotic symptoms and hallucinations.

It used to be thought that insomnia was harmful because it deprived one of the activity of sleep. It is now realized that insomnia is harmful because it deprives one of dreams. Great personality disturbances result if people are robbed of the opportunity to dream. Few people can endure more than 72 hours of being withheld from their dreaming states. Subjects who persevere finally begin to experience hallucinations. The mind appears to create its own stimulation in the form of fantasy when the normal channels of stimulation are cut off. One of the dangers of alcohol is that it has been proven to shorten dream time. When an alcoholic withdraws from addiction, almost 100 percent of his or her sleeping time is spent dreaming. This is because the person who does not participate in dreaming recovers REM sleep on subsequent nights in the exact amount of time as that lost during the previous night's deprivation. Interestingly enough, deprivation of non-REM sleep does not appear to create a need to make up lost sleep. Perhaps our body, in its wisdom, knows something that our mind has not yet begun to fully comprehend.

Hypnogogic Dreams

There is one type of dream not technically defined as a REM dream. The "hypnogogic" dream belongs to the mysterious realm between wakefulness and dreaming. It is characterized by quick random hallucinations which can often take the form of faces or country scenes. Each can continue for a significant period of time.

Scientists do not consider this category a part of the family of true dreams because one remains consciously aware of all that is going on around him. The scientific view is that this is simply a movie of memory pictures of the past clearing the brain cells, if you will. However, a metaphysical perspective would be that during this twilight period, your mind acts much like the radio tuner flipping randomly among stations. The various stations are thoughts, feelings and images that other people have had in the past, present and future times. It reflects a type of random tuning into different realities.

Children and Dreams

Newborn infants spend 50 percent of their sleeping time in REM sleep. In premature babies, that percentage can rise to as high as 75 percent. By age five, the percentage of REM time is 25 to 30 percent. In adolescence, the rate drops to 20 percent. The dream time remains at approximately this level until about age 60 when it is reduced to 15 percent. While there remains no conclusive scientific means in which to determine the content of an infant's dream we do know that small children's dreams are very different from those of adults. The majority of small children's dreams contain the presence of various animals, especially tigers, lions, snakes and spiders. (See chapter on "ANIMALS.") As the child grows older, the percentage of animals appearing in dreams decreases. By the time children reach adulthood, they will dream of animals less than 8 percent of the time.

Animals and Dreams

One interesting aspect of REM research concerns animals. You might have noticed your cat or dog showing signs of REM sleep when their eyes twitch or their breathing becomes irregular during sleep. This has led researchers to hypothesize that most animals do, in fact, dream. Reptiles and snakes, however have never been shown to dream even though they spend some 60 percent of their time asleep. Interestingly enough, if you separate mammals into two groups, the hunted (includes rabbits, sheep, deer, elk, etc.) and the hunter (includes dogs, cats, man, etc.), the hunters usually spend from 20 to 25 percent of their sleep time dreaming. The hunted sleep less with only 6 to 8 percent of their sleep time spent in REM dreaming.

Research with animals suggests that the phenomenon of dreaming must have an essential evolutionary value. With only one exception there is no single mammal that does not dream. The exception is the dolphin which possesses a most unusual sleep pattern. Instead of REM sleep, dolphins sleep with only half of their brain at a time. It is my opinion that perhaps the dolphin is the keeper of a secret of sleep. To the advanced yogi, there is very little difference between the dream state and the waking state. It may just be possible that the dolphin has unwittingly melded the dream boundaries at the cellular level.

Dream-Inspired Scientific Discoveries

While there is continued scientific research and investigation being conducted with regard to the realm of dreams and sleep, dreams have long been associated with creative inspiration by those in the scientific community. Descarte, the man who first postulated Rational Empiricism, came upon his theory as a result of a vivid dream. Rational Empiricism is the theory underlying the development of modern science.

The man who understood the molecular structure of benzine made his discovery as a result of dreaming of a snake biting its tale. This resulted in the ring-like shape of molecular structure. He once counseled his fellow colleagues, "Gentlemen, learn to dream!" Einstein, when asked about the inspiration for his theory of relativity, replied that it came as a result of a dream during his youth. In this specific childhood dream, he had been riding on a sled, and as the sled sped faster and faster, it seemed to approach the very speed of light. The stars were distorted and were transformed into astonishing colors and patterns. In that moment, Einstein was profoundly aware of the immense power of their transformation. He related that not only did this dream inspire his discovery of relativity, he felt that his entire scientific career could be seen as an extended meditation on that particular dream.

The man who developed the structure of the Periodic Table of Elements, dreamed of it in the shape of chamber music. Niles Bohr dreamed he was at the races. As he observed the marked lanes on the racetrack within which the horses were running, he constructed the analogy of fixed and specific orbits of electrons circulating around the atomic nuclei. This led to the development of the formulation of his quantum theory and, later, was the reason for his winning the Nobel Prize.

Another dream-inspired technological innovation is the story of Elias Howe, inventor of the sewing machine. Howe had become frustrated with his numerous attempts to invent a machine that would, in fact, sew. He fell asleep at his workbench and proceeded to have a nightmare. In this nightmare, African cannibals were chasing him. Unable to elude his captors, Howe was bound and taken to their village where he was tossed into a pot of boiling water. While the water churned around him, Howe was able to break loose and climb out of the pot. As he attempted to climb over the edge of the pot, the natives prodded him back into the caldron with their sharp spears. When he awoke from this dream, Howe was extremely disturbed. He couldn't help thinking of the spears and recalling how odd it was that they had holes in the points...holes in the points...holes in the points. That was it! It was as a result of this dream that Howe was then able to design a machine with a hole in the point of the needle which could sew through layers of fabric. This still remains the fundamental design of all sewing machines. In fact, the discovery inspired by one man's dream catapulted us into a new level of economics and the machine age.

I put my conscious mind to bed with sleep,
subconscious mind awakes, speaking to me in
perceptions, images, wafting in and out of my memory.

M. Anne Sweet

WHAT PSYCHOLOGISTS SAY ABOUT DREAMS

Open gate slightly creaking in the wind, each melodic creak beckoning as if to say, "Enter please, come this way!" To a psychiatrist, dreams are more than an electrochemical process. Each one is a precious seed. A seed that can be nurtured and fertilized so that it will sprout, grow and bloom. And, these blossoms of the night can be carried back on whispered wings to give fullness and understanding to our waking hours.

Therapists feel that dream symbols are the secret keyhole through which spontaneous productions of the human psyche pour into consciousness as a way to keep emotional balance during waking life. Dreams are a way for us to work out those difficulties of normal waking life that are suppressed instead of experienced during the day.

In my private practice, I have discovered that it isn't the trauma that we <u>have</u> experienced that blocks us. It is the trauma or difficulty that we <u>did not</u> allow ourselves to experience totally and completely that creates barriers in our lives.

Once, in Hawaii, when I had hurt my foot running into a hidden stump, my mentor, the Hawaiian kahuna, told me to put my foot against the stump and put the pain back into the tree. As I put my foot against the stump, I was astonished to feel a release of pain and a soothing wave of relaxation fill my foot. I thought it was more kahuna magic. In a primordial way, it made sense. The tree stump had given me the pain so I was giving it back.

When I mentioned this incident to a psychologist friend he said, "You are so dumb! You can't put pain back into a tree stump. What you are doing is allowing yourself to experience the pain that you were suppressing. By re-enacting the situation that caused you the pain in the first place, by putting your foot to the stump, you can feel and release what you didn't allow yourself to feel when it first happened. By suppressing physical pain or emotional pain, you sustain it. When you really allow yourself to feel totally and completely or, if you like, become "one" with your pain, there is no separation between you and it...it disappears."

To relive is to relieve, and dreams are a safe way to relive and relieve the feelings and sensations that you don't process or experience during the day. You can use your dream state to release waking barriers.

Dream Analysts

Psychological study of dreaming has its roots in the late 1800's. In 1861, a therapist named Scherner brought forth the idea that daytime objects or emotions could be objectified in a dream. For example, lungs could be seen as balloons and anger could become a raging fire.

In 1877, Strupell, another dream explorer, stated that dreams were escape mechanisms. They were a way to avoid experiencing the world. He formulated the Law of Association and from this the Freudian theory of Association of Ideas evolved. Another theory explored during this time was that the function of dreams was similar to our eliminative processes. Their purpose was to rid us of useless thoughts. Dreams were also theorized as being signs of wish fulfillment. Other analysts purported dreams to be memories from one's childhood, or complexes, or sexual desires, but it was Freud who united the different theories into a viable therapy.

Sigmund Freud

Freud, (1856-1930) encouraged his patients to talk at length about their dreams. He suggested that they notice the thoughts that those dreams evoked. His free association of ideas technique evolved from working with his patients in this way. Freud felt that dreams were a form of either repression or wish fulfillment or both. He felt that a person could only reach walled-up emotions through free association. Even dreams with painful contents were analyzed as fulfillment dreams. He divided the images in dreams into three types: the ego, the id and the superego. The ego reflects our conscious self, the id is associated with our primitive instincts, and the superego dictates our social conditioning.

Freud thought that during sleep, the ego was absent and the id, that savage creature that is our basic primordial urge toward sex and self-preservation, came forth. To protect the ego and the superego from these latent sexual desires, the id camouflaged these latent sexual desires by producing symbolic dreams in the hope of preventing a shock to the dreamer. The function of a dream, in Freud's theory, was to preserve sleep. Therefore, our irrational wishes were disguised as other things to deceive our self-censoring superego. Freud viewed dreams as a compromise between the suppressing forces of the id and the repressing forces of the superego. Dreams were a secret code to be figured out. The classical Freudian symbolic language was very narrow for it mostly concerned our primitive instinctual desires. The vast majority of Freudian symbols were disguises for the various forms of the sexual drive. Freud felt that even if the experiences during the day triggered dreams, their primary energy came from a childhood experience usually regarding sexual frustration.

Carl Jung

An associate of Freud who found the Freudian approach rather limiting was Swiss psychologist, Carl Jung. Jung felt that the sexual drive was important, but it wasn't the determining factor in dreams. In Jung's approach, a dream object could be exactly what it was. A snake could be just a snake rather than always a phallic symbol. Jung paid attention to the actual form of a dream rather than branching off into free association. Jung felt there was no censor at work in the mind. Dreams were the revelation of the unconscious wisdom of the individual.

Jung also felt dreams were a way to delve into the collective unconscious. To test his theory that there was a collective unconscious common to all cultures and societies, he used mythology. Traveling to Africa and to the United States, he studied African blacks and native American Indians. In his studies, he became convinced that there were two layers of consciousness: the *collective unconscious* and the *personal unconscious*. He felt the *collective unconscious* contained archetypal symbols that represented the volume of wisdom of all humanity. He called those primordial images ancestral memory archetypes and felt that the individual inherits these just as he inherits physical characteristics. We inherit primary psychic mental essences from a collective psyche. To Jung, our *personal unconscious* was recognizable material from our past that had been forgotten or repressed.

Jung noted that archetypal images appeared in the dreams of people who were in situations that were life-threatening or life-transforming. When a person was experiencing illness, undergoing specific types of stress, or releasing an attitude or belief system, Jung observed that these images would appear. When a new orientation was needed, it was as if the person was connected with the life force energy that was moving within him. Jung felt that the archetype was a primordial image that met a need of the moment. He stated that true archetypal symbols were never invented. Someone could not consciously sit down and create a symbol. The symbols were already in the subconscious of all people.

Jung liked to work with a series of dreams, associating one with the next and so on to unravel his patient's difficulties. Freud, however, concentrated more on one dream at a time in his therapy, using them as isolated incidents. Both had success with their patients and their theories were appropriate for the time.

Alfred Adler

Another associate of Freud, Alfred Adler, also broke away from using his techniques. Adler felt that the major source of influence on a person's character development was his struggle for power. He introduced into our language such terms as "sibling rivalry," "inferiority complex," and "superiority complex." He felt that people were looking for meaning in life and that values and purposes were as necessary for life as sex and power drives. Adler (1870-1937) did not focus on the concepts of the unconscious as Jung and Freud had. He saw dreams more in terms of wishful thinking, daydreams and wish fulfillment. He did not see sex as an underlying cause as did Freud. He felt that dreams were influenced by our urge for power.

Erich Fromm

Psychotherapist Erich Fromm said there was one universal language from which the human race developed that was the same for all cultures throughout history. This forgotten language was the symbolic language that appeared in dreams.

Fromm divided symbols in dreams into different categories: conventional symbols, accidental symbols and universal symbols. Conventional symbols to him were symbols with only one actual meaning like a stop sign or a plus sign or minus sign. Accidental symbols were symbols personal to the individual in the dream, or personal to a group of people, but not real to people in general. Universal symbols were those found to be common throughout the world, as water representing emotion and intuition, and fire representing energy, power, purification and transformation.

In silence the channel opens, astral guides incognito,
energy of the universe travels with one purpose--
slips through, whispers its message and slips away.

                              M. Anne Sweet

WHAT METAPHYSICIANS SAY ABOUT DREAMS

Standing at the tip of the jetty's long rocky finger that extended far into the tranquil sea, I was experiencing a deep sense of contentment. Low-lying, opalescent clouds hugged the horizon, merging cobalt blue sky with the serene azure Hawaiian sea.

Without warning, terror pierced my heart. An immense surge of water and foam roared up from the sea and a rabid wave cascaded over the jetty. As I desperately attempted to cling to the jagged rocks, I was ripped from my hold and dashed into the frigid sea. Every ounce of strength was draining from me as I struggled to stay afloat. A powerful riptide sucked at my water-logged clothes. Searing pain penetrated my lungs as I inhaled saltwater. I was being drawn unmercifully down into the dark foreboding sea....

Sweating and trembling uncontrollably, I sat up in bed... fumbling for the light...any light.

A nightmare...an especially real and vivid nightmare! A long sigh of relief embraced me. It was only a dream. I nestled into the cool comfort of my sheets, images slowly fading from my consciousness as I returned once again to a deep sleep. The morning disclosed no hint of the night's terror. In fact, I retained no conscious memory of the dream at all.

As I was waking, a phone call interrupted the stillness of the morning. It was an invitation to go to the beach. It was such a clear, perfect day! My friend stopped by and we drove to an unfamiliar beach. There was a long jetty stretching into the sea. As we scrambled in exploration along the rocks, not even the smallest hint of the previous night's terror came to mind. I perched at the end of the jetty gazing at the horizon where a lazy cloud melded the crystal sea and sky into one endless universe of blue. Without warning, my conscious thoughts were flooded with the memories of the night before. With a desperate sense of urgency, I grabbed my friend and we quickly made our way back over the rocks that had taken us so long to maneuver. Puzzled, yet compliant, she scrambled to the shore's safety. From the security of the beach, we watched in disbelief as the calm sea suddenly began to churn, sending a powerful wave crashing viciously over the jetty where we had stood only moments before.

I credit the dream of the night before with saving my life. I had had no previous knowledge that I was going to the beach, had never been to that particular beach, and had never seen pictures of it at any time. In the realm of science, this dream would probably be considered a coincidence. A scientist might rationalize that given the vast amount of dreams occurring for an individual, statistically, there is a chance that one would come true at some point in time. The metaphysician, however, would consider this a true dream of prophecy.

In times long past, dreamers attributed their nightly visions to external forces. They believed that God, angels, nature spirits, gods and goddesses, various entities and the spirits of their ancestors would visit them in the night hours, presenting themselves through dreams. Ancient dreamers deliberately invoked these influences by incubating their dreams. They acknowledged great spiritual truth and enlightenment gleaned during the dream state, utilizing dreaming for telepathic purposes, prophecy, astral travel, communication with the dead, and ESP.

Metaphysicians believe that dreams are not only neurons firing in the brain, as the scientists believe, or psychological release for unresolved difficulties of the daytime, but that dreams are a way to touch the inner realms. The recent popularity of the Carlos Castaneda's books regarding the Mexican mystic, Don Juan, exemplifies the renewed interest in this belief system. Don Juan stated that dreams were aids to the development of psychic and mental powers. To increase these abilities, he affirmed one need only remain conscious while dreaming, learning how to control the dream itself. Maintaining consciousness during the dream state has been referred to as "lucid dreaming." (See chapter on "LUCID DREAMING.")

Edgar Cayce, aptly named the "sleeping prophet," has often been considered to be the grandfather of metaphysical and psychic interpretation of dreams. The waking Edgar Cayce was known as a gifted professional photographer, and admired as an amicable Sunday school teacher. The sleeping Edgar Cayce, however, possessed a far broader and more colorful reputation. He was a gifted psychic able to give valuable information that had a profound effect on the individual lives of thousands of people.

The sleeping Edgar Cayce was a medical diagnostician and a visionary. The fascination with his life and work was reflected when, in 1954, the University of Chicago awarded a Ph.D. based on a thesis study of his work. In the thesis, Cayce was referred to as a religious seer.

When Cayce was a young boy, he would fall asleep with his head resting on his school books, only to awake the following morning discovering he had absorbed information he had never consciously studied. As a result, Cayce was able to advance rapidly in school. This gift faded, however, and Edgar Cayce completed only seven grades. (I have found that I am able to experience only moderate results with this Book Sleeping technique. If you find this technique works well for you, please write and let me know.)

When Cayce reached the age of 21, he developed a gradual paralysis of the throat muscles which in turn threatened the total loss of his voice. Though several doctors were consulted, none were successful in discovering the cause for Cayce's condition. As a last resort, Cayce requested a friend to assist him in moving into the same level of sleep that had once enabled him to memorize his school books as a child. His friend gave him the appropriate suggestion, and at once Cayce entered a sleep-like state. (See chapter on "DREAM GAZING.") Within this level of consciousness, he recommended medication and manipulative therapy for his own condition which, in turn, successfully healed the paralysis and restored his voice.

As news traveled of Cayce's gift, many doctors in Kentucky began to use Cayce's unique talent to diagnose their patients. They discovered Cayce needed only the name and address of a patient in order to disclose in a dream state valuable information regarding that individual. By the time Edgar Cayce died in 1945, in Virginia Beach, Virginia, he had given thousands of people information over a period of 43 years. One in twenty of his readings refers to dreams. Cayce regarded dreams as a kind of problem-solving exercise. He referred to dream incubation as a way to present solutions to waking problems.

Cayce continually illustrated how various dream symbols attempt to develop awareness within the dreamer himself. He felt that symbols may signify that it is time to develop new beliefs, to take more responsibility for life, to be more accepting or to expand horizons. Cayce clarified that all dreams were not necessarily problem solving in nature, but often assisted in the self-transformation process of the dreamer. He advocated that certain series of dreams were devoted to developing new qualities within the dreamer such as humility, non-judgment, self-acceptance, love and courage.

Edgar Cayce believed that some dreams were representative of a new energy or change in a person's life, and that certain dreams could even prophesy the future. Cayce possessed the gift of dream interpretation. For example, one woman wrote to Cayce relating a dream wherein she saw five chrysanthemums resting on the grave of her husband's father. Cayce responded that, within five weeks time, her husband would have an experience of being taught by his deceased father through the medium of dreams. Cayce affirmed that the experience would be a joyful one. Within five weeks, the dreams did, in fact, come to her husband. Perhaps Cayce's greatest gift was his intuition with regard to health and dreams. He advocated one could not only receive signals of impending physical imbalances while in the dream state, but that one could also receive the cures within dreams.

Once approached by a woman who sorrowfully stated that she had dreamed she would never be able to conceive a child, Cayce reassured her that she most definitely <u>would</u> give birth to a child. He advised her to release any literal interpretation of the dream, and counseled that the dream was simply encouraging her to take careful preparation for motherhood, especially with regard to diet and in her belief patterns. These were the areas in which she required a new birth in order to conceive the child she so desperately wanted. Shortly thereafter, this woman became the joyful mother of a healthy baby.

Cayce was consistently urging his clients to solve their problems through their own individual interpretation of their dreams. The work of Edgar Cayce made such an impact that it remains the foundation of a great portion of modern metaphysics today.

Another aspect of dreams and metaphysics is the realm of reincarnation and karma. Reincarnation affirms that our true essence is not a mere body, but rather spirit. As spirit, we incarnate repeatedly in various bodies in order to learn and grow. Karma consists of the central concept that whatsoever you sow, you reap. This law of cause and effect governs one's

31

experience over collective lifetimes. As you balance karma during waking life, you are also able to work through and culminate karmic lessons through the vehicle of your dreams. (See chapter on "DREAMS FOR PAST LIFE RECALL.")
There are many reports of dreams wherein someone who has died is reassuring the dreamer that the deceased is alive and well, and that there is no further need to grieve. Occasionally, the deceased will instruct the dreamer in some matter-of-fact concern of daily life. Let me share a powerful example of this from my own experience.

I was working on Union Street in San Francisco at a healing center during a very rich and rewarding time in my life. My shiatsu (pressure-point therapy similar to accupressure) was at a peak. Every time I pushed a pressure point, I would experience a galactic synchronization with other points on the planet and the entire universe. My Zen training, with its disciplined commitment to focus, enhanced my ability to achieve a tremendous sense of clarity with each point I pushed.

One evening as the San Francisco fog was settling in for a night's slumber and I listened to fog horns wailing in the background, the phone rang. Upon answering it, I heard a friend on the other line speak hesitantly, with a voice full emotion. "David's dead." David, another healer and a medical doctor also worked at the center. He had a youthful exuberance and passion for life which permeated the entire center. The first thoughts rushing into my consciousness were those of disbelief...not David! He had had so much to live for. His practice was thriving, he and his wife had just purchased a beautiful home in Mill Valley, and they were joyfully anticipating the birth of a child. Why David?

That night in my dreams, a beckoning presence seemed to flutter at the edges of my consciousness. As I stumbled through the next few days, consumed by a sense of numbness, I began to experience strange phenomena. When walking through various rooms in our Marina flat, the lights would flicker on and off. Vaguely I thought about calling an electrician. My dreams at night were filled with an elusive sense of urgency. I did not, however, connect any of this with David. I merely assumed it to be part of my own grieving process.

Just before Christmas, my shiatsu group gathered in my living room for a class. My valiant little Christmas tree was radiant with its perky miniature lights. As the class began on this particular evening, the non-blinking lights on the Christmas tree began to blink on and off. I simply explained to the group that we had been having trouble with our electrical system and that we could ignore it. With great persistency, the lights continued to blink methodically. Turning our attention once again to the tree, an individual in the class asked it, "Are you trying to tell us something?" The tree lights responded with methodical blinks. It finally dawned on me that David had been attempting to make contact with me through my dreams in order to provide comfort and information to his grieving wife. With unfailing determination, he was endeavoring to contact me during my sleeping hours as well as through our electrical system. We continued to ask questions in which he responded with the blinking lights. In this manner we were able to garner information that he wished us to pass on to his wife. As soon as I gave his wife the necessary information, the dreams ceased and our electrical system returned to normal.

A psychologist would probably analyze my dreams during this time as a way to process and release my grief. The metaphysician, however, would perceive that David was indeed attempting to communicate with me in order to give me information. For me, the metaphysical interpretation is validated by the occurrence of the blinking lights, and the fact that the information to be relayed to his wife was valuable to her, information of which I had had no prior knowledge. Communication with deceased friends, parents or other family members is a skill that can be learned through dream incubation.

Another type of metaphysical dreaming is the flying dream. A psychologist would identify dream flying as a psychological sense of freedom expressed by the symbol of flying. To a metaphysician, however, dream flying is nothing more or less than astral projection. Astral projection, simply defined, is when one's soul literally leaves the body, connected only by a single cord, to explore other realms and dimensions. (See chapter on "DREAMS FOR ASTRAL TRAVEL.")

Another common metaphysical belief is that while we are dreaming, guides come forth to give us valuable information and insight. A guide is generally a discarnate being with whom you have been connected in a previous lifetime. This being continues to be interested in you, working with you to provide guidance which benefits the evolution of your soul. Guides will often come during the night hours. When the conscious mind shuts down during sleep, guides have easier access to your inner self. (See chapter on "DREAM GUIDE.")

DREAM WEAVERS

Ancestors, you have crossed over,
epic journey of the night,
to weave the fabric of our dreams
reflections of our innermost realms.

Deft masters of the dream loom
ever mindful of the texture and dye
of one thread against another,
we follow the footsteps of your crossing

M. Anne Sweet

"And it shall come to pass afterward that I shall pour out my spirit on all flesh; your sons and your daughters shall prophesy, your old men shall dream dreams and your young men shall see visions."

Joel 2:28

ANCIENT DREAMERS

Somewhere in the window of your memory hover those elusive moments just out of conscious reach. These are things so real that you can sense them waiting there, and in response, you reach out to touch them only to find they quickly slip beyond your grasp and vanish. These moments are beyond the world of form and illusion. They dwell in the midst of the crack between two worlds.

Throughout history, in every culture, there have been those rare individuals who have stepped through that mysterious veil to listen to messages of the night. These Dream Weavers have carried back with them precious gifts through the dim portal into normal reality. They have woven delicate web-like dreams in the silent spaces to lead the destiny of men and nations alike.

Though many of the adventures of these nocturnal mystics are recorded only in the bosom of the ages, a few records have found their way through history. In ancient China, within the Shang Dynasty, Emperor Woo Ting, (1324-1266 B.C.), disturbed at the loss of his trusted counselor, made a ritual offering to Shang-Ti, Ruler of the Gods. He asked the god to reveal the successor of his deceased counselor. The Emperor then slept and dreamt of the face of his new counselor. He searched the entire country looking for the reflection of that face seen in his dream, yet to no avail. Then, upon circulating the dreamed man's portrait throughout the empire, the Emperor discovered one man whose face matched the portrait. Now this man was only a common workman, yet the Emperor's belief in the validity of dreams was so deep that he made this commoner the new prime minister of his empire.

In ancient Greece, researchers believe 300 to 400 temples were erected for the purpose of practicing dream control. These temples, thought to be in existence for over 1000 years, were used as facilities of physical and emotional healing. Within these temples, divine help was evoked from the gods. Hypnos, the god of sleep, was said to fan mortals with his wings to induce slumber. Then Zeus would give Morpheus, a god of dreams, warnings, prophecies and inspirations to send to humanity via the winged messenger, Hermes.

The seeking of special dreams to invoke the powers of the gods is called dream incubation. (See chapter on "DREAM INCUBATION.") In ancient Greece, incubation occurred when one slept in a sacred place after having gone through a ritual of purification. The purification usually involved abstinence from alcohol, meat and sexual relations, along with an offering made to a selected deity.

Many of the sacred Greek shrines such as Delphi, the Shrine of Apollo, and the Temple of Epidaurus were dream oracles, or places where the deities were thought to reveal the secrets of inner knowledge. It was to these shrines that the sick would journey hoping that Asclepius, the god of medicine and healing dreams, would appear to them in their sleep. It is recorded that Asclepius offered advice in the form of herbal remedies and, on occasion, even awarded instantaneous cures. He was thought to appear to his patients in their dreams, mixing potions and applying bandages to the sufferer's body, and in some instances, even summoning sacred snakes to lick the ailing areas. Those desiring cure would sleep among nonpoisonous snakes, as snakes were thought to be the symbolic carriers of healing. The association has carried forward in the modern symbol of two intertwined snakes signifying healing.

It is interesting to note that in the yoga tradition, a coiled snake represents the kundalini life force embodied in the base of the spine. The kundalini energy is believed to be the potency of the universe manifest within the human being.

Hippocrates, the ancient Greek physician and father of modern medicine, once said, "Some dreams are divinely inspired and others are the direct result of the physical body." He believed that the appearance of the sun, moon, stars and natural phenomena were significant to the understanding of a person's health and well-being. If the sky in a dream was very clear, then a person's body was thought to be functioning normally. If the stars, for example, were not clear or were falling from the sky, this signified a disturbance in a person's health. Hippocrates stated in his treatise on dreams, "It is a sign of sickness if the dream star appears dim or moves either westward or down into the earth or sea, or upward. Upward movement indicates fluxes (unusual discharges) in the head. Movement into the sea, disease of the bowels. Eastward movement, growing of tumors in the flesh."

These symbolic interpretations might not be appropriate for today, but it shows the respect that dream symbols garnered in ancient times. It was noted in those ancient days that prior to the onset of disease, a dream would occur with the symptoms of that illness. In fact, these dreams today are called "prodromic," which is derived from the Greek word, "prodromos," meaning "running before."

Galen, the second century Greek physician, as well as Aristotle, founder of the science of logic, both held that dreams reflect the bodily state, and could, therefore, be used to diagnose and treat illness. Plato believed the liver to be the seat of dreams, and ventured in his famous work, *Timeaeus*, that prophetic dreams were received through the liver. Pliny espoused that dreams were supernatural in origin. In ancient Greece, dream interpreters were in great demand, being consulted much the same as medical doctors are today. One of the items looked for by dream interpreters would be Dream Gates. In ancient Grecian dreams, two dream gates would appear, one consisting of ivory and the other of horn. If the dreamer saw the Ivory Gate, it was interpreted as a warning. If he saw the Horn Gate, the meaning was deemed to be prophetic.

Several ancient civilizations revered dreams. In fact, four of our oldest civilizations - China, India, the Middle East and Egypt - have all left documented records indicating their use of dreams.

Dream incubation was widely practiced in Egypt from 4000 B.C. to 2000 B.C. The Egyptian pharaohs held dreams in great esteem believing them to be vehicles of guidance from the gods. Between the paws of the Great Sphinx there is a slab of pink granite inscribed with the dream of a man who once became an Egyptian king. One day while he was sleeping in the shade of the Sphinx, the god Ra, the sun god, appeared to him informing him that he would one day become the ruler of all Egypt. Upon waking, he happened to notice that the Sphinx was covered with sand and was in disrepair. He made a commitment that if he ever were to become ruler, the Sphinx would always be kept in perfect condition. A few years later, true to the dream, he became Thothmes IV. Loyal to his promise, the ruler restored the Sphinx, and it has been maintained ever since.

The equivalent of Asclepius in Egypt was Imhotep. Inside the Shrine of Asclepius-Imhotep in Egypt, there resides records of the interpretations of various dreams. One is inscribed, "A bed on fire means your partner is unfaithful to you."

In ancient Syria, a special prayer for dreams was:

> "My gracious god, stand by me.
> My friendly god will listen to me.
> God Mamu of my dreams,
> My god, send me a favorable dream."

In the Middle East, a practice called "istigara" was used to receive a dream that would answer a question. The "istigara" was a special dream prayer said just before falling asleep.

Even the Old and New Testaments mention God's will would be made known through the dreams and the visions of the prophets. In fact, there are some 20 well-documented accounts of dreams which refer to divine guidance being given through dreams. In some cases, these dreams changed the course of destiny. Moses was instructed by God to listen for Him in his dreams. "Hear now my words. If there be a prophet among you, I, the Lord, will make myself known to him in a vision and will speak to him in a dream."

And, an angel appeared to Joseph in a dream and said, "Joseph, thou son of David, fear not to take unto thee Mary, thy wife, for that which is conceived in her is of the Holy Ghost."

In ancient Japan, dream incubation was practiced in both the Buddhist and Shinto temples. There were several Buddhist temples famous for being dream oracles. The procedure for obtaining a visionary dream was as follows. First, there was need of abstinence, and a journey was made to the holy site where an offering was given. Here the dreamer would remain for a specified time of either 7, 21 or 100 days. These numbers were thought to be significant. The dreamer would sleep adjacent the inner sanctum awaiting a special dream. It was felt a divinity dwelled in the inner sanctum. Often a healing dream would be requested (much as it would be in ancient Greece), and the Bodhisattva Kannon would appear in the dreams, healing ailments.

Regardless of the culture which practiced dream healing, it was always the reigning deity who would come forth evoking the cure. In order to penetrate the same inner spaces touched by these ancient dreamers see the chapter on "DREAM INCUBATION." This will facilitate creating your own dream temple and incubating dreams as was done in ancient times.

MALAYSIAN DREAMERS

Amid the languid steamy days and humid Malaysian nights, nestled by monkey chatter and squawking parakeets, was a peace-loving culture that, until recent times, reportedly relied deeply upon dreams. The Senoi people of Malaysia seemingly had discovered a way to live in harmony with one another. The most important concern for each village was the nature of what was dreamed during the night. Every morning, during the family meal, family members would relate their dreams. They didn't forget a dream, as each child was trained in the practice of recalling dreams from an early age. Children were instructed to confront any negative or evil spirit in their nightmares in order to become masters of their destiny in waking life. Commensurate with Senoi tradition, children were educated to fully experience their dreams even when faced with the frightening circumstance of a strange beast or the sensation of falling. To experience their dream state as a condition over which they had control was a fundamental part of Senoi dream training.

All family dreams were discussed in length. A family member who had experienced a powerful dream would be congratulated on his dream action while another member would be given specific suggestions in dealing with various aspects of a disturbing dream. Following dream sharing in the morning, family elders met in village council to continue further dream discussion, the outcome of which became the cornerstone of the villagers' work for that day. The tribal adults kept a record of those dream experiences which they felt collectively reflected their future. Of particular importance would be those dreams wherein they received new songs and/or dances. The tribe believed strongly that dreams were fragments of a person's psyche disguised in recognizable dream forms. Consequently, they were convinced that one primary advantage of dream sharing was the ability to avert danger before it actually occurred.

The Senoi, with their focus on dream-sharing, were known to be an an incredibly peaceful culture despite the abundance of warlike tribes living near them. Perhaps one of the most striking characteristics of this tranquil people was their amazing psychological balance. Reports collected by several researchers indicate that psychosis and neurosis were two conditions virtually nonexistent among the Senoi. One hypothesis is that the people's understanding and use of dream states was primarily responsible for this psychological balance. Research confirms that when a community works together in mastering dream states, there is evidence of less crime and antisocial behavior experienced within that community.

Woven intrinsically within the tribal life were some very specific rules pertaining to dream control. These can also serve as valuable guidelines for individuals exploring their own dream states. Some of the general rules of the Senoi system of dream control as outlined by dream researcher, Dr. Patricia Garfield, are:

1. Whenever there is danger in a dream, confront it.
2. Always be moving toward pleasure in your dream.
3. Always create a positive outcome in every dream.

Whenever a dangerous or frightening experience occurred within a dream, the Senoi people felt it was necessary to confront the danger, fighting it to the death, if necessary. It was believed that the death of a dream enemy could release the internal blockages that created the dream antagonist within the individual. If one had trouble in a difficult dream scenario, then it was advisable to call upon his/her dream guide or dream friends for assistance. (See chapter on "DREAM GUIDES.")

The Senoi also felt it was extremely important to continue moving toward pleasure in every dream. This pertained to all kinds of pleasure, including sexual pleasure. A person could not have too many dream lovers or too much sex in dreams. If anyone was experiencing light sensual contact in a dream, it became significant to expand those sensations even to the point of moving toward orgasm. The Senoi believed that guilt was an emotion never to be experienced with regard to dream lovers. These tribal people espoused that images within sexual dreams were merely the various aspects of self being integrated through orgasm, with orgasm symbolizing both self-unification and self-integration.

These Malaysian people also believed that upon completion of any activity within a dream, whether it was a dream battle or a dream of love, it was imperative that the dreamer ask for a gift. The gift was to be either useful or beautiful in appearance. Therefore, regardless of what occurred within the dream, it was possible to reconstruct the dream, creating a positive outcome, (even if this was done after awakening from the dream state).

Primarily through the work of Kilton Stewart, the Senoi people of Malaysia gained the reputation of being an extremely peaceful society that used dreams to create a sense of harmony within their culture. With the advent of World War II and the intervention of outside influences, the Senoi no longer practice their dream-based culture. Some researchers feel that the data on this tribe sounds too good to be true and an element of doubt has been introduced. Nevertheless, the dream people of Malaysia remain a powerful symbol of a community where dreamwork can be integrated as a basis for personal, social and cultural guidance and understanding.

In the mist of dawn, the shaman dances,
head bowed in the ritual of his forefathers,
chanting rhythmic incantations, solemn
invocations to the spirit of the lake.

M. Anne Sweet

AMERICAN INDIAN DREAMERS

The evening embers are darkening. The lone cry of a solitary owl pierces the cold stillness. In the silent shadows tribal members return to their teepees. The time of the big hunt is approaching, and tonight is set aside for dreaming. Tribal members hold close to their being the quiet comfort of awaiting the Night Guardians. These Dream Guides are called upon to lend assistance and guidance during the night. Their advice is sought as to where and when to hunt. Tonight is for dreaming. In the blackness, chilled starry diamonds sprinkle the curtained sky. A lone shooting star punctuates the silence.

In the morning there is a gathering and each dream is shared...and with each dream, certainty of the location and strategy of the hunt becomes clearer. The tribe knows that their survival depends upon these dreams.

A Native American proverb:

"Respect your brother's dreams."

American Indians all gave special meaning to dreams. Dreams were used almost universally to predict the future, manage psychological problems, heal sexual difficulties and cure ailments. Each tribe had very specific techniques in obtaining and in understanding dreams. The study of the use of dreams within American Indian cultures is a very complex one. This chapter only briefly touches on the American Indian use of dreams.

To the American Indian, there existed only a thin line between dreaming and waking states. These people believed Mother Earth was a real entity and a powerful source of strength, and that Great Spirit pervaded all things of nature. They believed it was during the evening hours that one could access Great Spirit, ancestors and inner guidance. As a result, Indians gave great power to the world of dreams.

In the Mohawk villages, it was common for dreamers to become so inspired by images occurring in their dreams that they would create poems or riddles. They would then give and receive gifts based on whether or not other members of the tribe could guess the riddle received in their dreams.

The Seneca tribe worked very intimately with their dream work. They demanded each dream be acted out either symbolically or literally. It was this particular aspect of their culture which made their conversion to Christianity by the early French Jesuit missionaries extremely difficult.

Each of the tribes of the Iroquois nation -- the Mohawk, Oneida, Onondaga, the Cayuga, Seneca and the Huron -- called the Six Nations, participated in its own unique daily dream ritual. They would gather each year for a special joint ritual some time after the first snowfall. These determined Indians set out on their pilgrimage, traveling great distances for the purpose of this gathering. When they arrived, they would each act out their own dreams wearing masks. Occasionally, they would wear costumes along with the masks. At other times, they would perform naked except for a mask. The yearly festival of this traveling ritual dream theater was known as the "Onoharoia;" it allowed many Ondinnonk to be acted out very theatrically. Many of the masks of the Iroquois Tribe were the

46

ritual masks used in these ceremonies. Young men would perform in these ritual dream dramas, traveling from Indian settlement to settlement for the purpose of acting out their dreams.

The Jesuit missionary, Father Raguemeau, in 1649, referred to these various dream rituals when he said, "In addition to the desires which we generally have which are free, or at least voluntary in us, we have other desires which, as it were, are inborn or concealed. These, they (the Iroquoi) say come from the depths of the soul, not by knowledge but by means of a certain blind transporting of the soul to certain other objects.

Now they believe the soul makes known these natural desires by means of dreams, which are its language. Accordingly, when the desires are accomplished, it is satisfied; but on the contrary, if it not be granted when it is desired, it becomes angry . . . often revolts against the body, causing various diseases. They call this 'Ondinnonk' - a secret desire of the soul in a dream."

The people of the Iroquois confederacy believed so strongly in the importance of Ondinnonk that they felt someone would become sick and even die if his dreams were not acted out.

In Australia, the aborigines believe the entire universe is a composite creation of dreams. Their society is built around the importance of these dreams. Virtually, all their daily activities are regulated by the sharing of dreams and their interpretation. Numerous anthropologists have noted the phenomena of the aborigine tribes determining future actions based on the dreams of tribal members. The aborigines believe that everything was a dream before the coming of white men.

Australian Aborigine Poem:

Speak of the dream time.
It is that time before white man came.
That reality.

Dream Guides

Central to most tribes was the concept of a guardian or guide whom one could access during the daytime as well as during a dream. A psychologist, perhaps, would rationalize a guide as a gestalt conversation with an imaginary being who, in truth, is really an unacknowledged aspect of oneself. However, to the American Indian, the guide was very real. Their dream friends were as real as the friends whom they could touch during waking hours. Frequently, Indians would fast in order to gain a dream guide, a special dream, or a dream song (a song presenting itself to them during sleep.) Dreamers would sometimes compose dream songs without fasting. However, lack of food may, in some unknown way, enhance this mysterious creative process. Perhaps the thin air unique to the high mountains and rocky places preferred by the Indians as places to fast also influenced the quality of their dreams.

Research indicates that when an individual is involved in extremely quiet pursuits, he is more apt to experience a greater number of dreams than when involved with busy social activities. He will also have longer REM cycles each night; as much as 60 percent more REM sleep. Increased isolation seems to cause an increase in dreaming. Total isolation can even produce hallucinations in normal persons. Physical inactivity is also a variable in causing increased dreaming.

The Papago Medicine Woman Chant:

How shall I begin my songs
In the blue night that is settling?

In the great night my heart will go out.
Toward me the darkness comes readily.

In the great night my heart will go out.

American Indian Use of Dreams

American Indians had a variety of practical uses for their dreaming. In addition to discovering time and place for hunting and planting, they also utilized dreams to determine names. They would incubate or ask for the name of a new child, and the name would come in a dream. (See chapter on "DREAM INCUBATION.") Frequently, creative dances and songs came during dreams. Numerous cultural artifacts are believed to have their origin in dreams. The decorative patterns on blankets, paintings, jewelry and clothing are also thought to have been conceived during dreams.

Common Traits of Indian Cultures

The following traits are evident in all native cultures which possess a high regard for the status of dreams:

1. Dreams are considered vital to success in life. This particular attitude made it easier to recall and interpret dreams for the ancient American Indians, and it is also true for us today.

2. Supernatural figures appear in dreams granting special powers or giving important information.

3. Shamans, medicine women and men, are expected to use their dreams in acquiring knowledge.

4. Dreams are induced by utilizing techniques such as sleeping alone in a power spot or a sacred place, or by fasting.

Interestingly enough, research indicates that 80 percent of all hunting and fishing societies use dreams to seek and control supernatural power, while only 20 percent of all agricultural and animal-raising societies use dreams for this purpose. Thus, it appears the more dependent a tribe was on the activities of hunting and fishing, the more likely it would be to use dreams.

Dreams are relics of the human mind. In the recent past, American Indians had a direct path to their dreams. The American Indians knew that as they lived close to nature, and moved in harmony with all cycles of nature, it was far easier to access the mystical world of dreams. They were able to directly access the meanings and images of their dreams. Now, as our societies have moved farther and farther away from nature, we have forgotten the ability we once possessed in accessing our dreams directly and easily.

We can glean wisdom from the ancient American Indians. Take some time off -- a day, two days, or a week -- and spend time in nature totally away from electricity and machines. Allow time to be spent relying on your own resources. Get back in touch with the cycles of nature. Spend time in the moonlight, allowing the moon to bathe you. Drink from cooling streams. As a result of this gentle respite, you will find it much easier to access your dreams.

DREAM MAKERS

In the beginning, the attempt of our crossing
is clumsy, unsteady, the way is
mysterious and unclear, our dreams
are woven of thick coarse wool.

Along the way, we find the vestiges
of our ancestors, ancient dream weavers,
left as guideposts, illuminators, lighting
our way, refining the quality of our weave.

M. Anne Sweet

*The reason we can't see around
the corner is so we don't miss
the beauty here and now.*

Karl Bettinger

DREAM RECALL

Your dreams can provide you with fantasy, adventure and
romance. They can serve as a mystical key to foretell the
future and provide the enchanted key to unravel the past. Your
dreams can rival Hollywood in providing you with
entertainment, but with *you* as producer, director and STAR --
all giving truly Oscar-winning performances. However, if you
want to recall your dreams, you will need to remain cognizant
and alert at all times or you will forget the roles you have
played. You also will forget the other actors and the
significance of each one. And, you will undoubtedly forget the
lines you spoke even before returning "home." Just as it
requires skill in an actor to recite from memory his lines in a
play, it also is a developed skill for a dreamer to recall his
dreams.

The single most important element in being able to remember
dreams is motivation. To acquire that motivation, you must
first perceive your dreams as worthwhile; regard them as
valuable messages received from your subconscious. It is
imperative you believe they deserve to be heard.

Contemplate each dream as if it were a brilliant gem with each lustrous facet reflecting a clear and remarkable new insight into yourself. View each dream as if it were allowing you to gaze deeply from a rich new perspective into the shimmering jewel called you. And from these different perspectives, you will unwrap great wisdom in understanding yourself. Therefore, if you begin to regard your dreams as valuable and useful, you will want to recall your dreams, and will discover you have the necessary motivation to do so.

Dream Recall Blockages

If you are unable to remember your dreams at present, perhaps some attitude is blocking your ability to recall them. To discover the possibility of such an impeding attitude, participate in the simple process outlined on the next pages. This will facilitate your becoming aware of and releasing any choices, even those hidden away in your subconscious, which may be blocking your dream recall.

During this process, you will be given a list of some of the more common attitudes that make dream recall difficult. One or more of the beliefs might be appropriate for you. Take time to read the list thoughtfully <u>out loud</u>. If any one of the statements seems to "fit" or feels "right," be ready to jot down your experience.

On a separate sheet of paper, note the following headings, leaving room for a sentence or two after each:

ATTITUDE:

Thought response:

Emotional response:

Body response:

Affirmation:

Your Thought Response:

If you have read a specific statement (attitude) that seems true for you, notice the <u>thoughts</u> you are having in response to that statement. Observe what you are thinking in terms of any distinct denial or affirmation. Note whatever thoughts occur to you as a result of hearing yourself say this attitude out loud. Above all, remain honest with whatever thoughts come into your mind. Keep in mind there is no right or wrong thought. This exercise is simply being used to assist you in recalling your dreams.

Your Emotional Response:

Observe your emotional response upon "hearing" the statement. What specific emotions does the attitude in question generate within you? Remember, do not judge your response, simply notice it. *The very act of examining attitudes will allow them to be released.*

Your Body Response:

Notice your body's response. Even when it seems difficult to be conscious of thought or emotional responses, your body will often send its own clear messages. It *is* responding, though subtly at times, to the attitudes spoken, and it is possible for you to become aware of these responses. As you state the attitude, practice learning to recognize even those slight changes within your body. It might only be a small tightening in the center of your chest or a twitch in your left eye. Your body is always giving you clues. Learn to listen to it. It can be used as a valuable indicator of any concerns still blocking your dream recall.

Your Affirmation:

The last heading on your list, "Affirmation," will be something you create for yourself. An affirmation is a positive thought that reaffirms the direction in which you want your thoughts to go. Find or create your own affirmation that will release the attitude which may be blocking your ability to recall your dreams. Attitudes form pathways that thoughts travel. They are like well-worn pathways you consistently choose, without thinking, as you cross a field of golden grasses. If a person has the attitude, "Dreams are of no consequence," every time the word "dream" comes to mind, it is as if the mind runs down the path labeled, "Dreams are of no importance." This path can become so "worn" that it, in turn, requires conscious effort to create a new path.

Likewise, a positive thought or affirmation, "My dreams are valuable and important," will begin to create a new pathway and eventually, if affirmed often enough, the new pathway will replace the old. When a thought regarding "dreams" occurs, the mind will now begin to travel and reinforce the thought that dreams are valuable. As a result, it becomes easier to recall dreams.

At the end of this section there are some suggested affirmations to enhance dream recall.

Are you ready to begin? Good!

Attitudes that Block Dream Recall

Say these out loud.

> –I don't feel that dreams are
> important.

> –I'm not really sure I actually want
> to know what is in my subconscious.

> –I need sleep. Dreams interrupt my
> being able to get a good night's sleep.

> –I might learn things about the
> future that I don't want to know.

> –Maybe we are not meant to
> remember.

> –Sexuality in dreams is disturbing.

> –I might have nightmares.

> –I feel out of control in my dreams
> and that's uncomfortable for me.

> –I might open myself up for psychic
> intervention.

> –It's distressing to do things in my
> dreams that are inconsistent with
> my waking values.

–Something difficult happened in my
past and I don't want to think about
it or dream about it.

–It takes too much time and effort
to remember dreams.

These are only a few of the attitudes people who don't recall
dreams can have. As you are checking to see if any of these
are appropriate for you, see if there aren't other attitudes as well
that might apply to you. Remember, just becoming aware of
and exploring attitudes very often is enough to cause them to
begin to dissipate so that dreams can be recalled more easily.

Following is an example of how your experience might appear
on your chart:

Attitude: I don't feel that dreams are important.

Thought response: I feel that they are important to <u>other</u> people who are
having problems.

Emotional response: When I say this attitude, I feel some irritation and
even some anger.

Body response: After saying this attitude, I notice that I am not
breathing very fully and my lower neck muscles
feel tight.

Affirmation: There is <u>great</u> importance to dreams and my dreams
allow me to unlock unseen potential within myself.
I enjoy dreaming and I remember my dreams
easily.

Affirmations that Promote Dream Recall

–I enjoy dreaming and I remember
my dreams easily.

–I deserve sexual pleasure and it's
 enjoyable to experience dream sex.

–My emotions are valuable and I
 appreciate my emotional dream
 life.

–I have all the time I need to
 remember dreams and to assimilate
 them.

–I accept my past unconditionally,
 and know that everything that has
 ever happened to me in my life was
 necessary for me to get where I am now.

–My dreams give me valuable
 perceptions into my life that allow
 for more balance and joy.

–Dreaming allows me to be more
 creative and I love recalling my
 dreams.

–I do not judge my dreams. I know
 that every message from my
 subconscious deserves to be heard.

–Dreaming gives me valuable
 information about the future.

–I give myself permission to
 recall and understand the
 deeper meaning of my dreams.

–There is _great_ importance in dreams and my
 dreams allow me to unlock unseen potential within
 myself. I enjoy dreaming and I remember my
 dreams easily. So be it!

Diary of Dreams...Your Dream Journal

"I never travel without my diary. One should always have something sensational to read in the train." Oscar Wilde

A Dream Journal is a record of your inner journeys, your inner quest for self-understanding. Recording just one or two dreams, however, will not provide you with nearly enough information. Carl Jung felt that true self-knowing came from observing and interpreting a series of dreams over a long period of time, perhaps even years. He felt that in this way one could begin to weave a tapestry of the recurring themes pervading his life. As you continue your daily dream journal, you will begin to gain a comprehension of your life's ultimate destiny. Your diary of dreams can literally become your personal Book of Wisdom.

Dreams are forgotten very easily (usually within ten minutes from the time of awakening) and it takes an enormous amount of willpower to be able to pull them back into conscious thought, if at all.

Research into the area of sleep and dreaming has revealed that dreaming is accompanied by rapid eye movement (REM). Sleepers awakened during REM sleep were experiencing the middle of a dream. Sleepers awakened during bodily movement immediately following REM sleep could recount a completed dream. Five minutes after REM sleep, the sleepers remembered only fragments of dreams. Ten minutes after REM sleep, the sleepers were shown to have practically no recall at all. Thus, it is literally within the first few seconds that a dream is still vivid. Consequently, it is imperative that you write down your dream immediately upon waking while it remains fresh in your memory. Write down as many details as you can recall. (Lucid dreams, however, because you are a conscious participant, will remain in the memory for a much longer time. See chapter on "LUCID DREAMING.")

To Record Your Dreams You Will Need

1. **An easy-flowing pen**
2. **Notebook, journal or a tape recorder, preferably a dictaphone**
3. **Flashlight or night light (If using a notebook)**
4. **Easily-seen clock**

Easy-flowing pen

Be sure you have a pen that can write easily without pressure such as a felt-tip pen or an easy-flowing ball point pen. Use a pen rather than a pencil to record your dreams as it writes too lightly for notes taken when you are very sleepy. Place both pen and diary right next to where you will be sleeping.

If you prefer pens that have their own lights, these can be bought at medical supply stores. A less costly way to accomplish this is to purchase a penlight and tape it to your pen.

Notebook or journal

The best kind of nighttime journal is a tight, spiral wirebound notebook. A loose-ring notebook is not as useful, as the papers can slide and move while you are trying to write.

Divide your notebook into two sections. On the left side, you will write the date, hour and all the details of your dream. On the right side, you will note your own interpretation. (See example.)

It is important to write the date in your journal ahead of time as this sets up a positive expectancy for you to record your dream on that date. Recording the date can also allow for you to notice a realization later concerning a particular dream on a specific date. For example, you may have had a powerful dream on October 24th and then later realized it was the date of your mother's birthday. While not being consciously aware of it at the time, nevertheless, your mind was responding to the emotions and feelings you have in regard to your mother. Later, having this information may provide you with clues and valuable insights in regard to yourself and your relationship with your mother.

Also in preparation, you might want to jot down in your journal the heading, "*Dream One.*" This again sets up a positive expectancy to have more than one dream during the night. As soon as you have recorded your first dream of the evening, and before you go back to sleep, note in your journal, "*Dream Two,*" in order to set up the expectancy of a second dream.

When recording your dream, also note feelings you noticed you had in the dream. It is essential that you write down your memories quickly because literally in seconds the dream will begin to fade. Jot down predominant colors, symbols, key words, themes, and emotions. Try not to get stuck on some detail to the detriment of recording the rest of the dream. If you had heard a poem or an interesting verbal expression or phrase, record that data first. Later record the visual parts you remember. The visual images tend to be retained longer than auditory stimuli, so it is a good idea to first record anything you <u>heard</u>.

For individuals who find it difficult to come to enough conscious awareness to turn on a flashlight or a tape recorder, there is an *eyes-closed technique* you can use. As you awaken, feel for the notebook that is next to your bed. Then with your eyes still closed so that you are allowing yourself to be very much involved in your dream state, begin to write. You will have to experiment with finding a way to keep from writing over what you have already written. One method of avoiding superimposing writing is to extend the little finger of the writing hand as a guide in finding the edge of the paper; this gives you some definition of where you are. You can either use it as guide on the top of the page or on the side of the page. As I have difficulty reading my own handwriting when I'm fully awake, this is not the best technique for me. I awaken to unintelligible scribbles that give me no clue whatsoever as to the night's drama. Nevertheless, some find this technique valuable, so I have included it for this reason. Later, you will need to transfer what you have written onto your two-sided notebook so that you can write your interpretation beside it.

This is how to set up your Dream Journal:

Dream 1

–Date
–Time
–Location

–Note Absolutely
everything that you
can remember, every
word or image. Write
the first thing that
comes into your head
even if it doesn't seem
like a dream.

–Note your feelings
while involved in this
dream.

–Record anything
you heard.

–Note colors, symbols,
key words, themes,
and emotions

Here is where you write
your interpretation of
the dream.

(See chapters on
"DREAM
INTERPRETATION
AND MEANING.")

This is an example of a Dream Journal entry:

Dream 1

—Date: December 7th
—Time: 4:20 am
—Location: Home

My car isn't working properly. I look under the hood and notice that the radiator is empty. I keep adding water and it keeps coming out of a hole in the bottom.

The feeling is of being frustrated.

Interpretation

The radiator is the cooling device of the car. If it's empty, then the car overheats. My car seems to symbolize my body or me. Also, water represents spirituality. I keep emptying spirituality out of myself. If I keep doing this, I will overheat and I won't be able to run or function. I feel that this dream is telling me to spend some time being still and attuning to my spiritual side. I think it also means drink more water. (I later found out that my steering fluid had leaked out during the night giving the dream a psychic aspect as well.)

Tape Recorder

The advantage of a tape recorder is that you can usually stay in a deeper brain level and thus stay more in touch with those vivid dream images than when you are writing your dream down. For those who have a hard time falling back to sleep after writing down a dream, a tape recorder is an excellent tool. It can enable you to record more detail in less time than if you are writing. A disadvantage to using a tape recorder is that you will later need to transcribe the dream if you are going to keep a running record of your dream progress. Another disadvantage is that often in the night it may seem that we are communicating clearly, but we can be dismayed to find in the morning that we are not able to understand our midnight ramblings. Very often your voice will sound as if you have come from another dimension and, in fact, you have. If you use the tape recorder method, you might consider getting the small hand-held type that is used for dictation. These are easier to use in the dark than the larger models.

Flashlight

A flashlight is necessary if you are recording in a journal. The small battery-operated lanterns (not hand-held) sold in camping supply shops seem to work the best. Using one of these will keep you from having to juggle the flashlight as you try to write.

Easily-Seen Clock

It is valuable to note the time of occurrence of your dreams so that you can begin to see patterns in your dreaming, especially if you are working with my Chinese Meridian Dream System.

To begin to record your dreams:

–Put your tape recorder or journal
next to your bed with flashlight and
pen and visible clock.

–Lie in a position that allows your
spine to be straight while you
program yourself for dream recall.

–Choose one of the "Before Sleep
Techniques"

–Sweet Dreams!!!

Before-Sleep Dream Recall Techniques

These are techniques done before you go to sleep to assist dream recall.

1. Tibetan Dream Meditation

As you lay down to go to sleep, <u>intently concentrate on your desire for dream recall</u>. Now focus that intention as if it were in the back of your throat. You might imagine a glowing blue sphere in the throat area and within that blue orb imagine putting your desire for dream recall. Hold that visualization until you fall asleep. Using this technique, you may find that your dream recall is greatly increased. It is interesting to note that this ancient Tibetan technique has an interesting physiological parallel. Research has shown that it is this very area in the back of the throat (the stem of the brain) which controls the activation during dream states.   Thus, by connecting with this potent area before sleep, we are beginning the stimulation of dream activity and dream recall.

2. Water Technique

Drink half of a full glass of water before retiring and as you are drinking this water, affirm to yourself, **"Tonight I remember my dreams."** Upon waking in the morning, if no dream recall is evident, drink the remaining half of the glass of water, saying to yourself, **"My dreams are recalled, now and through the day."** Very often drinking the second half of the glass of water stimulates dream recall. Sometimes that recall will occur spontaneously during the day.

3. Third Eye Technique

This is another technique using water for remembering your dreams. Put a bowl of water next to your bed. Right before sleep, dip two fingers into the water and lightly touch your throat. Then rub these two fingers on your forehead in the area of your third eye (the area between and slightly above your eyes). As you rub this area, affirm recalling your dreams. The next morning again touch these two areas with water. Very often this will stimulate recall.

4. Spiritual Assistance

Relax your body with your spine straight. Let your mind become still and receptive. Pray to God or ask your dream guide for assistance in remembering your dreams. (See chapter on "AMERICAN INDIANS.") Strongly affirm that you *will* remember your dreams and repeat this to yourself several times before falling asleep.

5. Creative Visualization

As you begin to fall asleep, visualize yourself waking up, looking at the clock, noting the time and intently writing down a dream. Then, continue this visualization forward in time until you are seeing yourself waking in the morning and writing down another dream. Visualize yourself looking and feeling very satisfied because you have successfully recorded your dreams.

6. Cherokee (Tsa La Gi) Indian Technique

This technique has several parts and is an excellent method to use to not only remember but to obtain a vision dream.

a. When you enter the area where you will sleep, smudge the area with sage, cedar, juniper or sweet grasses. Smudging means to offer or hold the smouldering herbs so that the smoke of the burning herbs goes toward each of the sacred directions - north, east, south and west, and to Mother Earth and Father Sky (below and above). Smudge around yourself for purification. This smoke ritual is an ancient method of dedication and purification. It was felt that there could be direct communion with Great Spirit through smoke. One's prayers would go up through the smoke and Great Spirit would send prayers down to the person through the smoke.

b. As you are in bed, review each action of the day moving backward to the time when you awoke in the morning. Then move forward in time from the morning of that day reviewing and correcting each situation. For example, if you judged someone, review the situation...but this time with understanding in your heart. See yourself speaking kindly with that person.

c. Say a prayer giving thanks for the goodness in each day and affirm your intention to live a balanced and compassionate life.

d. Imagine a double helix of upward spiraling energy spinning through you as you count backward from ten to one affirming you will remember your dreams. Your very last thoughts before sleep are the thoughts that very often will affect your dreams.

e. Give yourself some task in the dream such as looking at your hands or lifting your arms to the sky (life affirming) in the dream as a way to increase dream ability.

f. Give thanks in the morning for all that you have received.

After-Sleep Dream Recall Techniques

1. Rolling Technique - Research has shown that dreamers will usually roll over or change positions immediately after a dream. It is thought that this assists the brain to move into a different brain wave pattern. If you didn't recall your dreams, while you are still in bed roll into a new position and sometimes this will spontaneously generate dream images. It seems that perhaps the dream is coded into the position that you were in while you had it and a gentle rolling can initiate recall.

2. Conversation - Immediately after waking up share with someone about what you remember. Just beginning to talk about your dream will allow more of it to rise to your consciousness.

3. Writing - When you write your dream in your dream journal, just write whatever you remember even if it's only a word or a feeling. If you don't remember, then write the words, "I don't remember my dream" and very often this will stimulate dream recall. Or write down what your *feeling* is about not remembering and often this is a clue to memory.

4. Imaging - Imagine that it is the night before and you are getting ready for bed, brushing your teeth, lying down and going to sleep. Then allow yourself to just watch the images and feelings that occur...even use your imagination. (Where do you think imagination comes from anyway?)

5. Doodle Technique - If you didn't remember your dream, begin to doodle. Just begin simply doodling in your dream journal. Very often this triggers associations and sparks your memory.

6. Color technique - In this process, get a sense for what color your dream *felt* like and begin coloring or imaging that color to incite recall.

7. Gestalt - Put out two pillows. Sit on one and say to the other. "O.K., dreams, why aren't you coming into my memory?" Then move to the other pillow and answer. An example would be, "You are always in such a rush in the morning I never feel that I have the time to come forward." Move back and forth between each cushion as the dialogue continues. Notice the different voices and body positions for the two pillow positions. This exercise can be done in writing as well.

8. Mood savoring - So you didn't remember your dream? With your eyes still closed notice the mood you are in. Savor that mood like you would a fine wine. Indulge in that mood. Make it more. This often keys the mind into dream memory.

Dream Recall Hints

1. Write it down. No matter how sure you are that you will remember the dream, you most probably will not. Write it down.

2. Don't move. When you write in your dream journal, after a dream, try to move as little as possible. Dream research has shown that movement very often will impair recall. It has been found in dream laboratories when people roll over as they are awakened from a dream, they have a more difficult time remembering their dream. (Use the Rolling Technique only if there *isn't* any dream memory.)

3. Watch those flashes. Often a dream doesn't appear but we will have a vague feeling that a dream is just around the corner of our mind. It is as if it is delicately perched on the edge of our consciousness waiting for some familiar element in our waking life to stimulate recall. These images can be so fleeting that it takes being subtly conscious of the images that suddenly pop into our mind. Watch those images that flash into your mind during the day.

4. Beware of the fragment trap! Even if it's only a dream fragment, record it. It can be an important missing link for self-understanding.

5. Record each dream as it occurs. It is difficult to record all your dreams in the morning. Laboratory tests have shown that even if someone does remember all their dreams in the morning, they are less vivid and detailed than if they are recorded individually as they occur. Just imagine watching four or five movies over an eight-hour period and then trying to remember them all at one time. Your memory is more exact if you remember and record them as they occur.

6. Sleep for shorter periods but sleep two or three times a day. If you can change your sleeping patterns so that you have five hours of sleep at night and then one or two naps you will feel more refreshed because you are constantly refreshing yourself and you will recall your dreams much more easily.

7. Read and study as much as you can about dreams. Where intention goes energy flows, and as you increase your awareness in the area of dreams you will increase dream recall.

8. Name that dream! When writing in your dream journal give each of your dreams a descriptive title. These are good as reference guides when you review your dreams.

9. Wake up naturally. Train yourself to wake up before your alarm. Waking up to an alarm often alters the quality of your dream.

10. Hard case? If you are still not remembering your dreams, find a way to sleep more lightly. Drink a lot of water before bed so you'll have to get up during the night to go to the bathroom. Sleep in a chair. Any way that you can figure out to sleep lightly contributes to your dream recall.

11. Even nightmares! Write down all your dreams, even nightmares and dreams that you <u>don't</u> feel good about, not just the "good" dreams. We are not just "good." We are whole...a balance of light and dark, yin and yang "good" and "bad." We are total infinite beings. It is important to honor and accept all aspects of ourselves. Each dream is important. As you write your dream down remind yourself that this dream is <u>indeed</u> important.

12. Resist the urge! Resist wanting to explain away the dream by relating it to a late-night snack, a television show that you saw right before bed or a book that you were reading.

These events were just triggers for you to touch into a deeper part of your psyche. Fifty other people seeing that same television show would have fifty completely different dreams. Similarly, if you are awakened by a dog's bark and you dream that you are surrounded by raging wild dogs, someone else, under similar circumstances, might dream about his favorite childhood dog bounding toward him. Even though each dream can be explained by the dog barking, each dream nevertheless has important symbols for the individual dreamer.

13. Don't feel guilty if you didn't remember a dream. Guilt will only hinder your future progress. And if you do feel guilty, don't feel guilty about feeling guilty.

14. Meaning? You don't need to find out the meaning behind each and every dream. Often just reviewing a dream several times will greatly contribute to inner balancing. Love and enjoy your dreams, interpreted or not!

15. Fun!!!! You don't have to record all your dreams. If you don't feel like it...don't do it. Dream recall and recording should be fun!

The sun is shining warm flickers on the waves
I float above the beach, moving on a thought...
a sound draws me across the bridge...
I shut off the alarm!
Quick! Back across the bridge to...to...where?
I must have been dreaming...

DREAM AIDS

Potions, totems, nature's rhythms and cycles have been an integral part of the healing and visionary art of the shaman, kahuna, seer, magi, druid, medicine man and medicine woman. Throughout ancient lore and recorded history, there has always been reference to power objects used to facilitate the art of divination and inner knowing. These viable tools for inner exploration can also be used to assist in discovering more of your dream realm.

STONES

From the earliest time in the history of this planet, stones have been held in great esteem. The aboriginal people of the world, and mystical secret societies have passed on their unique use of stones to assist in understanding the unseen realms.

The stones that are discussed here are a few that may be used to assist dreaming. It's important to remember that of themselves these stones can do nothing. It is your intention that activates them for dream use.

Moonstone

The moonstone, with its moonlike, silvery-white light undulating on its surface, is sacred in India. It is thought to bring good fortune. It is used as a gift for lovers and is believed to arouse tender passion and give lovers the ability to see into the future.

In many cultures it is felt that this stone changes with the phases of the moon. As the cycles of the moon are connected to dream cycles, the moonstone connects us more deeply with our inner dream states.

Moonstone is also soothing to the emotions. It can enhance physical and emotional balance for women during their menses. As the cycles of the moon are very connected to dream cycles, the moonstone connects us more deeply with our inner dream states. Sleep with a moonstone near you or tape a small one on your third eye area. It is important to dedicate your moonstone to your dream life.

Selenite

This very translucent crystal is ruled by the moon. It is named for Selene, the Greek goddess of the moon. This very powerful stone is used to gain understanding of one's personal truth. It can allow for a deep calming and the attainment of profound inner states. It symbolizes pure spirit and can be used for spiritual advancement. A selenite is also an alchemic key to the past and the future.

Selenite is aligned to your crown chakra and is a powerful tool for developing intuition and telepathic powers through your dreams. Use it for stimulating dreams of mental and spiritual clarity. It also can be an excellent stone for telepathic communication during the night. It, too, should be dedicated, before sleep, to assist dream recall as well as to gain spiritual understanding through dreams.

Pearls

Not technically a stone, pearls are excellent to use in regard to dreams.

Pearls are ruled by the moon. They originate from the oyster, a living species found in the sea. Not only does the moon affect the tides and the creatures of the sea, she also greatly affects our dream states. The very formation of the pearl is conducive to dream states. The layers are deposited in a concentric manner. The spherical shape, the soft luminescent color and the multi-layers are all symbolic of the nonlinear nature of dreams. The concentric fashion in which they weave through our consciousness symbolizes the dream state. Pearls come from the sea and, even upon land, maintain their connection to the fluidity, the ebbing and flowing, and the intuitive nature of water and the sea.

Pearls from the ocean are more potent for dreams than are freshwater pearls because salt water is a better conductor of electrical energy. The fact that saltwater pearls originate in the ocean means they are eternally connected with the sea. That alignment allows for a better intuitive connection with your bio-electrical flows. The greater the bio-electrical flow in your body, the more intense and vivid your dreams will be. Having pearls in your dream space will assist in experiencing dreams that are intuitive in nature.

Crystals

Crystals have been used since the beginning of time as objects of wonder and as a means of understanding and viewing unseen worlds. Their mystique spans time and culture alike.

The scepter of the Scottish Regalia is topped by a crystal globe. Sir Walter Scott said that among the Scottish Highlanders, crystals were called "Stones of Power." There are references to the power of crystals in Greek and Roman writings. Ancient Egyptians in the XII Dynasty used crystals for viewing inner dimensions. Shamans in Australia, New Guinea, Africa and the Mayan area were all shown to have used these amazing stones. In ancient Japan and China, rock crystals were thought to be the congealed breath of dragons. Since the dragon was emblematic of the highest powers of creation, this indicates the high esteem placed on the crystal by the Orientals. Almost every major culture with an esoteric understanding has used quartz crystals for "seeing."

American Indians were especially adept in their use of crystals for power dreams. Apache medicine men and medicine women used crystal for inducing visions and in finding lost property. Cherokee shamans used crystals for vision quests, healing and inner "seeing." They would sit with their crystal friend, burn cedar and offer prayers in a dedication asking for a dream or vision to guide them.

Many metaphysicians believe that crystals were also used for dream work in the ancient continent of Atlantis and that through the use of crystals, a person could travel through time and space during his dreams.

Crystals are basically magnifiers and transmitters. They are used in radios. In fact, silicon, which is in the crystal family, is the basis of computer technology. It allows for the processing of enormous amounts of information by transmitting electrical current over its crystalline structure. As there is a bio-electrical current within human beings, we can literally avail ourselves of the power of crystals to "transmit" or enhance dream states by transmitting our intention through its crystalline structure.

To utilize crystal for expanding your dream states :

1. The right crystal - Obtain a rock crystal that "speaks" to you. This means you intuitively know that this crystal is for you and your dreams. It is preferable to have a crystal that is used just for dreaming and nothing else.

2. Cleansing - The best way to cleanse a crystal dedicated to dreams is to leave the crystal outdoors on a clear night when there is a full moon. Place the stone so that the moonlight may shine directly on it all night. If that is not possible, you can:

    a. Rub your crystal with eucalyptus oil.
    b. Let your crystal soak in water and sea salt.
    c. Place your crystal outdoors in sunlight for at least five hours.
    d. Place in the ocean or a running clear stream for an hour.

3. Dedicating the crystal - To dedicate your crystal, hold it up to your third eye and say a dedication, either quietly or aloud. Program your crystal for only one thing at a time. Some sample dedications are:

"I dedicate you, Dream Crystal, to dreams that allow my spirit to soar so that my waking life is more joyous."

"I dedicate you, Dream Crystal, to dreams that will empower me with a positive vision of myself and a strong belief in my own self-worth."

"I dedicate you, Dream Crystal, to dreams that will enable me to develop my own unique creative skills"

"I dedicate you, Dream Crystal, to dreams that will allow my relationships to heal."

"I dedicate you, Dream Crystal, to dreams that will give me powerful insights into my future."

"I dedicate you, Dream Crystal, to dreams that will assist in the healing of myself and others."

"I dedicate you, Dream Crystal, to dreams that will deepen my connection with Spirit and God."

It is not necessary to dedicate it again. However, if you are going to change the programming, cleanse and re-dedicate it.

4. Dream Door - Put your Dream Crystal in a special place when you are not using it. You can put it in black silk to hold the energy or you can place it in a special location where you can admire it during the day.

At night, place it near your sleeping area. Just before sleep, hold the crystal to your third eye and imagine that your consciousness is melting into its fluid light structure. Imagine that within this shimmering orb of moon-satin light is a Mystical Door to your dreams. See that door opening. Know that you have opened the mysterious door to your inner realms. Then keep your crystal near you during the night.

Amethyst

Amethyst is also in the crystal family. Its rich purple reflects the ability to move easily from one reality to another. The color associated with the third eye is purple and this magical stone can be used to open the third eye area to gain spiritual dreams. It is a calming and emotionally balancing stone. As it calms the mind and emotions, our innermost nature can come forth in our dreams.

It is also excellent for people who have recurring nightmares. To use it for this purpose, place your amethyst on your forehead, in the area of your third eye, and program it for a deep and calm sleep. It is also an excellent stone to place under your pillow for "sweet dreams."

Dream Pillows

Whether or not there is some special ingredient within herbs that facilitates dreams, or whether it is a behavioral response connecting your dream desire and the aroma that is a constant reminder during the night remains unknown. In aromatherapy, inhaling the scent of the herb mugwort is thought to open the third eye (the door to dreams). Smelling it while sleeping is not only thought to assist you in remembering your dreams, but to reveal dreams of the future. When you sleep with a pillow filled with mugwort, a connection is established between the fragrance of the herbs and your desire for a special dream. What is important is that using a dream pillow really works.

Other herbs that can be used in dream pillows are borage and yarrow.

The best way to prepare a dream pillow is to:

1. Make sure that the herbs are of the highest quality and optimally pesticide-free.

2. Use a natural fiber when making the pillowcase. The very best fabric to use is silk as this is an excellent conductor of bio-electrical energy.

Wool is also excellent. Many meditators and yogis meditate on wool or sheepskin because this helps them align with the bio-electrical energy flows of the planet. Using wool or silk for your dream pillow will allow you to experience dreams that are more potent because you will be more bio-electrically balanced.

I suggest using lavender or purple-colored material because these are the colors of the portal to dreams and they will contribute to the power of your dream pillow.

3. Use your dream pillow only at night for dreams so that is the only thing you associate with it. You might keep it in a special box or covering and only take it out at night for dreaming. The fragrance will then be an intimate reminder of the alignment between you and your dreams.

4. Hold the pillow close to your nose as you drift off to sleep. Keep uppermost in your thoughts the desire for a dream. In the morning, deeply inhale the fragrance of your dream pillow. Very often this will revive the memory of a dream.

The Chinese Clock

Chinese, Japanese and Indian cultures have all traditionally thought of time as a nonlinear, circular process (as opposed to the Western concept of linear time). In Chinese medicine, the day is divided into hours assigned to different organs.

Gall bladder time is between 11:00 p.m. and 1:00 a.m. It is interesting to note that two of the most potent dream herbs, mugwort and yarrow, are also valuable herbs used to stimulate bile production from the gall bladder. It is not a coincidence that the same herbs used to induce dreams are also gall bladder herbs. Most individual have their first dream of the night within gall bladder time (11 p.m.- 1 a.m.). In addition to the innate dream-inducing qualities of these herbs, inhaling their aromas or drinking these herbs in a tea, stimulates the governing organ (gall bladder) which allows your body to move into alignment with the natural rhythms of the universe. When your body is in alignment with the natural cadence of the universe, you will have more powerful dreams.

If you are falling asleep during the gall bladder meridian time, just before going to bed rub your fingers on your temple area above your ears as a way to further stimulate your gall bladder meridian.

Notice what hour you go to sleep, then enhance your dream states by stimulating the corresponding meridian points before sleep.

Fall asleep.................................... **Stimulate**...............................
9:00 -11:00 p.m............................ Rub behind your ears.
Triple Warmer

11:00 p.m.- 1:00 a.m.....................Rub above your ears.
Gall Bladder

1:00 - 3:00 a.m............................. Rub the area over the liver.
Liver

3:00 - 5:00 a.m............................. Rub indention between upper
Lungs   ribs and shoulder.

5:00 - 7:00 a.m. ....Rub fleshy part between
Large Intestine   forefinger and thumb.

7:00 - 9:00 a.m. ....Tap lightly under the eyes.
Stomach

9:00 - 11:00 a.m. .... Circular pressure over spleen
Spleen

11:00 a.m. - 1:00 p.m. .... Rub the arm pit area.
Heart

1:00 - 3:00 p.m............................ Deep pressure around
Small Intestine   outside base of little fingers.

3:00 - 5:00 p.m............................ Rub the area where the
Bladder   eyeglasses rest on the nose.

5:00 - 7:00.p.m............................. Rub the center of the sole
Kidneys   behind the ball of the big toe.

7:00 - 9:00.p.m............................. Massage middle fingers.
Circulation/Sex

For more information about how to understand dreams utilizing the Chinese Clock Method, see the chapter on "CHINESE CLOCK."

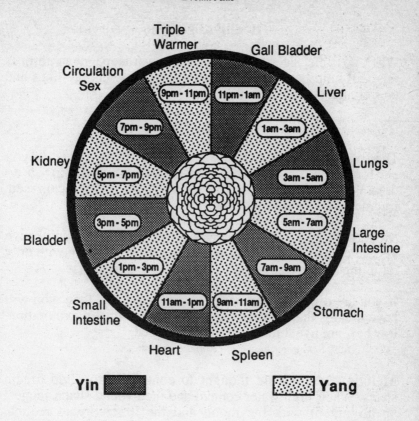

Triple Warmer

Gall Bladder

Circulation Sex

Liver

9pm - 11pm

11pm - 1am

7pm - 9pm

1am - 3am

Kidney

Lungs

5pm - 7pm

3am - 5am

3pm - 5pm

5am - 7am

Bladder

Large Intestine

1pm - 3pm

7am - 9am

11am - 1pm

9am - 11am

Small Intestine

Stomach

Heart

Spleen

Yin

Yang

Bodily Alignment

When possible, sleep with your head towards magnetic north as this will help better align your bio-electrical energy lines and thus contribute to better dream states.

Food and Drink

The foods you eat can greatly affect your dream states. If you eat foods you have trouble digesting, this will contribute to dreams that are "hard to digest." These dreams can seem fragmented, and will not flow.

Modern research has shown that pressure in the digestive system creates restlessness and causes us to wake up with only rambling dream fragments.

If you are digesting and assimilating your food, then you will have dreams that you can "assimilate." For dream exploration, it is best not to eat immediately before bed.

Melons - Melons are thought to contribute to vivid dream states. Their high water content and their round shape suggest an alignment with the moon and the inner dream realms. Perhaps melons contribute to dreams because they act as diuretics causing you to sleep lightly thus remembering your dreams more easily. Perhaps, however there is an inherent quality within melons that contributes to dream recall. Nevertheless, melons seem to assist some individuals in recalling dreams. For digestive purposes, eat the melons separately from other foods. "Eat them alone or leave them alone," is the current maxim.

Vitamin B6 - Taking a dosage of vitamin B6 shortly before bed not only can contribute to a restful night's sleep, it often will contribute to dream recall.

Alcohol and drugs - Alcohol and most drugs repress dreams. The person who regularly goes to bed intoxicated robs himself of restful sleep as well as of dreams. The ancient Greeks, masters of the art of interpreting dreams, declared that anyone entering a Dream Temple needed to abstain from alcohol for three days prior to entering. They felt that clear dreams were difficult to obtain if someone were heavily under the influence of alcohol.

Moon Water - Drink water that you have left outside in the moonlight. Be sure that the moonlight shines directly onto the water, not on it through the glass. Drink this moon water just before sleeping to contribute to dreaming.

Dreams conceived in the womb of our knowingness,
sensed first as a heartbeat deep within,
then a vague suggestion of movement grows
evermore prominent until it is fully born.

M. Anne Sweet

DREAM INCUBATION

The mother crane cautiously peers out though the rushes as the cold Canadian winds whip at the lake creating angry uneven waves. Beneath her lie three perfectly-formed eggs, warm and snug as their mother protects them from the ferocity of the elements. Sunbeams slant through a dark cloud, a chilling rain falls...and the eggs are safe. The evening darkens. The moon's reflection in the water is broken and broken again and still it is there. Through the long dark night the eggs incubate. The faint sky of dawn accents the sounds of water dripping down the marshy reeds. Beneath the mother crane...three feeble yet jubilant young birds.

Just as the mother crane incubates her eggs to allow them to come to birth, you can incubate your dreams. You can direct your dreams by consciously intending to do so, bringing to birth the seed that was planted. Actually, this idea is commonly accepted. We tell someone who is "stuck" in a problem to "sleep on it." Then, in the morning, as if by miracle, there is the answer that was needed.

Dream incubation is the concept that one can consciously guide the course of his dreams from the waking state. For example, a problem presented during waking hours can be resolved during sleeping hours, simply by making a conscious choice to do so.

Perhaps you are in a dilemma with one of your children. You might suggest, "Dreams, give me information that will help me resolve the difficulty I am having with my son." Or, "Dreams, what would be a valuable career move for me?" Or, "I need information with regard to my weight. Why am I having difficulty losing weight, and what can I do to assist myself in this situation?" Or, "Dreams, I have not been feeling well lately. Is there any specific nutritional guidance which will facilitate me in creating good health?" Each of these is an example of dream incubation. You can even inquire about dreams experienced the previous night with regard to specific understanding. "Dreams, why were there kangaroos in my dream last night? What was the meaning of that dream?"

You have perhaps heard the expression "sleep on it" in connection with problem solving. Sometimes, seemingly putting the problem in the background and getting a good night's sleep can lead to a solution or a resolution through a dream. Developing this communication with your dreams can give you answers to many questions in your life.

Almost everyone who studies dreams concurs that they allow us to get in touch with hidden parts of ourselves, tapping wisdom far greater than anything we are aware of on the plane of normal consciousness. Dream experts differ, however, on the meaning of the information that comes forth. Some believe it is from a source external to ourselves such as our guides and or God. Some are convinced it is our higher self. Other dream experts feel it is simply a segment of our own psychological makeup which we are not in touch with during normal consciousness. Nevertheless, through incubating dreams, it has been proven repeatedly that one can receive information that will assist during the waking state.

It is the goal of us, the dream makers, to translate these non-physical, non-material expressions into images that make sense in our three-dimensional, linear consciousness. The goal in dream incubating is to be able to create a dream that makes as much sense as possible, that is very clear and understandable. Hence, a dream that demonstrates the value of dream incubation.

One can also incubate dreams for the purpose of testing possible future probabilities. By imagining possible conclusions, one can examine future actions as well as compute the outcomes. This enables one to experience an outcome without actually taking an idea to its completion in waking life.

When you incubate for dreams, it is often likely that you will experience profound emotions in the dream state and in waking life. Enjoy your emotions as you would enjoy a symphony. Be willing to experience the full gamut of your emotions. Allow your feelings to ride the waves of the high and low periods that present themselves to you. Breathe in the excitement when listening to the crescendo and decrescendo of your own majestic symphony. Enjoy the anger, caress the sadness, experience the boredom, celebrate each nuance and variation as they occur. Enjoy all aspects of your dreams, including the humiliation, the fear, and the anger. Each is an integral thread in the weaving of life.

One can even incubate dreams simply for the enjoyment of it just as you would experience a first-run movie, a video or a favorite television show. Incubate dreams just for the fun of it! They do not always need to be scrutinized for the significant meaning in your life.

If there is some area of your life experience that you would like to explore, or if, perhaps, you desire a psychic perception in regard to yourself then dream incubating might be valuable. Here are some simple guidelines:

1. Choose a time when you are not too tired. Make certain you will have plenty of time in the morning to process the information given during the night. Choose a time when you have had no drugs or alcohol.

2. If there is an issue that you want to incubate first begin to contemplate the specific issue. Consider the solutions already presented, get in touch with the feelings and emotions you have concerning this issue. Weigh what you may need to release if that issue were resolved. Ask yourself, "Am I willing to have this resolved?" "Am I willing to let go of this difficulty?" Consider how different life may be if that problem were solved. Once you have evaluated the issue from the perspective of your emotions, your thoughts, your attitudes, perhaps even body sensations, ask your dream guide one or more of the following questions. (See chapter on "DREAM GUIDE.") "Dear Dream Guide, help me understand the difficulty that I am having with this individual. Show me a solution for this particular difficulty." Or, "Help me understand why I am afraid of speaking in front of crowds, and what should I do to resolve this difficulty?" Or, "Dream Guide, give me an idea for a magazine article."

3. Place your journal or your tape recorder beside your bed. (See the chapter on " DREAM RECALL.") Make sure your spine is straight. As you fall into a deep sleep, repeat your request several times - "Help me understand my fear of the dark, etc." As you are falling asleep, imagine that you are releasing all the thoughts, attitudes and feelings you have had regarding that issue. Simply concentrate on your question, repeating it over and over to yourself. If you notice any distracting thoughts, simply allow them to filter in and out of your awareness, always returning to your question. "Dreams, help me understand my fear of flying. Tonight, I release my fear of flying." Hold these thoughts in your mind until you drift off to sleep.

4. And now, simply fall asleep. Incubated dreams usually occur the very same night you have requested them. Occasionally, they will occur the following night. Trust any information that is revealed whether or not it appears to make sense at the time. Write any and all items received immediately upon waking. Be patient in waiting for the understanding. Frequently it is not until the following day or even the next week when you are able to make any association

between that dream and the issue from which it was incubated. Nevertheless, there is within that dream, the answer to the problem or the dilemma you are facing. Any incubation efforts which you perceived as failures often, in fact, prove to be quite valuable. Go ahead... give your Dream Guide the benefit of the doubt! Trust that there is a higher part of yourself that has already solved this dilemma.

Dream incubation is often a valuable tool in releasing difficulties with regard to relationships. For example, Alice was given a horse by her father, and the horse somehow seemed symbolic to her. Consequently, she incubated a dream that would assist her in understanding what the horse represented. The dream revealed a past lifetime Alice had with her present-day father. (See chapter on "PAST LIFE RECALL.") In this past life he had left her, and had done so riding away on a horse. Alice realized that the horse symbolized painful abandonment for her. Alice shared that as a result of this one dream, she was able to release a great deal of anger directed at her father. This opened the door for her to create what is now a deep and more loving relationship with her father.

Incubation can also be used to receive information not previously known to you. One example of this was when I was preparing to teach a course regarding manifestation. It was a new course I was adding to my seminar curriculum. I had been incredibly busy the week before and had been unable to spend much time preparing for the workshop. Early one morning the entire seminar appeared before me in a dream and while it was still in my conscious thought, I leaped out of bed and frantically wrote down all the details of the seminar. The information given was so extensive that we were unable to cover all of it during the day-long seminar.

The idea of dream incubation originated in ancient Greece. Research indicates that there were 300 to 400 temples built in honor of the god Asclepius. These temples were in active use for nearly 1000 years, beginning at the end of the sixth century B.C. and culminating with the end of the fifth century A.D.

Dreamers would go to a sacred place, the dream temple, to sleep for the purpose of receiving a useful dream from a god. There was the belief that by sleeping in holy places and appealing to a god, they could obtain profound answers to their inner questions. To participate in modern day dream incubation, it is not necessary to sleep in a sacred place nor appeal to a specific god. However, I do find that if I honor my place of sleep as an inner temple, and if I appeal to Spirit, this assists me in both the vivid clarity and the contents of my dream incubation. If possible, locate a beautiful place in nature as was done in ancient times and create a sacred sleeping chamber. You might also consider creating a moon ritual. (See chapter on the "MOON.") After selecting your own form of ritual and purification, call upon the Great Spirit, God or your Dream Guide to lead you through the night hours asking for the dream you desire. Ancient Indians, Chinese, Japanese, Egyptians, Hebrews, and Moslems all practiced dream incubation in places of rare beauty found in nature.

With regard to dream incubation, anticipate having all your dream expectations met. In ancient times the dreamer would participate in purification rites, sacrifices, rituals and ceremonies. However, the same effect can be produced if you have a clear intention when you incubate your dream. The manner in which you phrase your dream incubation statement is very important. Instead of, "I hope that tonight I understand why my relationship with my aunt is going through difficulty," say, "Tonight, I understand my relationship with my aunt." Your dreams will respond in clarity proportionately to your intention.

A narrow pathway, cut like a river gorge,
the path as clear and shining as the river,
winds and turns on its course between the
rocky terrain of waking and the
soft pastures of sleep.

M. Anne Sweet

LUCID DREAMING

Have you ever been dreaming and then suddenly become conscious that you were, in fact, dreaming? In lucid dreaming, the dreamer is aware that he or she is dreaming during the dream.

You have probably experienced some degree of lucidity. Perhaps you have been involved in a frightening dream only to find yourself thinking, "Hey, I'm OK, this is only a dream!" When the dreamer realizes that some segment of the dream is only a dream, it is called "prelucid dreaming." A fully lucid dream is one in which the dreamer definitely recognizes that he is dreaming. These dreams tend to seem more real and more vivid than normal waking reality. Also, the sense of sound, sight, taste and smell seems intensified.

Though lucid dreaming has received much attention from the metaphysical community in recent years, it is not a new idea by any means. In Eastern cultures, lucid dreaming has always been an esoteric element of the spiritual practices of Taoism, Buddhism, and Hinduism.

The Tibetan Buddhists have expanded the practice of lucid dreaming into an art form. Tibetan Buddhists believe that dreaming is a way to connect more deeply with one's soul. They feel that each time we dream, we are experiencing the condition of our soul essence. If we die while dreaming, the dream will only continue. The ancient text, *The Tibetan Book of the Dead,* gives instructions on how to pass through the different dream dimensions that occur after death. These dimensions are called Bardo states. If you are unable to maneuver your way through the Bardo states, you are forced to reincarnate into another life. However, if you **are** able to successfully weave through these dream states, you most surely return to God and total oneness. Obviously, then, lucid dreaming to a Tibetan Buddist is of utmost importance. It is considered a means to release oneself from what they consider "a world of suffering." Tarthang Tulku, a modern-day Tibetan teacher, states, "Dreams are a reservoir of knowledge and experience, yet they are often overlooked as a vehicle for exploring reality."

The value of lucid dreaming is enormous. When individuals begin to have the experience of lucid dreaming, the truth of who they really are and their personal reality expands. They begin to feel more expansive, as one does when taking in a lovely, deep breath of air, and this feeling begins to affect other aspects in their life. Personal limitations begin to dissolve and there is a sense of being more in control of personal destiny. Intuition and imagination during waking hours are noticeably increased.

One of the goals of lucid dreaming is to transport your waking consciousness into your dreams and your dreaming consciousness back into your waking life without feeling a break. The purpose for this continuity in consciousness is that it allows the dreamer to recognize that the world of the waking self is a self-created dream as well. If you are working with lucid dreaming, an excellent affirmation to keep in mind is, **"All that I see I can dream. All that I dream I can see, and I am aware of all of my dreams."**

Lucid dreaming can be regarded as a spiritual evolutionary process, a step toward remembering who you are and what your true destiny is. An Arabic mystic said, "A person must control his thoughts in ? dream. The training of this alertness...will produce great benefits for the individual. Everyone should apply himself to the attainment of this ability."

Cultivate the skill of lucid dreaming much as you would any other ability. Just as the ability to type, swim or paint can be developed and fine-tuned with practice, so can the ability to lucid dream. It takes a certain amount of discipline at first, but it becomes easier, and in time, even effortless.

1. Lucid Dreaming Techniques: As you are going to sleep, say, "Tonight I am aware and conscious that I am dreaming." Use the techniques in the chapter on "DREAM RECALL" to recall your dreams, and as you remember a dream during the night, while you are drifting back to sleep, say, "During my next dream, I remember that I am dreaming." Sometimes repeating the phrase, "I am dreaming,...I am dreaming,...I am dreaming," as you fall asleep will contribute to having lucid dreams. Having made a conscious choice to experience lucid dreams, be vigilant and consistent and, over a period of weeks, it will begin to happen for you.

2. Applications: Once you are adept in recognizing that you are dreaming while in that state, begin to alter the circumstances of your dream. Deliberately choose some action you can take. Start with something simple. The Mexican mystic, Don Juan, told Carlos Castaneda to try to look at his hands while he was dreaming. Other simple dream actions could be picking a flower or opening your arms to the heavens in delight or hugging a tree. Become the hero or heroine of your dreams. You don't necessarily need to force your visualization, but simply be in your dream with awareness.

Stanford University psychologist, Stephen LaBerge, a proponent of lucid dreaming, has developed sensors which detect the eye movements that accompany vivid dreams. A pulsing red light is activated to be used as a signal to remind the dreamer that he is actually dreaming. Though mainstream sleep and dream researchers may be skeptical of this controversial technique, it demonstrates once again the interest being generated for a deeper understanding of our dreaming selves.

*I close my eyes and walk down the gentle rolling hill
into the valley of my inner universe, a quiet place
for daylight dreaming, a crystal ball through which
I can watch myself move, ask questions, receive answers.*

M. Anne Sweet

DREAM GAZING

"Dream gazing" is similar to daydreaming with an added dimension...it is daydreaming with discipline. It is one way to access the mystical world of dreams through your waking consciousness. As you glide deeper into the inner realm, the world of dreams begins to blend subtly with the world of daily living. Just as it is possible to alter your waking life through your dreams during the night hours, one can also use daytime dream gazing techniques in your waking hours as a means of facilitating your waking life.

Richard Bach was interviewed as to how he came to write the magical book, *Jonathan Livingston Seagull,* Bach stated, "I saw a very brilliant visual kind of dream while awake. I vividly saw a little seagull flying alone at sunrise, very much like the first major photograph in the book. And I didn't have to ask what his motivations were. Why he was doing what he was doing. All in a split second, I knew. It was like a great block of knowing we have in dreams sometimes -- you just know.... So, I grabbed the nearest thing, a green ball point pen and some old scratch paper and I wrote. My wrist got tired trying to keep up with it. It was like a motion picture.... We all hear voices and see visions but it happens at night and usually we forget about them when we wake up and we call them dreams ...."

Bach was referring to the ability to dream while you are awake, which I call "Awake Dreaming" or "Dream Gazing." To dream gaze, first allow yourself to become very relaxed. Suspend your normal thoughts. Letting them go frees your mind and body alike to release all tension. Then simply imagine a dream. Create any dream you like, allowing it to be as unpredictable as one that would occur during sleep.

Start simply with perhaps a very short, one-minute dream. Then, write down exactly what the dream contained. This is especially valuable if you have not been recalling your nightly dreams. You can become familiar with the world of dreams through dreaming during the daytime hours.

Another advantage of dream gazing facilitates dealing with a difficult waking scenario. You can create or imagine a dream simply by suggesting, "In regard to the situation or difficulty, I am now going to create a dream." Allow your mind to wander freely while you create this dream. Carefully notice the symbols and feelings that begin to well up. This will begin to assist you in resolving your burdensome issues. (See chapters found in section on "DREAM MEANING.")

For example, let us hypothesize that your elbow is giving you a great deal of pain because of an injury or illness. Consequently, you imagine a dream where you are scrambling through a jungle. You are terrified because a huge black panther is right behind you in swift pursuit. You leap toward the safety of the dense underbrush and when you look up, you are looking into the golden eyes of the panther! Without a second's warning, the panther jumps, grabbing your elbow in its jagged teeth! You hear the fragile bone snap in two! There is excruciating pain. You are aware of an overwhelming sense of dread and abandonment filling your entire being. You realize you are totally alone with no one to help you. There is no one to whom you can call for help. No one.

To look at this waking dream, write down the details and look at the different aspects of it. First, you are in the jungle. The jungle may represent your primitive nature, your primordial self. The panther is chasing you. What does the panther represent? Perhaps it symbolizes the unconscious, the dark side of yourself or shadow. There is a fear of encountering your shadow, the primordial reflection of yourself. As the panther rips into your elbow, your elbow is feeling immobilized. You also sense being unable to move. Perhaps your "awake dream" represents the fear of the primordial part of yourself which is preventing you from moving forward in life. Perhaps you are feeling restricted in life because of that fear. As you are nursing your elbow, you are filled with an awful sense of aloneness because no one is coming to your rescue. By beginning to understand the underlying causes of your awake dream, you may often begin to feel relief of the problem.

In exploring your "awake dream" more closely and in understanding the symbology, perhaps you discover that the fear in the dream represents your apprehension in moving out into areas that are unknown to you. Then, as you begin to affirm and strengthen your belief in yourself, i.e. repeating to yourself something like "I am able to move into the unknown easily and effortlessly," you may find that your elbow has greater movement and freedom.

Dream gazing is the most powerful and useful dream technique that I personally use. It enables me to move to the very heart of any difficulty and immediately facilitates an expedient resolution.

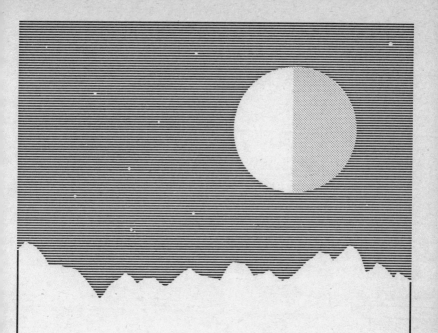

DREAM WORKERS

Apprentices of subtle craft,
we have gathered much in the following
of this age-worn path;
journeymen to the Loom Masters,
we spin the tapestry,
pictorial odyssey,
crystallized visions,
loving designs of the heart.

M. Anne Sweet

Dream window, throw open the shutters to the sunrise,
a view of the distant road to be traveled, an event
far, far away; but something tells me I must
start closer to home, the garden waits to be tended.

M. Anne Sweet

DREAMS FOR "SEEING"

I raced down the beach, pebbled stones cut at my feet, tears stung my face as the wind whipped at my clothes. A distant thunder storm marked the sky with jagged scars across weeping clouds. Finally, I fell to the ground, sobs of anguish and anger wrenched my entire being. As if to lessen the turmoil, I clutched at a cold, sharp rock, tightening my squeeze until its surface edge carved into my hand. With every heaving breath, I wanted to die. Betrayed...I had been betrayed. If only death would take me on its solemn black wings.

I cried until until tears dried up within me. Empty, and vacant, I got up and walked home. As I lay in bed, a dense fog of utter loneliness suffocated my entire being. I had never felt so alone. Gradually the gripping tension lessoned, and I reluctantly drifted off into a restless sleep.

Hazy, dark shadows slipped in and out of my dreams...homeless spectres aimlessly wandering...forever in the chasm of the night. In the distance, I could see a brilliant light. As I was drawn to its soothing glow, shrouded formless beings tugged at my arms. Wrenching away from their bony grasp, I glided gently to the light., its beacon a welcome relief to my hollow heart. Face or form eludes memory, but my awareness still retains a feeling...and a voice. "You are to weep no more. You have passed the second barrier and you will never need to return this way again. I am with you...I am with you...I am with you." The sound of the voice echoed within me, resounding with strength and power as it gathered energy much like that of an approaching storm.

Slowly the image faded, and I fell into a deep, sweet sleep. I awakened feeling so refreshed. The night's storm had cleared the sky and golden sunlight filtered softly through my bedroom window. I stretched and reached to touch the light...caressing its liquid warmth on my fingers. I felt so new. Something had lifted during the night. My fear had melted and there was an awareness of the beginning of a new day. Something mystical had occurred during the midnight hours. Someone, somehow had come and soothed my aching soul. At a crossroads in my life a visitor, vaguely familiar to me, had pointed the way...and that made all the difference.

Most individuals can recount at least one dream which provided them with a new understanding of life or that helped them during an especially crucial period. These dreams appear to reach beyond the ordinary boundaries set by most dream analysts. They are monoliths speaking of an ancient wisdom and a deeper magic. These were the prophetic or visionary dreams of old. They originate from the well-spring deep within us where God resides. These are dreams not necessarily ordered or commanded, but rather reaching out to us in times of need. They lend assurance and guidance through the "dark night of the soul." The prerequisite in tracing the thread which leads one to vision and prophesy is an open heart, the willingness to ask...and to listen.

Visionary dreams are different in character than precognitive dreams. A precognitive dream allows you to glimpse into the future. Dream researchers state that forewarning dreams are fairly common. Even Freud reported cases of precognitive dreams. One thoroughly documented case of a precognitive dream is the story of Clinton H. Elliott.

Back in the mid-50s, Elliott dreamed that his sister would die in a matter of six weeks which, in fact, she did. This wasn't particularly amazing except for the fact that it added credence to his claim that he dreamed he also would die soon. When he received this message, he informed his family and friends and began to put his affairs in order. He calmly made plans for his family's future with his absence in mind. He even told his wife the kind of funeral he desired. At 66, death was easily a possibility, except that he was remarkably healthy. He spoke of his coming death to his friends, including those with whom he worked. He was employed in the construction of the tunnel being built under Boston Harbor. One could guess that his belief in his impending death might contribute to a slow, dwindling death; however, this was not the case. Elliott died by accident...and it was a very strange accident. He was at his worksite discussing his future death with the other workers, who, needless to say, were a bit skeptical. As Elliott went off his shift, an enormous crane that had been checked thoroughly by the safety inspectors less than an hour before, suddenly jerked and collapsed, pinning Elliott beneath the twisted steel, killing him immediately. It was a totally unpredictable accident to everyone except Elliott. He had dream-predicted his own death.

Though almost all death dreams indicate psychological release or death of old beliefs rather than actual physical death, in this case Elliott <u>was</u> able to see into the future through his dreams. Dreams laden with prophetic import may often lead to historical consequences. The Duke of Wellington was inspired to restore the Alhambra in Spain as a result of a dream in which he saw this beautiful Moorish Palace disintegrating. The American President Roosevelt declared that Washington D.C. needed a new airport because he had had a disturbing dream that foretold of an accident due to the disrepair of the existing airport. Cornelia, the wife of Caesar, received a premonition dream of her husband's death and tried to forestall his attending the fatal meeting of the Roman Senate.

Often our personal guides will give us information in our dreams. However there are also Disseminating Guides who, rather than work with only one individual, serve a purpose similar to broadcasting units in the sky. When an idea whose time has come emerges, these guides begin broadcasting that information. Individuals that have their psychic antenna tuned to that station will receive the information. This is exactly why inventions or discoveries will occur at the same time, in several unrelated parts of the world, often within days of one other. When someone is sleeping he is less mentally defensive so he is more receptive to the information that is being broad-spectrum broadcast from the psychic realms. Hence, many discoveries have been made by chance during sleep.

Often dreams are a means for those who have died to communicate with us. It seems easier for us to hear them through the vehicle of our dreams. It is usually more for our sake than for theirs. There is usually something that we are have not completed in regard to this individual or perhaps something that we didn't communicate to that person that has been a stumbling block for us in our life. The visitation will often clear up those blocks. There are occasions, however, when there is some message or warning that these loved ones feel that we need to hear. Keep in mind, however, that just because someone has died, it does not necessarily imply that he has grown in wisdom. If someone is as thick as two planks nailed together when he is alive, he possibly will continue to be as thick as two planks when dead. So even if it is a true visitation from someone you know that has passed, remember to weigh the advice that is given against your own good judgement.

If you need to resolve an issue with someone who has died or feel the need for his comfort or solace, "call" him just before drifting off to sleep. The way to do this is to feel that you are touching his essence. Allow yourself to experience the connection you had with him while he was still alive. As you are going to bed hold his essence close, and ask for him to come to you during the night. It can be a way to ease the loneliness when someone has gone.

Some individuals have remarkable success with alien encounters during their sleep. As the vibrational intensity of the planet increases, the number of UFO sightings will dramatically increase. Even now many best-selling books and top-grossing movies concern the topic of aliens. Either we are more receptive to their tentative venturing, or they are becoming far more persistent. Nevertheless the UFO phenomenon is here to stay. It will become increasingly prevalent in our lives and will begin to play a more significant role in our dreams. For the most part these are benevolent beings that offer valuable advice and guidance. Remember, simply because someone is from another planet does not mean that it knows what is best for you. It might come with lovely lofty messages but always make sure that, first and foremost, you follow your own inner guidance.

There are some very specific methods that you can use to increase your ability to have psychic dreams. The first step is to incubate for your dreams. (See chapter on "INCUBATION.") In other words decide what area of the psychic realm that you want to explore, and then program yourself before bed. You can incubate for alien communication or even for a visit to another "dimension." Other dimensions are co-existing universes that we can gain access to just by slightly tuning the dial of our reality radio. (An interesting aspect of dimensional travel is the similarity of reports among those journeying to these other dimensions within their dream states. I've discovered that even people who live in different countries will consistently describe similar dimensional experiences.) You can also incubate for past life exploration, astral travel, or to enter the realm of fairies, sylphs, gnomes, and angels.

Whether or not these are "real" or the figments of a collective mythological consciousness is irrelevant.

The value comes from the experiences that are obtained during the night. The test is:

1. Are the messages gained during the night valuable?
2. Do they contribute to your waking life?
3. Do they <u>expand</u> your inner horizons?

Perhaps Einstein was musing on this expansion in his statement;

"A human being is a part of the whole, called by us the 'universe' a part limited in time and space. We experience ourselves, our thoughts, our feelings as something separated from the rest, a kind of optical delusion of our consciousness. This delusion is a kind of prison for us. Restricting us to our personal desires and to affection for a few persons near us...our task is, perhaps, to free ourselves from this prison by widening our circle of compassion to embrace all living creatures and the whole of nature in its infinite and eternal beauty."

I'm often asked how can you tell if a dream is a precognitive dream or just a psychological balancing of inner concerns? The following criteria has assisted me greatly in making this discernment.

1. The dream is in color or the colors are unusually vivid. A precognitive dream isn't always necessarily in color, but it can be one of several determining factors.

2. You will get the message in three different ways during the dream. The message will appear in three separate, but distinct forms within one dream.

3. There will usually be a round or circular object within the dream. This can be an object like a ball or a round plate or a circular mirror, etc.

If a dream, that seems precognitive, fits all three criteria there is a very good chance that it is a foretelling dream. Sometimes you will get a precognitive dream with all the criteria and yet interpret it incorrectly. The following letter is an example of this process:

"Dear Denise,

The following is what I believe was a prophetic dream. I used your method of Dream Interpretation to decipher this dream and it met all three requirements of a prophetic dream. 1. There were three parts. 2. It was in extremely vivid color. 3. It contained a significant object that was round.

I had been interviewed for a different job within my company a few weeks before this dream and I was awaiting further developments. This is the dream; it was in three parts.

First, I dreamt I received some news about a job. I was quite excited about it. Then there was a sudden change. In the second part of the dream I was in an office. A couple of men, who were my new bosses, were talking. I looked down and noticed I was wearing a hideous pair of pants. They were bell-bottoms with green, black and white striped designs. I was extremely embarrassed and tried to make myself inconspicuous. I wanted to change into another pair of pants without the men seeing me. In the third part of the dream I was in a big gymnasium. There was a huge piece of paper covering the entire floor. It was my new job to fold and unfold the paper into different configurations like Origami, the art of Japanese paper folding. My co-workers and I created various shapes by folding them. One of them was a huge round hoop or a ring shape.

I was awakened by the telephone ringing. It was my mother informing me that the office wanted me to come in for a second interview. She had been calling repeatedly but I had not heard the phone.

As I drove to the interview, I was thinking this was going to be a piece of cake. I was sure I had the job because I so clearly had had a prophetic dream in which I got a new job. The interview was difficult. The guy asked technical questions that I was unable to answer, and he cut me off every time I tried to tell him about myself. I remembered feeling embarrassed by the entire situation.

A week later I found that I hadn't gotten the job. When I heard that news I thought maybe it wasn't a real prophetic dream after all, but later I realized that I just hadn't interpreted it correctly. In the first part of the dream I received news about a job. That happened. I was called in for that second interview. The second part of the dream I was feeling inadequate and self-conscious which is exactly the way I felt in the interview because I could not answer the technical questions the interviewer asked me. The paper-folding part was a little more obscure but that part was also prophetic. My search for another job is a large convoluted task. I keep turning opportunities over in my mind, pulling them apart and putting them together in various ways symbolized by my folding and unfolding the paper.

I learned from this dream that the obvious interpretation might not always be correct, especially when I am too attached to the interpretation. I was so excited about the interview that I jumped to conclusions and did not take time to listen to my feelings or really study the dream. I thought you'd be interesting in hearing this dream.

Shine on Brightly,

Karl

The way that Karl learned from his dream, including the realization that he was trying to fit his dream to his expectations rather than looking at what the dream was trying to tell him without adding to it, was a valuable lesson. Dreams for "seeing" will allow you to expand your inner horizons and as you expand your inner horizons your outer boundaries will also expand.

*Ancient partners, we
have long walked separate paths,
knowing our spirits
would meet and, remembering,
be drawn together again.*

        M. Anne Sweet

PAST LIFE RECALL

The gondola gracefully swayed through the soothing Adriatic waters just off the coast of Venice. The oarsman bellowed off-key arias as we gently glided past one island after another. One particular island seemed to glisten more brightly than the others in the distant haze. As I pointed the island out to my amiable singing host, he gently nudged the gondola in that direction. This beguiling gem in the sea seemed to be beckoning mysteriously to me. With hand signals, I told the oarsman that I wanted to get out and explore.

As I stepped onto the dock, a slightly balding, round Franciscan monk came scurrying out to greet us. He spoke some English and offered to give me a tour of the entire island, which consisted of the Franciscan monastery and its grounds. As I followed his jolly form, I was swept away by an overwhelming feeling of *deja vu*. I was so comfortable on this small island. I felt as if I knew exactly what was around each corner, even before we reached it. Images and forgotten memories flooded my consciousness. How could it be that I knew my way so clearly? I had never heard of this island. Suddenly, as we rounded a new corner, I viewed a scene far different from the one I was "remembering." Without being able to help myself, I explained, "Oh, this is new!" With an astonished look the monk replied, "It is new to the original structure...but it is more than six hundred years old." To my amazement, I had unearthed memories of being a monk living on this lovely island over six hundred years before. Thus, my journey into past-life exploration began.

Have you ever had the eerie experience of being in a foreign town and sensing a familiarity too uncanny to describe? Or, have you ever listened to a particular piece of music and instantly found yourself transported to another time and place? Perhaps you have met a stranger and experienced an instant rapport which you didn't understand, or you've met someone new and taken an immediate dislike to him. Maybe, you have had a dream in which you found yourself in a foreign place, or in foreign clothes, and yet experienced a tremendous sense of familiarity? It could be that you were being reminded of someone or some place from your childhood long forgotten, or could it be that you have lived there before? Perhaps you had been in that foreign town in a different body, in a different time? Could it be that you had known that stranger in another existence....in another incarnation? Could it be that this dream is a key to your past lives?

The concept of reincarnation was present long before recorded history. In fact, two-thirds of the people in today's world ascribe to the belief of reincarnation. Reincarnation is the idea that the soul is eternal and as such, returns to the earth plane again and again, through rebirth in various bodies, in order to grow and learn. Each lifetime provides a myriad of experiences that allows one, as spirit, to become stronger, more balanced, more loving and eventually, to unite with the all-pervasive spirit known as God.

In one life, you may live in poverty to learn humility and resourcefulness. In another lifetime, you may be extremely wealthy to learn to deal with money fairly and in a positive fashion. In one life, you may be blind in order to learn inner sight, and in another one be athletic, enabling you to experience and fully understand physical strength. You may be a woman in one life and a man in another, or be Caucasian in one and Oriental in another. Past lives are not so much building blocks as they are a jigsaw puzzle with each life contributing to our evolution in being more whole, complete and balanced.

"As ye sow, so shall ye reap." This is the law of karma. Karma is the fate we create for ourselves as a result of our actions in this lifetime as well as in other previous existences. The idea of karma gives us a clearer understanding of why one individual experiences adversity throughout his entire life while another has an easy path.

Reincarnation and karma provide us with a clearer picture of our purpose and mission in the present, through our understanding of previous lifetimes. They also give us a better understanding of our destiny in the universe. Life is not a one-time affair nor is it a series of meaningless experiences strung together haphazardly. Rather, it is a mystical on-going journey, that allows you to emerge as a conscious, loving being. The search for your soul may be the most important enterprise you have ever undertaken.

Throughout history, celebrated philosophers have pondered the vast mysteries of life, birth and rebirth. The first record provided by historians concerning reincarnation was discovered in ancient Egypt. Those ancients believed the soul to be immortal; when the body perishes, the soul enters into another human body.

The ancient as well as the present-day Hindus are another example of a community of people which believes that the soul is immortal and inhabits one body after another in search for its true divine nature. In the centuries preceding Christ, Buddha shared wisdom regarding the cycle of reincarnation, the great wheel of life and death. Buddhists, similar to the Hindus, strive to be released from the death/rebirth cycle by attaining nirvana or oneness with God. The Essenes, an early Jewish sect, are said to also have believed in the concept of reincarnation.

The Greek philosopher, Pythagoras, in 500 B.C., wrote of reincarnation and, in fact, gave descriptions of his personal recollections of his various incarnations. Plato also believed in reincarnation and the continued evolution of the soul. Napoleon Bonaparte once admitted to being Charlemagne in a past life. Voltaire, the French philosopher, observed that, "It is not more surprising to be born twice than once." And the Spanish painter, Salvadore Dali, confessed that he was the great Spanish mystic, St. John of the Cross. Even such diverse, new-world personalities as Benjamin Franklin, Ralph Waldo Emerson, Henry Ford, Walt Whitman, Henry Longfellow, Henry David Thoreau, Thomas Edison and General George Patton all ascribed to the teachings of reincarnation.

Benjamin Franklin, in fact, in one reference to past lives, wrote his own epitaph which has since been titled "the most famous of American epitaphs." It reads as follows:

> "The body of B. Franklin, Printer.
> Like the cover of an old book,
> Its contents torn out and
> stripped of its lettering and
> gilding.
> Lies here, food for worms, but
> the work shall not be lost.
> For it will appear once more
> in a new and elegant edition,
> Revised and corrected by the
> Author"

There are volumes of excellent books on the subject for those who are interested in seeking proof of reincarnation. My purpose here, however, is not to refute any remaining doubts regarding past lives, although I firmly believe in them. Rather, I merely intend to illustrate that your dreams can serve as a doorway to your past. By stepping through that door, you may expand the quality of life beyond your expectations.

To prove beyond reasonable doubt that the images in people's dreams that seem to be from the past are, in fact, actual memories is not nearly as important to me as the results produced when someone spontaneously experiences these past pictures. Altogether too much valuable time has been lost by those who are fearful of being deluded by what otherwise must be acknowledged as an amazing capacity of the human mind.

The value of discovering your past lives is immeasurable. Spiritually exploring past lives and other dimensions are ways to tune into inner guidance. The practice of exploring the distant past leads to personal integration and even to a harmonious unification with the flow of the universe. You find yourself more often in the right place at the right time. Some develop a strong relationship with their guides while others experience spontaneous spiritual awakenings.

Therapeutically speaking, to release psychological problems without exploring the source beneath surface symptoms is much like attempting to cut weeds with a lawn mower. The problems will resurface again and again until one dissolves the very roots which created the difficulty. Perhaps someone who compulsively eats may discover that in another life she starved to death and that fear has resurfaced to create an inappropriate desire for food in this life. By experiencing a past life either in your waking or dreaming state, you can begin to release the decisions made in times gone by that are still affecting you today.

Children are especially adept at recalling their past lives in the dream state. When my daughter was only eight years old, she shared with me a remarkable dream in which she was a black man in the United States during the time of slavery. She described, in detail, how her pants were ragged at the edges and how she would till the soil with a dilapidated hoe. She confided that some of her present-day friends were also black slaves in that lifetime. Perhaps one of the most curious factors regarding this experience was that one of her friends, whom she had described as being in this dream, unknown to her, had a

113

similar dream wherein she was also a black slave in the deep South of the United States.

In order to connect with your past lives during sleep, it becomes important to utilize the variety of techniques described in the chapters on dream recall. Each evening repeat to yourself before retiring, "Tonight, I dream of a past life. Tonight, I dream of a past life. Tonight, I dream of a past life." Continue to repeat this phrase as you drift off to sleep. When you first begin, you perhaps will find that you only receive a mere wisp of a memory which could be from the past. To receive more clarity with regard to this past life, during your waking hours use your imagination to expand what you have received, regardless of how insignificant it may seem. For example, let's say you saw an ornate helmet in one of your dreams. Upon waking, imagine the kind of person who might have used that helmet. Imagine where he might have worn it as well as the circumstances surrounding his life. Imagination is an invaluable resource in unwrapping your past.

Imagine a past life associated with your dream images, and more often than not you will begin to discover who you once were. On many occasions, individuals who have obtained vivid dream past-life experiences have actually traveled to one or more of the places they "remembered" in their dreams. They have then discovered that their dream perceptions were accurate! Past-life recall can be fun in the dream state as well as enormously rewarding during your waking life.

Body abruptly whipped away, leaving my spirit
to be caught and drawn up by a current of thought;
heart and spirit soar on the wings of an eagle,
plunging dives, circle then uplift again on warm winds.

M. Anne Sweet

ASTRAL TRAVEL

I soared, frolicked, and galloped with ecstasy to the lofty ceiling of my bedroom, and then dove for the comfort of my soft teddy bear. With a burst of glee, tumbling and twirling, I soar to the ceiling once again with reckless abandon, taking a moment to hover over my rag doll cradle. My mother opens the bedroom door, "What are you doing, Denise?" she asks. Innocently I respond, "Oh, nothing, Mommy." "That's nice!" she murmurs and closes the door. Once again, only momentarily disturbed, I am again jumping off the bed, arms outstretched, my body careening wildly through the air.

When I was a child I was always leaping from the end of my bed, tumbling and flying through mid-air. I really believed that I could fly. I didn't know that I was astral traveling. As I got older, I forgot the ability to consciously fly. In my dreams, however, there were relics of this abandoned memory. Occasionally, I would discover myself in a dream soaring over the rooftops and racing to the stars. In my twenties, I enrolled in a week-long course focusing on astral travel. There, I was once again able to reclaim a degree of that skill which had given me such great joy as a child.

There is one category of dream experience not included in the definitions of either dreaming or lucid dreaming. It is commonly referred to as an "out-of-body" experience. An out-of-body experience is one where the awareness of your soul being is literally separated from your physical body. This usually occurs during sleep. Numerous esoteric religions and philosophies are founded on this experience. In addition to a sense of separation from the physical body, there is also a self-awareness which is extremely vivid. This is quite different from a dream though it is not uncommon. In fact, during sleep, the sensation of a quick jerk might be indicative of a difficult re-entry into your body. Individuals often have out-of-body experiences, yet fail to recall them.

Dreams with regard to flying or being in an airplane frequently accompany out-of-body experiences. Also, individuals who actually fly or are pilots in their waking life are often inclined toward out-of-body experiences. Research indicates that people who as children felt they could fly, or spent time jumping off objects such as trees, also have a tendency toward out-of-body experiences.

There are records of out-of-body experiences occurring throughout history. Descriptions of these experiences are similar whether they took place in India, Egypt, South America or even in the Mid-Western United States. Vivid out-of-body experiences are frequently triggered by an accident or a near-death experience.

In rare instances, they are generated by a deliberate attempt to consciously leave the body. Most people find that these experiences dramatically alter their belief concerning the nature of personal reality. They also tend to be extremely joyous experiences for the recipients. The authenticity of such out-of-body experiences can be verified. They are not that uncommon. In fact, specific studies reflect that at least 25 percent of adult humans recall having at least one out-of-body experience in their lifetime. Many did not realize that they were having out-of-body experiences until the phenomenon was defined for them.

There appears to be no research of any kind indicating that damage may result from a person consciously leaving his body. In truth, it is a very natural occurrence. An interesting occurrence in connection with the out-of-body experience is that, when you are in this frame of reference, you do not experience time or space as you generally know it to be. Another interesting phenomenon is that you may notice when you first leave your body, you seem to remain in substance very much in your present physical form. However, the longer you are separated from your physical body, the weaker that memory becomes, and your "being" appears to transcend into a cloud-like vapor or some other amorphous form.

There are certain variables which seem to influence the out-of-body experience. Alcohol appears to be a definite deterrent to experiencing this phenomenon. One thing that seems to increase the ability to leave the body is the way you position your body, particularly if you lie in the magnetic north/south direction with your head to the north. The north/south alignment is also valuable in regard to sleeping deeply. If you desire a very restful night's sleep, placing your head toward the magnetic north is ideal. However, if you want to feel energized, placing your head toward south works best. For astral travel your head should be toward the north.

In the Carlos Castaneda books, Don Juan, Castaneda's mystical teacher, instructs him in the art of lucid dreaming, as well as astral travel. (See chapter on "LUCID DREAMING.") "Every time you look at anything in your dreams, it changes shape," he told Carlos. "The trick in learning to set up dreaming is obviously not just to look at things, but to sustain the sight of them. Dreaming is real. When one has succeeded in bringing everything into focus, then there is no difference between what you do when you sleep and what you do when you are not sleeping." Don Juan went on to mentor Carlos in astral traveling during the dream state.

Oliver Fox, in his book, *Astral Travel*, speaks of his own experience. "Instantly, the vividness of life increases a hundredfold. Never had sea and sky and trees shown with such

117

glamorous beauty. Even the commonplace houses seemed alive and mystically beautiful. Never had I felt so absolutely well, so clear brained, so divinely powerful, so inexpressibly free! The sensation was exquisite beyond words."

When I initially began astral traveling, I would remain close to my home. I observed myself wandering through the different rooms in our house. Curiously, my traveling would often be in a different time frame, it would be daylight instead of evening. The astral dimension is an arena that is outside of the space/time continuum. As I gained more confidence in this area, I began to experience floating and eventually flying. At the start, I would venture only a few feet above the ground because I still retained the fear of my physical body falling. As I grew in my confidence, I was spreading wings and transcending the earth in an ecstasy of flight.

My first adult recollection of astral travel was a frightening one. It was a very humid, tropical night in Hawaii. Early one evening, I spent time with a good friend casually discussing the art of astral travel. This was an activity in which neither of us had participated. We jokingly said we would meet each other at 3:00 a.m., selecting a predetermined location. Before I retired, I said to myself, "Tonight, I will meet Susan at 3:00 a.m. by the waterfall in the upper Manoa Valley." This was a good midpoint area with which we were both familiar.

It was about 3:00 a.m., I awoke aware of a very strange sensation. Although the room was dark, I felt a kind of rocking, floating experience as if I were drifting on a float tube in a swimming pool. I was startled. The ceiling which is normally six to seven feet above my bed was now only inches from my body. I was weightless...without substance. What was this? What was happening? I couldn't quite understand why I was hovering so near the ceiling. Was it a dream? No, I was fully conscious. Yet, it seemed so very real. I was so light, so free. Then almost as an afterthought, I rolled over gently, noticing my bed was below...with me in it! The terror of observing my own body was so frightening that I immediately zoomed back into my body with a harsh jolt. The shock was so profound that it took a long time before I ventured out again.

It was as if I was split into two different persons. The part of me that I identify with as "who I am," was free, light and floating. The other "being," the part that I associate with my physical body, was somehow me, but not me, lying on the bed, a mere physical shell. This experience was only the beginning of many explorations into the nature of astral travel and out-of-body adventures.

History has given us many examples of astral travel. In the first century A.D., the writer, Plutarch, told of a soldier in Asia who, while unconscious, roamed for three days in another dimension. Native tribes have always taken out-of-body experiences for granted. The shamans, American Indians and African witch doctors have all practiced rituals enabling them to escape from their physical bodies. The Australian aborigines would go into a trance and venture on an astral journey whenever their tribes needed guidance. This was evidenced in the movie, *The Right Stuff*, where the aborigines were assisting the astronaut as he was maneuvering through difficulties with his space capsule. Legends from prehistoric days share the secrets of those who left their bodies and communicated with the gods.

Even the church, throughout time, has recorded these out-of-body experiences. Saints such as Anthony of Padua and Alphonsius Liguori were seen elsewhere while their physical bodies remained in the church or monasteries. The scientific mystic, Emanuel Swedenborg, visited many dimensions, scripting detailed accounts of what he had envisioned. Thomas Quincy reportedly left his body while smoking opium.

It is said that Napoleon, shortly before his death, traveled astrally from St. Helena to Rome to inform his mother that he was dying.

The British Society for Psychical Research, formed in 1882, studied astral traveling, as well as other psychic phenomena.

Richard Hodgson, William James, Sir Oliver Lodge and others from the society investigated many of these cases. A number of universities throughout the world are now involved in research that can assist advancement in this field. New research has designed out-of-body experiments in which the sleeper astral projects to another building and then describes what he sees during his visit.

Many out-of-body experiences are described by soldiers during war when they have literally leaped out of their bodies to escape from the horror of gunfire or the excruciating pain of explosives. Occasionally, people leave their bodies to simply visit a friend or a loved one. A mother will travel to see her daughter, a father his son. St. Augustine related the story of one man lying in bed who suddenly looked up to see a philosopher friend standing in his room. They began to discourse on Plato. When the two men met the following day the man inquired about the experience. The philosopher responded simply, "I did not do it, but I dreamed that I did."

The sixth century B.C. philosopher, Hermotimus, of Clazomenae, like all Greek philosophers was curious about the state of death, so he employed his skill in astral travel in order to investigate. He often fell into a trance, and wandered away from his body, becoming catatonic, even deathlike. On one of these occasions, his wife, annoyed with these astral departures, simply had him declared dead and his body cremated. According to Ceasar de Vesme, in "A History of Experimental Spiritualism," mediums reported in later years that Hermotimus was quite upset to come back and discover his physical body missing!

On a lighter note, in his *On The Delay Of Divine Justice*, Plutarch tells about Aridaeus of Asia being knocked unconscious and immediately taken from his body. While out of his body, he was able to see his uncle who had died in previous years. His uncle greeted him, assuring Aridaeus that he was not dead, and that his soul was in fact, firmly attached to his body. "The rest of his soul," explained the dead uncle, "was a cord connecting it to the body. So long as the cord still remained attached to his physical body, Aridaeus would still be alive." Aridaeus could also see a marked difference between his double or his astral body, and the astral body of his dead uncle. His body had a faint shadowy outline while his uncle's was totally transparent. While observing this phenomena, Aridaeus suddenly became aware of being "sucked through a tube by a violent inbreath," and he awoke once again to find himself back in his physical body.

This tube is similar to the tunnel that many astral projectors experience when they are leaving and returning to their physical bodies. The astral body has different names in different cultures. The Hebrews call it "ruach." In Egypt, it is known as "ka". The Greeks knew it as "eidolon." The Romans called it "larva." In Tibet, it is still referred to as the "bardo body." In Germany, it is "Jüdel" or "Doppelgänger," or it is sometimes called "fylgja." Ancient Britons gave it various terms: "fetch, waft, tisk, fye." In China, it was called "thankhi." The "thankhi" left the body during sleep, and their records indicate that the astral body could be seen by others. Ancient Chinese meditated to achieve astral projection. They believe the second body was formed in the area of the solar plexus by action of the spirit, and that it then left through the head. Many of these ancient Chinese teachings were discovered inscribed on 17th century wooden tablets describing the phenomena of out-of-body experiences. The ancient Hindus defined this second body, the astral body, as the "pranamayakosha." Buddhists referred to it as the "rupa."

Anthropologists studying various native tribes find that this journeying with the astral body is a very common event. The cultural beliefs of the astral traveler determine the pattern of that experience. In Eastern Peru, the shaman imagines he is leaving his body in the form of a bird. Asian tribesmen view the silver cord, spoken of by modern metaphysicians, as a ribbon, thread or a rainbow. Africans perceive it as a rope and the natives of Borneo, as a ladder. Regardless of how the term is defined, it nevertheless appears to be a common experience among astral travelers that a type of silver cord remains that serves as a connection between the astral and physical bodies.

The scientific view of these dreams is that they are ancestral memories inherited from the days when, according to Darwin's theory, our predecessors were aquatic and airborne creatures. Psychologists refer to it as a type of depersonalization, or a means of avoiding being grounded in normal reality.

Conditions of Travel

In order to astral travel, there are two very important conditions to consider. The first is that you believe and appreciate the reality of an astral body, a second body. The second condition is to believe that you can astral travel and specifically focus your desire on leaving your physical body. Now, if it were an easy thing to consciously astral travel, it would be an everyday occurrence. However, it is my belief that anyone can experience the existence of an astral body if your intent is indeed great enough. Astral travel is something that most of us do anyway. We simply don't remember the experience. It can be a frightening experience, only in that we strongly identify with our physical bodies rather than our astral. The greatest barrier we encounter is fear itself.

Fear

Even the most "fearless" of us will discover, upon deeper examination, that at some time we have come face to face with the wall of fear. First and foremost, there is the fear of death - the fear that if we are separated from our physical body, perhaps we will die. Our automatic reaction may be to get back within the physical body quickly before we die, that this is where our life is, in the physical. We tend to have these reactions in spite of our emotional attitude and our intellectual thought process. Only after repeating the experience again and again can we hope to release the fear of death. It is much like beginning to swim and eventually realizing that your body <u>will</u> float, that you will not drown.

Another common fear is, "Will I even be able to get back inside my body?" I can say with absolute certainty that you will always be able to get back into your physical body. There is abundant evidence that those who astral travel are always able to return safely, one way or another. Fear of the unknown is also faced by many would-be travelers. There is no guide book. The healthiest way I know is to work through your fear by simply allowing it to exist and yet be willing to explore the unknown.

Astral Aids

The following are some guidelines to assist in your astral journeys. The first thing to do is relax. You might take some stress reduction courses or read about creative visualizations. This will help you to completely relax your body. You may also try some self-hypnosis or post-hypnotic suggestions that will help you to travel on the astral level. Visiting a hypnotist may assist you in setting a post-hypnotic suggestion. Meditation may also facilitate you moving into a very deep state of relaxation. Placing your head toward the north, and straightening your spine will also make a difference.

Next, move into the space between waking and sleeping consciousness. This is a very delicate balance. It is where you are not yet asleep, but are no longer awake. You might focus on an image or symbol that is unique and special to you. As you move more and more into a deep state of relaxation, begin to observe the kind of mind pictures or any light patterns that seem to randomly appear. Frequently these are referred to as neural discharges. Do not encourage or deny them, simply allow them to move through, acknowledging an even deeper state of relaxation while maintaining conscious awareness. You will perhaps recognize that you are deepening your consciousness because your body will begin to feel either extremely heavy or very light. Your sense of touch, smell and taste will begin to fade. Occasionally, auditory signals will also being to fade.

As you are in this very calm, relaxed place, with eyes closed, focus your awareness outside of your body. Begin to imagine that you are now at some point outside your body. If it is in another corner of the room, imagine that you are touching the wall. Be aware of the floor and all objects surrounding you. Imagine that you are in this place. Often, as one begins to leave his body, he will experience a tingling sensation, or hear a vibration. It is crucial at this point, simply to allow the vibrations to increase in their frequency. This will occur until the frequency is so high you will almost be unable to perceive it. For some, their body will feel slightly warmer.

The next step is to imagine that you are moving your right or left hand. Imagine yourself reaching out for and touching any object that is near while remembering that this is not your physical body, but your astral body.

Another way to enhance what you are doing would be to imagine touching the wall and then gently pushing against it. Then begin to increase the pressure to a hard push. At this point, it will appear as if your hand or arm is actually going through the wall. Then carefully withdraw your hand.

The ancient Etruscans used to take part in a rolling technique where they would enter into a very deep state of relaxation. They would literally imagine rolling out of their bodies as a means to leave the body for astral travel. Some travelers prefer a lift-out method. The important thing is that you experiment, discovering which method works best for you. Be gentle with yourself. Sometimes after long periods of practice without attaining any results, in that moment when you least expect it, you will experience your first out-of-body journey.

Returning to your Body

Once you have learned to leave your body, you are free to explore and examine anything and any place you desire. If you ever wish to return to your body, simply imagine moving either your fingers or your toes in your physical body. This will generally facilitate bringing your spirit back into your body immediately. You can also swallow or move your jaw to bring yourself back. A simple guideline is to activate any one of your five senses.

Once you are familiar with traveling in your own environment, one way to ensure a good initial experience is to imagine being with one specific person whom you love and enjoy. There is frequently a very intense energy and psychic connection between one's self and those he loves. Simply imagine yourself with your special person and see what happens.

Good luck!

Dreamtime weeping,
riding the cresting waves
of long-lost thoughts,
I heal my wounded heart.

Denise Linn

DREAM HEALING

My thin cotton summer dress rippled in the warm wind as I stood high above the vast blue sea below. I felt exhilarated as I stretched my arms toward the sky. I turned from my vantage on the chalk-colored cliffs that overstretched the sea and barefooted my way through the golden carpet of rolling grass. A lone seagull circled lazily overhead. His slow-cycling shadow whispered over the undulating grasses that moved in uniformed response to the commands of the ocean breeze. In the distance was a black cottage. There were no windows and no doors. It was completely black. Like heat radiating off a hot country road, its image seemed to waver like a mirage in the distance. As I approached the black cottage, I was aware that there was someone inside. Sue! It was Sue inside! "Sue, come out! It's so beautiful out here!" Inside I heard a timid feeble response, "I can't come out."

"Please Sue," I urged, It's so dark in there. You must come out into the light." There was no response, only the distant sound of thundrering waves greeting well-worn rocks below chalk-colored cliffs."

I awoke from my dream. Was it a dream? It seemed so real. I was left feeling slightly tired, even exhausted. That was the tenth time I had had the same dream in as many days.

Sue was a vivacious woman in her early thirties yet she was dying of cancer. Initially, when I was called in to contribute to Sue's healing, I was astonished to see a once-hearty woman reduced to a mere 98 pounds. She was as emaciated as a frail skeleton with stretched, taut skin over the bones, deeply sunken eyes and cheeks. Every day I went to Sue's bedside to assist in her healing process and every night I met Sue in my dreams. I assumed that my purpose in these nightly healing sessions was to encourage Sue to step into her own healing.

I'm standing outside the black cottage. As usual, the radiant rays of the sun bathe the summer grasses with fluid golden light. I place my hands on the peeling black paint of the cottage. "Sue. Please, Sue come out." A solemn, hollow voice from within states, "I can't come out. My husband is here."

I assumed that she was attempting to tell me, through the inner dimension of dreams, that there existed a submerged emotion concerning her husband that ultimately was preventing her healing. I realized I had possibly discovered the source of the emotional difficulty which may have generated the cancer in the first place. I began to work with Sue regarding undelivered communications concerning her husband. I thought this must be the path to her healing. We worked in depth with any and all difficulties that she might have felt were unresolved regarding her husband.

Sue continued to get weaker and weaker. This was hard for me to accept because everyone with whom I had ever worked had improved and regained health. I often contributed to the healing of those whom the medical profession felt were incurable, frequently with miraculous results. What was I doing wrong?

I stood on the chalk-colored cliffs inhaling the essence of the slumbering sea below. As I walked through golden grass, I could feel the warmth of the earth radiate up through the soles of my bare feet. The black cottage seemed to shimmer in the sunlight like a mirage of an oasis on the desert. I once again urged Sue to venture out into the light. Sue responded, "I'm not quite ready. My husband is keeping me here."

Sue's husband was constantly at her side. He never seemed to leave her, even for a moment. Sue began counting the days until Christmas. She had two beautiful children in their early teens and she desperately wanted to celebrate Christmas with them...she had to live until Christmas. The day after Christmas, the nurse asked Sue's husband if he would please leave the room, so she could change the bedding.

In that moment...when he left the room, Sue's spirit soared...and her body died. That night, again, I dreamed.

I stood barefoot, grounded on towering majestic white cliffs. The ocean had never seemed more radiant...more magical. It seemed to hold the very essence of life...the womb of all beingness. Shimmering diamonds of light danced on the ocean's surface. The air was heavy with the fragrance of sea and foam. I became aware of a serene presence standing beside me. Turning, I was greeted by a softly swirling goddess of light. "Sue?" I looked in the direction of the black cottage. There was only the vast horizon. I had only seen Sue when she was ill and emaciated. The woman beside me was completely whole and radiated an exquisite beauty. This lovely woman said, "They think I am dead. I am so alive. If only they knew. You see, Denise, death can be a healing as well. I am healed and I am well."

In that moment, I realized that it can be as healing to assist someone in dying as it is to assist someone in living. In my nightly urging for Sue to step into the light, I was making it easier for her to release her physical form. She had completed her earth plane incarnation and was ready to move on. Her husband's attachment to her had been holding her back. In the moment that he left the room, she went for the light, leaving her body behind.

Sue allowed me to see a deeper aspect of dream healing...an aspect that contributed to my daytime healing practice as well. Many people practice Dream Healing every night. Most are unaware of the fact they are doing so. Often, those who have incarnated to participate in Dream Healing will reincarnate around battlefields or areas where there is a sincere need for much healing. These beings will assist soldiers dying in battle to make the transition from living to spirit. In war-torn areas of Europe, there were a large number of Dream Workers who incarnated during World War I and World War II. These souls, from deep within their sleep, were assisting the wounded and dying to step into the light. They helped make that transition easier.

Dream Healing is not only a means of contributing to the dying, but it can contribute to the living. Frequently knowledge of our cure lies deep within our psyche...too deep to access during the daylight hours. A Dream Healer can contribute to another's healing simply by touching deep within the psyche in sleep. The same rules that are appropriate to daylight healing apply to Night Healing. Gaining an understanding of these tenets of healing will contribute to your own intention to join the ranks of the Healers of the Night.

Asclepius, the Father of Medicine, was believed to work his cures during sleep. He would appear within his patients' dreams, mix potions, apply bandages, and, at times, even summon snakes to come and lick their wounds or infected areas. The very symbol of modern medicine, Hermes' staff, is the symbol of two intertwined serpents or snakes. Dream healing is a very powerful way to heal yourself and those whom you love. However, before learning Dream Healing techniques, there are some very important tenets to remember in regard to healing.

1. We are all healers.

Within each of us there resides the ability to heal. When we remove the considerations and the doubts, each of us can tap into that gift. A common concern among those who are first entering the field of healing and dream healing is whether they know enough or have enough experience to heal anyone. My old Chinese teacher used to wisely say that a person will draw to himself those who want what he has to offer. So, whatever your level of ability, whoever comes to you, within his higher self he knows what you have to offer. And, what you have to offer is what that person needs at that time. Do not doubt that this is true. You have within you right now all that you need to heal. You already know enough.

2. We are not our bodies.

While this appears to be all too obvious to many, there are those who do not realize that it is upon this premise that great healing can occur. The body is an illusion. Remember that you are not working on the <u>body</u> or even on the astral network or the emotions. Rather, you are becoming aware of the true essence of another.

While it is possible to heal by deciding what is wrong and "fixing" it, a more powerful way is to realize we are not bodies; know all human beings are infinite, immortal, eternal and universal. Find that place within the person with whom you are working that is universal. Go beyond the idea of separation and find that place of oneness and connect to it. Remember who both of you truly are in that moment. There will be healing. The essence of healing is oneness.

3. What is held as a belief system does the healing.

It is not the method or technique in itself that heals. All techniques can work. Rather it is your belief or your faith in the technique that is being used on or by you that will heal.

131

For instance, it is a common thing in Western cultures today to "believe in" the practice of medicine by the medical profession. Many people put their faith "in their doctor" and in this way have found the place where they can best heal themselves.

4. There are two kinds of healing - causal and symptomatic.

In symptomatic healing, the healer can assist in elevating or focusing on the symptoms. However, unless the actual cause is addressed, the person with whom you are working can find the problems recurring or they will develop some other difficulty.

For example, if a young man has arthritis in his right hand, perhaps the underlying cause can be traced to earlier experiences with his father. If, when the boy was young, his father would swat the back of his hands when he was misbehaving, consider the range of emotions in play. While feeling enraged, the boy also loved his father, yet feared him. Perhaps in dealing with all these emotions, the child began to deny those feelings and just feet overwhelmed with powerlessness. He might have felt that he really couldn't get a handle on what was happening to him. Now, as a grown man, when he finds himself in a situation where he feels "helpless" or "powerless," where he "can't get a handle on things," his hands are affected.

A symptomatic healer, through utilization of the dream state and through using various dream techniques, can contribute to the man's gaining freedom of movement in his hand. However, unless that young man can release the underlying feelings of powerlessness, the arthritis can return or some other difficulty will manifest itself in another area of the body.

In other words, it is important not to think there is something "wrong" with someone and attempt to fix it. A more powerful way to heal is to see the divinity in that person, to remember the magnificence of the one with whom you are working. The healer who works from the vision of being able to see the individual as he truly is, can work with the <u>cause</u> of the difficulty and facilitate healing.

5. The body reflects consciousness.

Every emotion or thought that a person has ever had remains stored within the body. And, all the emotions that were denied or suppressed are stored in the body and as such, influence the health and well-being of the body.

Normally, as a person goes through life, situations arise that can cause him/her to feel angry, sad, joyous, etc. When that person decides that it is inappropriate to even have the emotional response (he is already experiencing), he can "go numb" or deny what is happening to his body. He can find some way <u>not to feel</u> whatever is going on with him. Each of these unexperienced emotions creates bodily difficulties. These difficulties are the body's way of putting attention on what needs to be cleared.

When there is a health problem, the emotions and situations that caused that difficulty are usually not those that have been experienced or felt. Rather, they arise from situations that have <u>not</u> been experienced. Those situations where a person went numb, or didn't allow himself to feel the pain, or grief, or anger. Individuals then tend to recreate like circumstances again and again, even lifetime after lifetime, until they finally fully experience what has been avoided.

6. All healing is self-healing.

The body always wants to heal itself. No technique or method ever healed anyone in and of itself. It is the body's response to that method that heals. Two people with the exact same difficulty can be given identical procedures and one will be healed and the other will not. This happens because all healing is basically self-healing. The person with whom you are working heals himself. You are the facilitator.

7. The only person you ever heal is yourself.

As a healer, you must turn your focus on yourself. The true essence of healing is oneness, and the greatest healers know intimately that it is only themselves they are healing. Each person with whom you work is a part of you, yourself. It is "you" in a different body. This is a universal law. Know that each person you have drawn to yourself for healing is a different aspect of your own being.

For example, if there is someone in your life who has cancer, a valuable way to start the healing process is to first look within yourself and try to discover, "Is there anything 'eating away' at me?"

As you begin to heal the emotions that are "eating away at you," this affects the person you want to heal. It will begin the healing process within him or her. It is important to remember that you are not healing that person. Each person you work with is allowing you to be healed by drawing attention to certain aspects of yourself.

My Hawaiian Kahuna teacher said it was a sacred thing and a great honor to be allowed to contribute to the healing of someone else. The honor is for you. It is yours. If you want to contribute to the healing of someone, and you notice that person is having difficulty receiving, then look within yourself. First allow yourself to know that you deserve love. Open yourself up to the deepening of this awareness. As you create that context for another's healing, you heal yourself.

As a healer, and particularly a Dream Healer, it is imperative not to feel you are sacrificing yourself. You must know you are not better than the people whom you are healing.

In any kind of healing, it is important to go beyond the dualism, and the feeling of separation. Reach that exquisite level of oneness. Remove the wall that you may sense between yourself and another, until you feel the unity that is between that person and yourself.

8. Disease and/or physical difficulties can be a gift.

Physical difficulties can be one way of learning. If the healer prematurely removes blockages before the higher self of the ailing person has learned whatever he needed to learn from the imbalance, it will be recreated. It is important regarding healing, to provide a safe space for the person to choose his own path. It is not for you, the healer, to arbitrarily take choice away from him. Ultimately, as a healer, you do not know what is best for another. It is not appropriate for you to decide what is wrong with someone and then just fix it. This response identifies with the belief in the illusion that a person is just his body. We are not our ailments.

9. Love is the ultimate healer.

An aspect of the definition of love is the unconditional acceptance of another's reality. This acceptance is at an even deeper level than one's personality or persona. It is accepting one's very essence. There is then nothing you need to do to bring about healing. Your presence is enough!!!

10. Health is a function of service.

Service is not seeing that someone else is in bad shape and deciding to "help" him. This idea of "fixing him" comes from forgetting that he is divine and in the process of choosing his own reality. It also sets you up as seeing yourself as better than another. It implies that you will help someone up but not quite "up" as far as you are. As you allow people to go beyond you, so you grow.

My Chinese teacher used to say, "It is a poor student who doesn't surpass his teacher." Hanuman, the Monkey God of India, said, "When I don't know who I am, I serve you. When I know who I am, I am you."

Do what you can to contribute to the world so that the world will be a better place -- not for the world's sake, as the world is perfect just the way it is -- but for your own sake. And, in the same way, do what you can for another, for your own sake, remembering the person is perfect as he is. Don't sacrifice -- ever. Service is not sacrifice.

11. A healer is compassionate.

As a healer, it is important that you maintain a balance by having a foot in each reality -- one foot in the reality of the physical world and one foot in the realm of the spirit. In the spirit realm, you know that the world is perfect. In this realm you know there are no accidents and each person has generated his own illness and is completely responsible for his life. However, by remaining in intense "spiritual" focus you may become cool and have a lack of compassion for the suffering of others. In contrast, by focusing intently only in the physical world, you become a player in a large drama. In this reality most people get "sucked into" the misery of the world and they begin to feel sorry for people. We forget that others are not their body or their problems. It is easy to get into this frame of mind and not see beyond the suffering. But, if you do this, you have forgotten who you really are.

It is important to be compassionate and to sympathize with a person's pain, yet remember his true essence. He is not ill; it's his body that is ill. Find this balance and you will be an excellent healer.

Intention

After gaining an understanding of these tenets of healing, you can begin to enter the realm of Dream Healers. The most important aspect of night healing or dream healing is your intention. As you prepare for sleep, be relaxed and comfortable. Use your Dream Guide technique or Dream Shield technique. Let your full intention be to contribute to the healing of the person you have in mind. To do this, first imagine him (or her) very clearly. If you are not visual, get a sense of him. (Each person has a feeling, an aura of his own.) Get in touch with that person's feeling. Hold his essence. Say his name within yourself. You might even visualize him as very happy. See him running, jumping, feeling really exhilarated. Then go to sleep. Where intention goes, energy flows. You may not even remember what good you may have contributed during the night; nevertheless, you will have begun to move into the realm of the Night Healer.

Often, my clients will tell me that they have been aware of me working with them in their dreams, and upon waking have discovered their symptoms are relieved. Occasionally I will have no recall whatsoever of having visited them in the night, or I will have only the faint glimmer of a memory. I have even told individuals I would work with them in the night, and then have forgotten to program myself before bed only to hear the next day how effective the night healing was. So don't be discouraged. It might be that you have been a Night Healer all along.

If you want to contribute to your own healing, as you go to sleep say, "Tonight I am healed. Tonight I am healed." Your body will reflect your dreams and your dreams will reflect your body. Your body will heal itself through your dreams. Your affirmations will contribute to that healing. It may not be necessarily true that you are creating an illness; however, your soul may be trying to communicate a very important message through that illness or disease. Use your dreaming states as a workshop to receive these communications.

Soul to soul we meet,
love weaves its thread between us,
I weep, the beauty
of the tapestry touches
and I am lonely no more.

M. Anne Sweet

DREAMS FOR LOVE AND SEX

His buttocks, firm and ripe as mangoes, move with confident grace as he saunters down the beach. His back muscles ripple with feline certainty as he takes long, languid strides. He hesitates...and turns to face me. We are no longer two strangers who happen to be walking on a lone beach in the same direction. We have entered into a conspiracy of attraction. The look is brief. It is only the suggestion of a glance. Still, in that silent moment, a tangible current fills me with his soul. I walk on....and smile.

I woke up from my dream feeling a mysterious inner glow. My dream lover encounter had been so brief, and yet so fulfilling. I sang through my entire day.

Dreams can be a pathway to ecstasy. They can be a way to expand love for others and love of self and can be used to work out sexual difficulties within waking life. They can even be a wonderful form of evening entertainment.

Sexuality appears regularly within the dream state. Physiologically, men have erections frequently during the REM dream states, and women's vaginal areas moisten during these times. It is a normal, natural part of our dream states. In ancient cultures, there was an understanding of this natural occurrence. In fact, the understanding of sexuality and sensuality was considered basic to the expression of all life. In the East, it was a means of expressing Unity with Spirit. Sexuality was looked upon as a path to mystical experience. An ancient Indian text states, "Sexual union is an auspicious Yoga which involves enjoyment of all the sensual pleasures and gives release. It is a Path to Liberation."

In the Orient, it was thought that the underlying reality to all of life consisted of two dynamic energies called yin and yang. Yin was the receptive feminine principle and yang was the masculine outgoing or projecting energy. Each was considered necessary for harmonization of life. Yin was embodied in the receptive energy of the moon. Yang was embodied in the projecting energy of the sun. Everything was considered either yin or yang, and all life was an interplay, a dance between these two forces.

Men and women were considered the highest expression of these two powerful energies. A healthy sexual union was considered a way to break through the illusion of duality - a way to attain liberation and to enhance health and well-being. Sexual union was considered a way to become closer with God. There is no greater power in the universe than the divine union of a man and woman dedicated to the expression of their higher selves. You can access this power in your dreams.

Guilt

A common occurrence when one has dream sex is to feel guilty about your nocturnal erotic experiences. It is important to remember that there is no cause for guilt in any dream relationship. In all ancient cultures with a metaphysical basis, sex was not opposed to spirituality or religion. Sex was an art form on a par with other art forms. It was a normal part of each person's education. It was important not to shroud the essence of sexuality with guilt. The Senoi, in Malaysia, believed it perfectly normal to have sexual feelings toward almost anyone within dreams. The Senoi were taught to move toward making love and to enjoy these dreams to the fullest. They were also encouraged to experience orgasm in their dreams. It was insignificant who or what the object of the love was. It could be an animal, an inanimate object, perhaps a friend. The Senoi believed that dream images were merely various aspects of the self that needed to be integrated and loved. You can, as the Senoi did, fully enjoy dream lovers.

Release any censorship of yourself. There is no such thing as incest or promiscuity in dreams. Your dream lovers are simply different aspects of yourself appearing in erotic from. The Senoi believe in letting go in their dreams and fully experiencing pleasure. This form of total release allows them to be free from repression and fears prevalent in our normal modern society. They espoused the more dream lovers you have the better.

In addition to letting go of guilt regarding your dream sex, it is important to release any guilt carried from past sexual activities. This guilt can be subconsciously activated every time you have sex. Guilt is always disruptive. To experience full sexual union in the present, it is essential to forgive yourself your past. When you maintain that you are guilty and your source of guilt lies in the past, you are not looking inward. To look inward is to know that everything that you have ever experienced was necessary for your growth and understanding. It was necessary for you to be who you are today. Even the thoughts and actions you may be ashamed of contributed to your being who you are today. As uncomfortable as those memories are, it is important to observe and release them. Forgive yourself. Any residue of guilt that you still cling to can be creating barriers for you. It is often processed and released in your dreams.

Whenever the pain of guilt seems to attract you, remember this. If you yield to it instead of forgiving yourself, you are deciding against inner peace. Therefore, say to yourself gently, but with conviction, "I accept who I am and what I have done as well as what others have done to me. I accept and forgive myself."

One valuable technique is to write down all feelings of sexual guilt. After they are all written down, burn them saying, "I release now and forevermore, my attachments to this guilt. So be it." Your dreams will reinforce the releases that occur in your waking life as a result of this process.

Opening the Dream Sex Channel

Another important aspect of sexuality is understanding how energy flows through the body. Within the body are energy centers called chakras. In order to maintain a healthy view of yourself, it is imperative to have a harmonious circulation of your life force energies. When these energies become blocked, self-esteem is lowered, disease occurs and vitality diminishes. Basic to this energy flow, is the flow of our sexual energy. This energy can be likened to our creative energy. Many times, people involved in a spiritual movement deny or block this vital energy. Sometimes they become so heavenly that they become ineffective in their earthly pursuits.

We need to maintain a balance within all our chakras or energy centers to be empowered in day-to-day life. The first chakra, the sexual center, is important to the maintenance of all the others. It is our connection to the earth. It is the home of the kundalini; that mysterious force dwelling at the base of the spine that yogis strive to awaken. It is what is referred to in the Orient as the "Fighting Spirit." This doesn't imply that one needs to pick a fight. It simply means zest and vitality for life. As this area opens, women discover that their menstrual flows become easier, hormones are vitalized, their skin becomes softer, clearer and they are rejuvenated. You have probably seen a woman who seems to be lit by her own glow. This is usually a woman whose first chakra is opened and clear. The first chakra opening in a man will cause him to feel more at choice in his life and he will operate from a perspective of greater clarity and certainty.

I emphasize that each of our chakras represent a different facet of ourselves and each deserves to be developed and opened, none to the exclusion of others. However, the first chakra is one easily ignored by those on a spiritual path, because of guilt or denial. This area is part of your god-given heritage. Use it. Allow it to open and your sexuality and your zest for life will increase.

One method to prepare for dream sex is to channel the sexual energy upward through the chakras and up through the top of the head, which in India is known as the aperture of Brahma. This can be done with the use of breath. Eastern mystical teachings stresses the importance of breath as a way to align and channel the creative sexual energy. Your breath should be slow and deep; a breath that extends your lower abdomen when you exhale and contracts when you inhale. This is a most natural way to breathe. It is the way we breathe when we are asleep. However, most people breathe just the opposite, with the chest expanding on the inhalation. Once you've mastered this deep type of breathing imagine a brilliant surge of energy entering at your feet, moving up through your entire body and out the top of your head. This exercise will begin to open your chakras which often leads to enlightening, transformational experiences during your sleep. Sexual dreams can sometimes be the opening of the Kundalini and many major enlightenments occur during sleep as a result of the opening of sexual chakra.

Once you experience this energy moving through your entire being, you might want to do the dream lover meditation found in this book. You might also fall asleep repeating expressions such as, "This night, show me the highest potential of sexuality. Tonight, let me dream of divine intimacy with my partner." Know that any dream lover you encounter will allow you to become a more fully integrated, creative person.

Dream Sex and Creativity

Western researchers would seem to concur with the Senoi use of pursuing pleasure in dreams. They discovered that an active sex life in dreams not only contributes to a sensuous waking life but also indicates self-actualization and confidence. Abraham Maslow, the noted American humanistic psychologist who presented the idea of self-actualization, said that people with potent dream lives are much more self–assured, independent, composed and competent. Also the dreams of a less assured person are more likely to be symbolic rather than the openly sexual dreams experienced by the the person with high self-esteem.

One researcher discovered a high correlation between sexual dreams and creativity. In a creative writing class, the instructor divided students into groups of the most creative and the least creative based upon writing assignments. Then data was collected from both study groups. The non-creative students had sexually passive dreams or nonsexual dreams. The more creative students had a higher proportion of overtly sexual dreams. The researchers concluded that freedom of sexual activity in dreams is related to freedom of creative thinking in all areas.

Interpretation of Dream Sex

Occasionally, women will dream of having a penis. Freudian psychologists call this "penis envy," and believe these dreams imply a secret desire on the part of the woman to have a penis. Rather than penis envy, these dreams can represent the female dreamer's desire for achievement of traditional male characteristics as they see symbolized by penises.

Certain dreams of sex are wish-fulfillment dreams, especially those portraying extremely satisfying sexual encounters when the dreamer has gone too long without sex. Occasionally, one of these dreams may literally revolutionize a person's sex life. In some dreams, one may dream of making love with an

144

individual of the same sex. This isn't necessarily latent homosexuality. Rather it is most likely a desire to attain those qualities represented by the lover. For example, if a woman dreams of making love with another woman who is very strong, this may reflect her desire to incorporate qualities of strength into her own character.

In analyzing your dream, notice where your sexual encounter takes place. It is not uncommon for sex dreams to occur in a Victorian house symbolizing Victorian attitudes. If you are having sex in the basement, perhaps you are experiencing submerged or subconscious feelings concerning sex, or maybe your dream is indicating some area of sexuality which you perceive as base. If your dream encounter is in the middle of a raging hurricane, this generally indicates you are experiencing powerful emotions with regard to your own sexuality.

Dream Sharing

One special aspect of dream sex is dream sharing. You can literally share a dream with a loved one. This exercise is enhanced if you are sleeping together because your auras are so intermingled. It is then easier to step into each other's dreams. Dream sharing can also be done from a distance. If you are separated from your loved one, it can be a way to continue your intimacy. For the most effective dream sharing to occur it is valuable to discuss it beforehand. Mutually agree to enter each other's dreams. As you go to sleep, affirm, with intention, that you and your partner will be together in your dreams. Often dream sharing occurs spontaneously without pre-programming. Perhaps you have had an experience of sharing a dream with your lover. The following morning you discover that you both experienced a similar dream. Dream sharing can be an excellent way to increase intimacy and to develop greater understanding within relationships.

Before beginning your dream sharing, it is valuable to do a simple meditation. This meditation is based on a Tantric Buddhism technique. First, sit in a comfortable position directly facing your partner. Make sure your spine is straight. This is extremely important for this particular meditation. Now, participate in the natural type of breathing described earlier. Remember, as you inhale your abdomen expands and as you exhale, your abdomen contracts. If you sense your chest expanding and contracting instead of your abdomen, simply imagine the presence of a balloon in the center of your abdomen. The balloon expands and contracts with each breath. It may take a short while to become accustomed to this type of breathing, however the results will be well worth it! It is a very natural way of breathing; this is the way you breath when you are asleep. Allow yourself to feel very relaxed. Then, imagine a current of energy originating in the center of the earth moving up through your spine and all the way up through your entire being. This is your grounding cord. Imagine this energy moving out the top of your head like a geyser, cascading down around you like a fountain. Look into the left eye of your partner and imagine a beam of energy flowing out from your own heart chakra (the energy center in the middle of the chest) into the heart chakra of your partner. Then imagine this same energy moving down his/her spine and penetrating the sex chakra. This extremely potent energy then travels from your partner's sexual area into your own, arriving in your heart chakra once again. This is called the "circle of gold technique." You may also reverse the flow of the energy. As you are doing this, allow yourself to experience the very deep and profound connection with your partner. Once you have completed this exercise, maintain silence and immediately go to sleep, programming yourself for an even deeper connection to occur during the night.

Children, still close to the knowledge of their souls,
play hopscotch in the schoolyard, leaping over
dragons and dungeons, one foot, two feet grounded,
finishing every battle victorious, unscathed.

M. Anne Sweet

DREAMS FOR CHILDREN

A golden pool of what once was butter floats in my morning bowl of oatmeal. My finger, finding a chip in the earthen bowl, idly plays with its rough edges. My ten-year-old daughter is in the middle of an engaging conversation concerning her exploits of the previous night. I am enjoying our family's breakfast dream sharing. When Meadow shares her dreams, a hazy look crosses her face as she vividly remembers the intimate details. Her dreams are usually long-winded sagas full of intricate details. They sometimes appear to span generations. She also pays close attention to details in her waking life. David's dreams are usually succinct and to the point - much like his personality. My dreams are usually active and whimsical.

When we take the time to share our dreams and assist each other in understanding their secret messages, the quality of the day is more balanced. For each of us, our dream sharing is extremely significant for the consolidation of our family energy. It provides Meadow with a sense of acceptance and a deeper understanding of herself. Meadow claims she is more apt to recall her dreams and use their messages when we take this time to share our dreams over breakfast.

It is not uncommon that, when a child relates a dream, an adult will non-verbally communicate the attitude that dreams are not to be taken seriously. When a child has a nightmare, we rush to reassure him saying, "Oh, it's just a dream. Don't worry about it. It doesn't mean anything."

Listening to your child's dreams, even in the middle of the night when you are longing to crawl back into bed, is an act which can have an inspiring and transforming effect on your child's life.

Dream Importance

The first step in working with your children and their dreams is to communicate to them the significance and value of their dreams. You will want to encourage a child's interest in dreams. Never _ever_ correct or criticize the child's behavior in the dream or belittle any feelings the child may have concerning the dream. Let children know you enjoy hearing about their dream exactly the way they dreamed it. Encourage your child to confront the scary beasts or other scary things contained within the dream. Assist him in understanding that it is all right to call upon his dream guide or his guardian angel to help him out of a threatening situation.

Savanna, one of my daughter's friends, told me she was afraid to go to sleep at night because she was afraid scary monsters would come in the dark. I gave her a pointed quartz crystal I had previously programmed for use as a Dream Crystal. I told her that, as she went to bed, she should hold the crystal in her hand and say out loud, "I command that all dream monsters leave now!" Savanna later informed me that since being given the Dream Crystal, she has not experienced any nightmares and can sleep peacefully through the entire night.

It is valuable for a child to feel empowerment through dreams. Let your child know he can have control over his dreams. If your children are experiencing difficulty in feeling powerful in dreams, and they have already attempted to change their dreams without success, it is important to continue encouraging them. Your children may feel worse about themselves because they have been unable to change a dream. If this occurs, have them either focus on acting out the dream or drawing a picture with a more powerful ending. Your emphasis should be on the flexibility and changeability of the dream. Use the time wisely to listen carefully and attune to what your child needs in the moment.

Also, communicate with your children that they can use dreams to develop a talent or ability which can in turn be incorporated into their daily life. They can say to themselves before sleep, "I'd like to become a better swimmer, skater or artist. Give me the dream that will help me accomplish this goal."

Dream Books

To begin working with your children and dreams, you might first obtain some "dream books" in which to record dreams. A dream book can be a notebook, scrapbook, diary or even a special set of homemade pages. Allow your children to select the book that really appeals to them. Let your children know that these are special books to be used only for their dreams. They can write the dreams themselves or, if they are too young, you can write the dreams for them. Then have your children create a drawing of the dream placing it alongside the story. Your child may wish to color a picture of how they were feeling or how they wished the dream had ended.

The dream book can also be utilized when children think of additional stories regarding their dreams; they can write or illustrate these stories in their book. If they had a disturbing dream, they can go back into the dream and rewrite the script making themselves the hero or heroine. Help them understand that it is definitely all right to go back into their dream and

149

have it end exactly the way they had wished it would. Let them know that even scary things in the dream can be changed.

Dream Interpretation

It is crucial for adults to give their children the time and space necessary to interpret their own dreams. It may be difficult at first for children to figure out what their dream means. Simply by allowing them to share the dream, they will be empowered in their waking life. As adults talk about the interpretation of their own dreams, the child will often feel safe in talking about his own ideas of what his dream may have meant. Dream guidance should be very gentle, and children should never feel that they are being pushed.

Nightmares

Children with recurring nightmares are helped if they can be given crayons and paper and encouraged to draw the beast that scares them. When a child draws the monster or scary creature, he can put it in jail, make it look silly, or even draw a Dream Guide that is bigger and more powerful. With this simple exercise, the nightmares often cease.

Dream Champions

If your child is having difficulty in either scaring off the monsters or believing that she can change any part of her dream, you may wish to become a "Dream Champion" for your child. By becoming a "Dream Champion," you actually begin to fight the battle for your child until she either feels safe or feels empowered enough to take the battle over for herself. For example, the adult can imagine the sword in his hand and say out loud, "Now I have the sword in my hand; the hairy monster is backing up. Look how afraid he is of this bright sword! I am so powerful the monster is starting to run away, but I won't let him just run because the magic silver in the sword is going to destroy him so that he never comes back to scare you again!"

150

If at any point in the drama, you can give the sword back to your child, do so. I find that once the child feels safe and has some sense of control, she will often want the sword and will "finish" the job herself.

Dream Sharing

One delightful way to introduce children to learning about their dreams is for them to have a Dream Visitation night. Recently, my daughter invited her friends, Savanna and Roslyn, to spend the night. These girls had never done any dream work previously. Just before they went to bed, I said, "Tonight, why don't you all share your dreams. Tonight, why don't you enter each other's dreams." The following is what occurred as told in their own words.

Roslyn's Dream

"Savanna and Meadow and I were walking to a rock shop. Savanna had brought her best crystal. I had brought an orange crystal I found on the way. Meadow had brought a crystal she had found near her home. When we got to the rock workshop, everyone was cutting crystals into quarters. We sat down and started to cut ours into quarters. Savanna was very mad because she had brought her best crystal, but she did it anyway. We cut them and then we had to glue them back together. Little chips were falling out. We were to glue those back in, too. When we got done, we took our crystals and wrapped them up in paper and took them home. Savanna still had her best crystal, but it wasn't like it used to be. It still had little chips out of it that she had forgotten to glue back."

Savanna's Dream

"Meadow and I were sisters. There was a man who had kidnapped a girl. I told Meadow about it. Meadow got so mad she threw him in the swimming pool. Roslyn was watching.

151

Meadow was mad because she liked this man and he had been pretending to be nice to her."

Meadow's Dream
(A condensed version...Meadow's dreams are epic novels.)

"A few days ago, two of my friends were spending the night and my mom said, 'All of you girls are to share a dream.' It didn't seem like we all shared the same dream, but we all dreamed about each other and I am going to tell you one of the dreams I had that night:

I was with my friend, Savanna, eating at her school cafeteria, and she started punching into the principal's computer. I found myself and her, in the principal's office punching all these things into his big computer. Savanna remembered that the principal had all these rules like, 'You'll have to die if you mess with the principal's computer.' Then she remembered that we had to stick our hands in a window thing. We stuck our hand in this window, but when Savanna tried to pull her hand out, something grabbed her hand with all these bones on it and pulled her in. I grabbed her foot and pulled her out. The principal began chasing us. We ran through all these things through the whole school. We had to do all these things or die. We finally got out.

Roslyn was there and all three of us ran to the town square. I asked them, 'Do either of you have a quarter?' They said, 'No.' Savanna said, 'A quarter is a lot of money!' I ran up the hill to town and called her mother, Sandra, to see if she could come get us. And for some reason, I was becoming quarterless during all this. Finally, my mom came and I told her the story about the principal, how he was chasing us. She started videotaping him and becoming friends with him. She was kind of the hero of my dreams because she made the principal all happy and then he forgot about shaking us. And then my mom picked me up and asked me how my day was and I said, 'Oh, nothing exciting.' And then Savanna and Roslyn were picked

152

up by Sandra. Everyone was safe and happy at the end of my dream."

(Meadow's note: "I think the meaning of this dream is to go ahead and take chances and it will have a good ending. Take chances in life.")

It was interesting to note that not only did the girls recall their dreams, but each dream had all three girls in it. Without going into any in-depth dream interpretation, it is also fascinating to note that two of the dreams (Roslyn's and Meadow's) had the idea of "quarters" in them, and two of the dreams had the idea of a male protagonist who was eventually overcome.

Meadow asked if she could relate a dream that she felt was very significant to her. I have included it because it demonstrates a method of dealing in a positive manner with a child's nightmares.

Meadow's Nightmare

"A month or two ago, I had a dream about robbers and this man, who used to be my mom's friend, was one of the robbers. I was so horribly terrified. That is my biggest fear - robbers, coming in and taking things and being there. It was probably the most scary dream I ever had and I was really frightened.

And then, after talking to my mom about that dream I got really scared just talking about it. So, she put out a pillow and she said to pretend that that was the robber, so I began chopping him and hitting him with my hands and beating him. Then, the next night, I had another dream about robbers in the house. But this time I had a plan. If we heard the robbers knock on the door, at the count of three, we would open both doors - the back and the front doors. We had it all figured out. I woke up and I was a little scared, and then I thought about killing the robbers, so I wasn't scared. I think that was a really good improvement, don't you?"

"Then right after that, I had a dream that me and my mom were where this man lives who had been the robber in my first dream, and we saw this beautiful house. And, that is where he lived. And my mom said, 'Oh, it's so nice to be back again.' And, I wasn't mad at this person any more and he wasn't a 'poo poo head' anymore. So, I think I've really changed through my dreams."

By showing Meadow that she could be in control of her dream states, (i.e. by hitting the "robber" pillow), she was able to feel more powerful than her dream enemy, and this feeling translated into waking life. Meadow is no longer afraid of robbers.

The man in the moon looked out of the moon
Looked out of the moon and said,
'Tis time for all children on the earth,
To think about getting to bed.

Mother Goose

DREAM MEDITATION

To become Loom Master is to weave
with the threads of the universe,
the thread of a thought,
of a breath on the wind,
drawn from the earth
from the moon and the stars,
a textile so fine, it is the
gossamer clothing of our souls.

M. Anne Sweet

Night comes.
I move along shadowed corridors of sleep
Gentle hand placed by my side
Companion Guide 'my soul to keep.'

G. Effort

DREAM GUIDE

The three meditations contained in this book are all inward journeys which you can either read to a loved one or make into a recording of your own voice, playing it back to yourself before sleep. This first meditation will allow you access to the powerful assistance of a Dream Guide. A Dream Guide was extremely valuable to the American Indian. Guides would usher these people through the night, assisting them in transporting gifts of wisdom back from the "other side." A Dream Guide is an entity who can guide you safely through the night. A guide can help you glean greater understanding of yourself and the inner dimensions. Your guide may be someone you have known in a past lifetime or one that you have been with in this life who has already passed on. It might even be the superconsciousness of someone who is currently alive. If your guide is someone alive at the present time, it could be the conscious assistance given by a guru or master, or it could be the unconscious help from another's higher self without his conscious awareness of providing such guidance.

Dream Guide Meditation

You are about to embark on an exciting journey to that inner place within yourself. Once you have tapped into this inner place you will have access to an inner source of great strength, power and peace. You are commencing a journey where you will encounter your Dream Guide.

To set out upon this journey, lie or sit in a comfortable position. Uncross your arms and legs, get as comfortable as possible.

Do this now. Good.

As soon as you are completely comfortable, allow your eyes to close softly. Now inhale. Completely fill your lungs with air....hold for three seconds...and as you exhale, feel yourself relaxing.

Take another breath....even deeper than before.... hold....exhale completely....and experience your entire body relaxing. Now, one final and deep breath. Hold three seconds and relaxxxxx.

Good. Now focus your attention on your left foot. Feel your left foot relaxing. It is now completely relaxed. Focus your attention on your right foot. Feel your right foot relaxing. Your right foot is now completely relaxed. With each breath you take, feel yourself deliciously, pleasantly relaxing.

Now focus your awareness on your left leg and feel your left leg relaxing. Feel it completely relax. Allow yourself to be aware of your right leg and feel it relaxing. Be aware as your right leg totally relaxes. Now imagine a warm wave of relaxation rolling up from your feet, extending up through your legs, your abdomen, your chest, up to your shoulders, down your arms and all the way out through the very tips of your fingers. Imagine one warm wave after another. Good.

156

Imagine your abdomen is a balloon. As you inhale, the balloon inflates. As you exhale, imagine you are letting the air out of the balloon. As the balloon slowly, slowly deflates, you become even more relaxed. You may do this now. Good. Your entire body from the neck down is now relaxed, warm and comfortable. Now focus your awareness on your neck muscles, allowing your neck to relax. Feel your jaw and face relax, completely relax.

Now, imagine yourself in a beautiful, natural environment on a star-shimmering night. It may be by the oceanside or among the silent spaces of trees in a lush green forest, or at the peak of a lofty mountain with the moon glistening off the snow like spun crystal. Perhaps you may imagine an enchanted meadow resplendent with fawns, fairies and unicorns. This may be a place you have been before, or simply a place that exists within your imagination. It is whatever is beautiful to you...whatever makes you happy and comfortable in being there. Do this now.

Imagine this moonlit, starry place as thoroughly as possible. Spend some time seeing yourself and experiencing this environment using all your senses. Listen to the still sounds of the night. Imagine yourself walking, running, dancing and exploring in every way this moonlit cathedral of the night. Make it as real as possible by using all your senses, create it so you can feel it. Use your sense of touch, smell and sight. Good.

Now, somewhere in this natural environment, imagine a still pool - still...deep...serene...clear. This is a quiet pond with moonlight secrets hidden in its depths...a spring-fed pool where you can see your own reflection, altered as if in a dream. Its surface is satin, glass-clear water...still water. This water is dedicated to your intuition, your clarity and your dreams. Take just a short while to really visualize the water. Then, as you are observing this still pool, you begin to notice a mist that is forming over its surface. This mist grows, beginning to swirl and dance as if it has a life of its own. Whirling, twirling and dancing, the mist reaches out until the entire environment is wrapped in this mystical fog. You feel totally comfortable, safe and serene.

As you stand bathed in the moonlit comfort of these mists, your intuition gently informs you that someone is approaching in the distance. As you sense the presence coming closer and closer, you are aware of great strength, great power, and of great radiance. A calm serenity radiates from this being as he or she comes closer...and still closer. You await this arrival with anticipation. You experience a deep connection with this being as your Guide continues to make its way into your presence. Through the mist, you can feel in every cell of your being the pervading love and absolute, unconditional acceptance that is given to you by your Guide.

Your Guide is coming forth from the Ages to provide you with insight, to give you assistance through the night, to allow you to access your own power and perfection in the waking hours. And now, your Guide is coming closer to you, stepping forward, each step bringing this being closer to your side. You sense your Guide being very close now. Such brilliant radiance. Such divine power. This being knows you intimately and has awaited your call through eons of time. Reach out now with your hands extended toward your Dream Guide. As you do, be aware, feel and experience your Guide's hand gently slipping into your own. In this moment you feel a relaxation so deep that it touches the very core of your being as you are guided into the quiet realm of the night. When you go to bed each evening, imagine your Guide's hand in your own. Know this Being is with you, now and forever, to guide and lead you through the mysteries of the night.

The mists now begin to clear, enabling you to clearly see the form and features of your Guide. If you are not able to visualize, then get a sense or feeling of your Guide. For example, you might not be able to see a waterfall, however, you can get a feeling of the freshness of the waterfall. Now, take some time to be with your Guide. You may wish to ask your Guide's name or other questions, or you may simply choose to sit with your Guide, wrapped only in the gentle silence of the moonlit night.

If you desire, your Dream Guide will come with you night after night during your sleep to assist you in dealing with difficulties presented during the day. Your Guide can also facilitate your learning greater wisdom for the future or from the past, as well as assist you in exploring other dimensions.

Say good-bye to your Guide.

At this time, you may wish to drift off to sleep. If you wish to return to normal waking consciousness, however, simply take a deep breath...and in your own time, and when you are ready, allow your eyes to gently open....

I open my heart to the Knowingness,
Conveyed through the years it brings love.
The joy of my soul overflows;
I spin and dance and jump twirling,
Leaping higher and higher, unlimited
for my spirit is free.
I cut myself loose from the puppet strings
which have danced someone else's dance for me.

M. Anne Sweet

DREAM SHIELD MEDITATION

A Dream Shield is a personal power object. It is a way to cultivate inner power and strength. It can be used to experience deep understanding of the Ancient Mysteries and will keep you and your loved ones protected. The symbols that you place on your shield are rudiments of your own individual mythology and will allow you to be more in alignment with your life's purpose. Here is a letter received from someone who accessed the power of a Dream Shield.

Dear Denise,

I wanted to let you know what happened after I took your "Past Life Seminar" where we did the "Dream Shield" technique. On Sunday night, after the seminar, I received a phone call advising me that my brother had died that morning after having a heart attack Saturday evening. I did not communicate with his widow directly because there has been lots of "stuff and junk" between us for over twenty years.

After the phone call, I talked with my good friend Gina. I commented that I probably would not attend the funeral, as I was fearful of having a family confrontation. I experienced a major quarrel some years ago at my father's funeral between this brother, his wife and I. Gina indicated that the funeral could possibly be a means of deep healing for myself and that I might not have such an opportunity for a long time. I told Gina that I would ask for dream guidance and follow that guidance. We continued to chat about other things and then I went to bed.

I consciously did not create my "Dream Shield" as I turned off the light. I recognize now, that my subconscious had already been programmed by the "Dream Shield" process that we had done earlier in the day at your seminar. I went to bed and slept soundly. I woke up at 4:30 a.m. very surprised. Dream recall is a very new process for me, as are visual pictures. My pillow was sopping wet, for I had apparently been silently weeping. I had a vivid dream where I was standing at the cemetery under a canopy and I was reading a letter of farewell. I felt extremely calm, healed and peaceful. I knew that everything was okay. I did not have any anxiety about recalling the letter for I "knew" that I could recall it at the office when I went to work later. Everything felt perfect and serene.

That evening I received the details of the service and asked Carol, my brother's widow, if I could have the time to read my letter. My request was granted without argument even though I could sense some attempt to manipulate me. It was as though I was "shielded."

On Thursday, at the funeral, I read my letter and felt an immediate sense of deep, deep peace with my brothers, both Fred, who had just died, and my other brothers. At the end of the reading, I placed a bouquet of rainbow-colored carnations on the casket. After the service, as we comforted each other, there seemed to be a feeling of deep compassion and a sense of true togetherness. His widow thanked me for the poem and asked me for a copy. The gathering afterwards was a very warm and friendly time both for our friends and family.

It was an extremely healing process and I had a real sense of completion. This was much more than I ever could have believed was possible.

    Love,
    Vi Randall

p.s. I've included the eulogy that I wrote for my brother as it was dream inspired.

Eulogy for Frederic

On November 8, 1987, the spirit of Frederic returned home. This is the fall or "earth" season, the time of dying, of gathering home all things that will nurture and sustain life through the dormant winter or "fire" season. This was Fred's season and he lived the essence well. He nurtured his family, he worked with his hands, and he enjoyed life to the fullest when in the company of his family.

Today, November 12, I honor the spirit of my brother, and I speak words of love and send him many rainbows to help him return to the Great Spirit from which all life comes. Father Sky and Mother Earth are in harmony on this day to grant him a safe journey. During the last year, his mother and older sister completed their journey and he now joins them. We will miss him as we have missed Elsia and Rondalyn, but to all things there is a season. A time to mourn. A time to cry. A time to be born. A time to die. This is our time to honor our brother, our friend, our soulmate in our own way. This is the time for our own reflection, a time to release our fears, our jealousies, our anger, our hate and mistrust. A time to acknowledge that we are all one family on this planet Earth. A time to come together, in spirit and harmony, to wish and grant each other the same love and peace that we wish Frederic. To his widow, I send understanding and love to sustain her during this transition. To his children, I send knowledge that their father taught wisdom and faith. To his brothers, strength and serenity. To all his friends and family, unconditional love.

Let each of us honor Frederic in our own way as he is laid to rest with his father. His physical journey has been completed but his spiritual journey continues. From Father Sky, I call upon the Wind to blow his spirit gently home. From Mother Earth, I call upon her to receive him home. May the spirits of Fire purify all thoughts, and may the spirit of Water, cleanse and wash away his hurts, anger and disappointments.

In closing, grant me forgiveness for my trespasses. I love you, Frederic, older brother and mentor. Thank you for being my teacher. I'll miss you.

Dream Shield Meditation

The Dream Shield Meditation is based on ancient dream techniques. This safe, easy technique is best done just before sleep. You can record this meditation on a tape to be played back to yourself before bed. Speak with a very slow, relaxed voice. You might want to include a musical background. You can also read it to friends or use it for clients.

To begin this process, first allow your body to assume a restful position, making sure your spine is straight. You may do this now. Good.

Now begin to take very easy deep breaths....nice, easy deep breaths. Inhale and exhale. That's good. It is almost as if you are being breathed. It's as if nothing else exists except for your breath. In and out. All your thoughts and cares are drifting away as you continue to breath in and out. With each breath you take, you find yourself relaxing more and more. You find yourself moving deeper and deeper within yourself. Imagine that you are flowing into your body with the oxygen as it enters your lungs. Then, you are flowing out of your body as your body exhales that oxygen. In and out. Each breath taking you deeper. It is as if you are drifting and flowing with the very gentle ebbing and flowing of the air that you are breathing. There is a rhythm, a balance to the universe and your breath is connecting you to that rhythm, that harmony. Breathe gently and evenly as you continue your journey into a very relaxed, yet aware, state. Allow your awareness to gently drift into your body and allow yourself to be aware of any tightness. Just notice it. Good.

Feel that tightness just melting away like ice melting on a warm summer afternoon. That's good. Drifting and floating. Drifting and floating. Now allow your imagination to begin to drift and float. Just drift and float and imagine in your mind's eye a moonlit night. You are walking along an ocean shore on a warm, softly-dark evening. Your entire body feels relaxed and you are moving with grace and ease. The soft sensuous sounds of the ocean are serenely lulling you into a brilliant deep, calm place within yourself. In the distance, you are aware of a great shimmering, sparkling and glimmering spot on the ocean shore. As you approach it, you can see thousands and thousands of crystals lying on the sand. Their luminescent beauty reflected by the light of the moon. Each crystal seems to have its own inner glow that is so magical...so mysterious. You walk through the myriad of crystals, each sparkles, so effervescent.......each is seemingly lit by its own inner light. In the distance, you see a particular crystal...a special crystal that seems to draw you to it. Reach out and pick up the crystal. The instant it touches your hand, it is as if thousands of tranquil electrical currents are surging and flowing through your body. Take a deep breath and feel the power that is enveloping you. This is your power flowing into your Dream Crystal.

As you put this Dream Crystal into your pocket, you begin to hear a deep, resonating tone. Touching the crystal has activated a powerful resonance within you. It feels as if your very being is beginning to resonate as well. Appearing before you in the moonlit night is a shield. It seems to be translucent at first. It is only a veil of light and sound, but as you stand and observe it, it becomes solid. As you observe this shield, this Dream Shield, you are aware that carved and engraved upon its surface is a symbol - a symbol that only you can see. No one should ever know what this symbol is. It is for you alone.

Now reach forward and grasp the shield. Feel the great sense of security and safety afforded you just by holding this Dream Shield. And as you hold this Dream Shield, you are in awe as you watch the environment begin to change. When you touch the crystal to the Dream Shield, you activate an ancient and powerful force field...a force field that has wanted to be activated for generation upon generation...a force field that will allow you access to the same dream powers the Ancients accessed.

And now the earth begins to shake beneath your feet. You feel great, mighty movements of earth. As you walk holding the shield, you observe the splendid scene of the earth being formed. Hills are moving and valleys forming. Mountains are pushed up into splendid jagged edges reaching for the sky. Observe as the substance of Earth is moving through its creation. As you stand observing this magnificence, it is as if you are one with creation...you are one with the elements of Earth. Earth is physical strength. It is being a part of the physical dimension. Touch your shield to the earth and let the earth empower your shield. Your shield has now been activated with the power of the element of Earth.

As you continue walking, the winds begin to rise. With more and more power, the winds are whipping around you and pushing through you. Hold your shield to the wind and let the element of Air empower and activate your shield. The element of Air unlocks our high ideals. It is the divine process of thought. Feel yourself strengthened as you become one with the element of Air.

And now the air becomes still...nothing is moving. Then you feel moisture, one drop, then another, then another falls. It is the beginning of the time of the Great Rains. Hold your shield over your head as torrents of rain begin to cascade down around you and your shield.

Be aware as the element of Water is activating your shield. Let yourself feel the strength of the element of Water. Water represents intuition. It is spiritual. It is fluid. Allow yourself to become one with the element of Water. Feel the great power of Water activate your shield.

And now, although the rains are subsiding, great bolts of lightning begin to punctuate the sky. Again and again powerful bolts of lightning streak through the atmosphere above you and thunder reverberates around you. Raise your shield high over your head with both feet firmly planted on Mother Earth. Feel the surge of a bolt of lightning as it strikes your Dream Shield. Feel the power and strength course through your shield, down your arms, through your veins, as the lightning grounds through your feet as your Shield is activated with the power of the element of Fire. Fire represents inner growth.

Your Dream Shield is complete. It has been activated by the elements of Earth, Air, Water and Fire. You are now ready for dream exploration and dream adventures.

Now you notice that you are beside a door. Take a short time to be aware of this door. Is it big or small? Is it old or new, ornate or plain? This is the mystic door to your dreams. Take just a moment to examine it. Your Dream Crystal and Dream Shield are the keys to open this door. Decide which area you wish to explore in your dreams. Do you wish to do problem-solving for a difficulty that you are having in waking life? Do you want adventure and romance? Do you want to explore the psychic realm? Do you want healing for yourself and others? Decide what you want to explore in your dream realm. You may do this now. Good.

Imagine you are holding your Dream Crystal to your third eye area, (the area that is slightly above and between your eyes). Dedicate your Dream Crystal to your dream quest. Hold your Shield with one hand and your Dream Crystal in the other and lightly touch the door with your Dream Crystal. The door begins to open. As it does, your shield and crystal become invisible, but still a part of your energy field. You are now welcome to enter the world of dreams.

You are remembering to accept unconditionally whatever occurs during this dream state. If you notice your mind making judgments, just thank your mind for its concerns and keep going. If you see dream enemies, confront them. Request a present from them. Always move toward pleasure in your dreams.

And now, step into the realm of dreams. Take a short while to explore the dimension of dreams. You may do this now. Use your imagination to enhance your dreams. You have a short while to do this. You may do this now.

Prepare to leave the realm of dreams. It is a realm to which you can return night after night. Begin your departure by taking a deep breath. I am going to count from one to ten and as I do, allow yourself to begin to return to normal waking consciousness. Or, if you so desire, drift off into a deep, restful sleep.

One - every number you hear deepens your ability to remember your dreams.

Two - your dreams are valid and you understand the meaning of your dreams.

Three - every dream you have, whether it is remembered or not, greatly enhances your waking hours.

Four - feeling rested and rejuvenated.

Five - you are very rested and refreshed and your body vibrates with excellent health.

Six - your ability to be in the right place at the right time is greatly enhanced by your dreams.

Seven - you are one of the light workers of the night and you contribute to the well-being of others during your sleep, even if you are not aware of it.

Eight - if you choose sleep, it comes soundly and easily.

Nine - you are more and more awake; more and more aware.

Ten - if you choose, you can now move to normal waking consciousness.

Sweet dreams!

In the meshing of our sleep, our dreams, is the meshing of our souls;
we share the butterflies of our hearts,
the birds of our childhood, called to us with love,
inner voices singing in harmony to the tune of their song.

M. Anne Sweet

THE DREAM LOVER MEDITATION

> *"I want a dream lover,*
> *So I don't have to dream alone...."*
> Bobby Darin

The dream lover meditation is designed to provide you with increased awareness of your own sensuality and sexuality. When your sexual/sensual energy is open and clear, you will naturally experience and enjoy life more fully. You can utilize this meditation during your waking hours, or you can use it just before sleep as a means of programming your night hours for sensual encounters.

My initial attempts at creating a lover from the land of dreams were less than the sizzling trysts I had anticipated. My first dream lover was a pale, withdrawn, insipid lad that looked about 15 years old (though he whiningly sought to convince me he was much older). This was definitely not what I had in mind. I terminated the dream. My endeavor the following evening centered around a robust, burly man (not my type, but a definite improvement over a spindly teenage love) with a noticeable bulge in his pants. Fortunately, with my *dream x-ray eyes*, I could see the oversized potato he had stuck in his pants in hope of luring me to his bed. I again made a hasty retreat. My next attempt was a dark, foreboding shadow of a presence who tried to force his attentions on me. Foiled again!

My fourth dream lover, finally, was more of a success. The dream was set in 18th-century Italy. This lover was neither too young nor too old. He possessed all the correct physical equipment. He was strong, kind and romantic...he was perfect! I even met his entire passionate Catholic family. He then informed me we could not make love until we were married, informed me we could not make love until we were married, and our marriage would not occur until after his older brother had married. Brother!!!

At least this last dream gave me a clue as to why I was having so many difficulties obtaining a desirable dream lover. My puritanical upbringing was making it unacceptable on a subconscious level for me to take a lover (any lover including a dream lover), in that I was already married. In discussing the situation with my husband, David, he shared that he had always had dream lovers, and felt that they were important for his own sense of well-being. In short, he encouraged me in my nightly endeavors.

I also knew that individuals with an active dream sex life usually were more creative in all waking aspects of their life. So, I intensified my efforts! After a few more feeble encounters, it became <u>definitely</u> worth the effort. I strongly recommend it! One immediate benefit was that my dream escapades greatly enhanced the sexual relations I had with my husband.

Often a man or woman secretly desires to have an affair, not necessarily because he or she experiences any lack in a present relationship, but because of a desire for change or some variety. Taking a dream lover (or lots of dream lovers) is one constructive way to fulfill that desire for diversity while keeping your present love relationship intact. It is also excellent for the single person, since a dream lover can appease the compulsive <u>need</u> to be with a partner. Consequently, you can be more at choice in your selection of a companion.

Preparation for Meditation

If you are using the lines below to make a tape for your own use or if you are reading them to another...first create a restful setting...phone off the hook, lights low. Be in a setting where you will have little or no distraction. Use a very slow, sensuous voice when doing this meditation. If you are making a tape, you may wish to have some music in the background. Select music that is very sensuous and arousing for you.

DREAM LOVER MEDITATION

To begin this dream lover meditation, first make certain that your body is completely comfortable and in a relaxed position. Good. Now, check to see that your spine is straight and your arms and legs uncrossed. That's good. As your body begins to move into very deep relaxation, notice that each breath you take is allowing you to move deeper and deeper within yourself. Simply watch your breath for a moment. You aren't encouraging your breath or denying your breath, just observing your breath. In and out...day and night...light and dark...black and white...male and female...yin and yang. There are two opposing, yet complementary, forces existing in the universe. In this moment, you are aligning and becoming one with those forces. In and out...keep watching your breath. Good. Now allow each breath to become deeper and fuller, deeper and fuller. Nice, deep, full breaths. That's good.

Now allow your imagination to take wing and see yourself in an enchanted, moonlit meadow. The moon is spilling out of the heavens in cascading waterfalls of light. A mist of scented jasmine caresses the slumbering ferns already curled up for the night. A dream owl hovers overhead, his silvery reflection in the stream below seen only by the stars. The surrounding trees murmur gentle secrets in their soft-footed shadows. There is a quiet magic in the air.
Now spend some time imagining yourself in this secret garden of the night. Make it as real as you can. Image yourself using all of your senses to experience this place of quiet beauty, and image yourself walking through the meadow. If you cannot visualize, get a sense or a feeling of being in the meadow. Your body feels very graceful, very sensuous, very relaxed and easy.

You notice that in the center of the meadow there is a bed. It is a sumptuous bed. It is so luxurious and voluptuous. The

171

You notice that in the center of the meadow there is a bed. It is a sumptuous bed. It is so luxurious and voluptuous. The pillows are soft and round and firm. Take some time to really imagine this bed, making it as real as possible. Make it your perfect bed. It might be a big, four-poster bed like your grandmother's feather bed or, perhaps, a canopied bed draped with gossamer, luminescent fabric lightly caressed by the warm breeze. What kind of bed is this? Really imagine this bed.

Now slowly and ever so sensuously, climb into this bed. Be aware of the opulent plumpness of the pillows. Feel the silky smoothness of the sheets as you slide easily beneath the covers. It feels so good to be in this bed. Fanned by the gentle fragrance of the night, you find yourself drifting off into a deep, deep, deep sleep. Deep.... deep..... deep.........sleeeeeep.

Somewhere in the magic of the night, you gently roll over and stretch. As you do, your hand brushes against a warm body. Your eyes are closed, yet you intuitively know this is your dream lover. While you tentatively explore the subtle curves in the mountains and valleys of your lover's body, twilight dances on your silhouettes and the entire heavens are a part of you. Deliciously warm waves of intimacy bathe your being. You caress and possess, and experience the faint, stirring breath of your dream lover softly in your hair. Take just a few moments to imagine the most exquisite...the most remarkable love-making. Feel your spirit, your entire being, soar to unlimited heights.

The dawn is approaching. As you lie nestled in your lover's arms, feeling such a lingering sense of deep fulfillment, you drift off into a contented sleep. When your eyes open, the sunlight is sending yellow needles darting through the joyous spaces of the forest trees. Your dream lover has vanished in the silent whispers of the night. A perfect rose graces your pillow.

At the end of this meditation, you can either move into the sleep state or move to normal waking consciousness. If you wish to return to normal waking consciousness, then count from one to ten and suggest that with each number, you feel more and more awake.

DREAM MEANING

At the outset of our night voyage,
I am hesitant, overwhelmed
by the immensity of the crossing;
innate wisdom of my inner sage
speaks reassurances to my childlike soul --
I breathe and step out, the journey
is given when the spirit is ready.

M. Anne Sweet

Drain pipes clog and septic tank backs up,
I hold in anger at the unfairness of a friend--
I tell myself the pipes are frozen from the weather,
and that my friend does what she must, I'm taking it too hard.
The weather warms--I talk to my friend and call the plumber.

M. Anne Sweet

DREAM SYMBOLS FOR LIFE

Golden sunlight streamed in through my frosty morning window. I sat watching the steam rise from my cup of peppermint tea, loving the way it danced in misty swirls like ethereal, disappearing sprites. Abby, my amber-colored cat, stretched lazily and curled up again, nuzzling her nose into velvet paws. Ruffling my fingers through her tawny, warm fur, I reached up and randomly flipped on the television set. As I took my first hesitant sips of hot tea, I watched part of a show focusing on a blind boy and the difficulties he encountered in life. Later that evening I decided to catch the late night news and *coincidentaly* saw the end of a show featuring a blind girl coping with her life. (*When you listen to the whispers, you don't have to hear the screams.*)

The next day, as I drove home after dropping my daughter off at school, I passed by a bus stop. Curiously there stood two blind men leaning nonchalantly on their white canes. (*When you listen to the whispers, you don't have to hear the screams.*)

Later, driving to the grocery store, a blind man unexpectedly stepped out into the path of my car. I slammed on the brakes, white-fisted the wheel and stopped just short of hitting this frail gentleman. I pulled over to the curb to collect my breath. I had not listened to the whispers and had almost heard the screams.

The universe every day, in every way, is trying to tell you something, just as your dreams are attempting to give you messages during the night. If you see a blind person in your dream, you might interpret that symbol as something you are "refusing to see" in your life. Your Waking Symbols are no less viable or significant. At the particular time in my life when I was being made aware of "blindness," there <u>was</u> something that I "wasn't seeing." My Waking Symbols were my higher self's way of letting me know. Unfortunately, I sometimes have to be hit over the head before I will slow down and focus my attention on what is being communicated. When I paused and looked more closely at the symbolic experiences I was having, I confronted and released what I had been unwilling to see or "what I was being blind to."

Waking life is no less an illusion than dream life. In my Zen training, both waking <u>and</u> sleeping images were considered illusions. We were urged to touch a deeper reality. Use the symbols that you notice in your waking life in the same manner in which you utilize you dream symbols. For example, just as your car may be a symbol for you and your body in your dreams, experiences relating to cars can be symbolic during your waking experiences.

One brisk September morning, Meadow, my ten-year-old daughter, and I were driving home from our country cabin. David had gone on ahead in our other vehicle. Stately, tall pines caressed the low-hanging clouds as we sailed over the high mountain pass and wound our way past vacated ski slopes. Suddenly, the engine in my car began to rev uncontrollably. I laid all my weight onto the brake, but my car continued gaining momentum, as it raced down the steep mountain road. I grabbed the emergency brake and yanked on it frantically as I turned off the engine. My car finally skidded to a stop.

When I was able to get a tow truck, the mechanic jumped out, looked over my car and easily started it up. "There doesn't seem to be any problem with this car, lady." I started the car and the engine sounded like someone had floored it. We towed the car 75 miles into town.

The next mechanic gave his diagnosis, "There's nothing wrong with this car, lady." Yet, when I got in and turned on the ignition, it almost ran through the back wall of the garage. *(If you listen to the whispers, you don't have to hear the screams.)* I finally discovered a mechanic who determined that the cruise control had broken.

What did my run-away car represent or symbolize to me? What was I trying to tell myself? To me, a car is a symbol of my body or my physical being. (See "car" in chapter on "DREAM SYMBOLS".) My car was racing out of control. It didn't have the ability to cruise. The only way it could operate was to get completely wound out. At that time in my life, I was completely wound out. I had a very intense seminar schedule and was spending most of my time thinking (or worrying) about the future instead of being in the present. My car's difficulties were telling me to slow down and smell the flowers, to set my life's course on "cruise control" and enjoy life.

Every day, in every way, the universe is trying to tell you something. A further example of this concept is the plumbing in my house. To me, plumbing represents my emotions. If the plumbing clogs or the pipes freeze, it's usually an indication that my emotions are backing up or are frozen. If I take the time to discover what it is that I am blocking emotionally and allow my emotions to run freely, the pipes will generally unplug. In like manner, I have noticed that when the basement begins to flood, it is usually when my emotions are running amuck and I am not taking the time to center and be still.

It's also valuable to notice the little bits of conversations you hear randomly in passing. One day, as I was being led to a table in a Chinese restaurant, I heard a snippet of conversation, **"...don't go ahead with the project."** Upon leaving the restaurant, I turned on the radio to hear a song, **"...don't go, Baby, don't go."** The newscast that followed mentioned, "...the engineers have been advised **not to go ahead with the project."** Was the universe trying to warn me not to go ahead with something? I had been scheduled to go to Washington, D.C. to work on a project, but listening to the subtle voices of the universe I decided not to go. It was a fortunate decision. The plane I had been scheduled to take was forced to land in Chicago due to blizzard conditions and no planes were able to get in or out of Washington, D.C. If I had gone, I would have missed my meetings and incurred a great deal of unnecessary expense.

The people in your life can also be symbols of your inner growth. I had moved to a new city and begun my practice. My first client told me that she was an agoraphobic. I had never even heard the term before. I found that it literally meant "fear of the marketplace" and was a term applied to someone who was afraid of going out into the world. Curiously, my *next* client was an agoraphobiac and then to my amazement, *my third client was also an agoraphobiac!* Three in a row!

When a symbol appears three times in my life (or in my dreams), I begin to listen very carefully. I knew that I didn't fit the classic definition of an agoraphobiac. I was comfortable in crowds ordinarily and could easily leave my home without feeling anxious. However, as I began to delve more deeply into myself, I noticed some raw truths. In our move, I had left behind many dear friends. My new environment seemed cold and hostile to me, and emotionally I had no desire to venture forth. The agoraphobiacs were waking symbols of my not wanting to venture out into my new environment. Once I became aware of these thoughts and feelings and began to take emotional risks, not only did I begin to enjoy my new city more, I noticed I began drawing clients that were more outgoing and, *coincidently,* my agoraphobic clients also began to get better. (See chapter on "DREAMS FOR HEALING.")

There also was a time when the majority of my clients were women who had not been able to get pregnant and were wanting to conceive. Knowing that I didn't want to have any more children, I was puzzled by this waking symbol. But, when I began to "give birth" to a new self-understanding, the women with whom I was working began to conceive, one by one.

Everything and everyone in your life, as well as in your dreams, is trying to tell you something...from the billboards you see to the formations you observe in the clouds, from simple things like losing your keys to the gifts you are given. You can use the symbols noted in this book as both dream symbols and waking symbols.

O dreams; Keep me by you!
Let your soft-footed shadows carry me
dancing through the midnight skies,
laughing to the outer edges of the universe.

DREAM METHODS

Each morning you wake with a light mist of a memory. Elusive fragments of dreams quickly disappear and the hazy clouds clear until you realize you are here...now...awake. Occasionally a dream is so vivid, you almost feel you could walk heartily back into it. Sometimes these dreams will continue to tug at your consciousness and you wonder what they mean for your life today, or yesterday, or tomorrow?

There are many methods that you can use to interpret your dreams. Each may take you on a unique pathway in understanding yourself and your inner soul. How you interpret the dream is less important than the meaning that you personally derive from it. You may look at each dream as a separate and new revelation, or view your dreams over time as a collective whole.

Here are some traditionally-used methods of dream interpretation. You might work with several of them or use one at a time. There is no "right" way or "wrong" way. Remember, have fun and find the one that works best for you.

Method 1: Make a Dream Journal. Record every dream that you remember for at least three months. Watch for recurring themes, people, places, feelings or situations. Important messages from the unconscious can be uncovered through this method. (See chapter on "DREAM RECALL.")

Method 2: Make yourself a Dream Dictionary. Make yourself a dream dictionary creating those symbols that are unique for you. Whenever you have a dream, write down the different symbols that appear in the dream. Then list the meanings that you personally assign to those symbols. As you begin to assemble a collection of your personal dream symbols put them in dictionary form. Refer to this dictionary each time you dream. You will find the more you use your personal dream dictionary the more insight you will gain into the symbols that you have listed. This is a powerful way to gain self-awareness.

Method 3: Watch that dream feeling. Find the feeling or emotion that you had as a result of your dream. Now look back over your life and remember the last time you had that feeling. Recall the situation which evoked that similar emotion. Most often it is either that particular situation or the issues underlying that situation that have evoked your dream. This can be a real clue to assist you to find the significance of your dream.

Method 4: Talk with your Dream Guide. Ask your Dream Guide for help in understanding and interpreting your dreams. This is the method that seems to work the best for me. (See chapter on "DREAM GUIDE.")

Method 5: Gestalt the dream. Go back into your dreams and take the part of each of the characters in the dreams. For example, perhaps you dreamed about a "man," a "child" and a "wood stove." To use this method you would say, "I am the wood stove and I represent ____ ." (Here you would say what "wood stoves" represent to you. Perhaps they represent "contained warmth" or perhaps they represent "family and friends.") Then you would say, "I am the child and I represent____." Continue to do this for each of the different parts of your dream until each one is clearly defined.

After you have defined the different parts of your dream in this way, have the different parts talk to each other. For example, you can put out three chairs. One chair represents the wood stove, one chair represents the child and one chair represents the man. Sit in the "wood stove chair" and talk to the other two chairs saying perhaps, "I represent family and friends and inner warmth and I think families should always be together as they are when they sit around wood stoves." Then, sit in the "child chair" and a likely scenario might be, "I'm the child and I don't want to be with the family sitting around the wood stove. I want to be outside so I can run and play. I don't want to be tied down. I feel confined and stifled when I sit around with the family." Continue with this process until you have a clearer sense of the true meaning of your dream.

Method 6: Draw your dream. Draw pictures that exemplify the feeling or the images that you have had in your dream. Utilize colors that reflect the tone of the dream. You do not have to always draw the exact images. For example, a black horse in your dreams does not have to look like a horse in your drawing. You can draw the feeling of "black," "movement," or "power." This exercise can begin to free you so that some of your unconscious feeling can rise to the surface.

Method 7: Use free association. This is based on Freud's most acclaimed theory. This consists of writing associations or the first idea that comes to mind for each part of the dream. This may give you clues to the major themes you are dealing with in the dream. For example, imagine that you dream about a rabbit. A free association might be: Rabbit -- Peter Rabbit -- my brother Peter who used to beat up on me -- "Hey, I'm feeling really beaten up by life these days!!"

Method 8: Pretend you meet a Martian. Pretend that you are telling your dream to an alien from another planet. The alien doesn't know anything about earth. For example, there is a broom in your dream. How would you describe this broom to your friend from Mars? You might say, "A broom is a long object that you hold close to you and then push away from you. It helps you get rid of things that you don't want." After you have described the broom to your imaginary alien friend, you might examine your life and notice if there is anything that you want to rid yourself of. It might be something that you are pulling toward yourself and then pushing away. As you begin to literally describe the parts of your dream to the alien in the most basic language, often the meaning of your dream becomes clear.

Method 9: Complete the plot. Go back into your dream in your waking hours and rework the dream in a way that you can end up the victor. You can change any uncomfortable part of it. You can be the hero. Conquer your dream enemies! Make your dream have a happy ending!

Method 10. Act out your dream! The Iroquois Indians regularly acted out their dreams in a drama or play fashion. You may do this in a group or do it on your own. The idea is to allow your body to physically act out the different aspects of your dream. This begins to integrate the meaning of your dreams more deeply into your physical reality.

Method ll: Utilize symbology. Go through the symbols in the Symbol Dictionary of this book. Find the symbols in your dream. Go through the colors, the numbers, and all the various symbols. Notice which ones feel right for you.

Method 12: Use the Chinese Clock Method. See chapter on "CHINESE CLOCK METHOD."

Method 13: Try the Kelly Method. Place your awareness of the dream in the right side of your brain. Play through the dream, staying in the right side of the brain. (This is the intuitive side of the brain.) Then shift your awareness to the left side of the brain. (This is the side of the brain which analyzes.) Replay your dream. Notice the difference in how your body feels when you rerun the dream on one side of the brain and then on the other. Notice how reviewing the dream will illicit different emotions depending on which side of the brain you use to replay it. You may also find that your interpretation of the dream will be altered depending on the side you choose.

The first dream of the year;
I kept it a secret
And smiled to myself.

Sho-u

SEASONS

The Earth Dimension is seasonal. Everything that dwells on the planet is affected by the seasons in one way or another. In ancient times the understanding of the power of the seasons was considered necessary to be able to understand the mysteries of life. In 250 B.C. a secret "mystery school" was founded in China that centered its teachings around the esoteric comprehension of the seasons. The teaching was preserved through secret societies of the Middle Ages and it eventually blossomed into the study of astrology. Each of the seasons has a profound affect upon our psyches and each season represents an integral part of who we are. Just as we have our cycles of learning and cycles of resting, we also have monthly cycles and yearly cycles. Dreaming also follows the cycles of nature during the year.

WINTER

Under the Winter moon
The river wind
Sharpens the rocks

Chora

Dreams during the winter months are the most powerful and the clearest. They directly concern your spiritual awareness. This is your time of inner growth, your time of going within, of looking within. These dreams are planting seeds for the year to come. This is the time when visionary dreams concerning war, religion and politics are most likely to occur. You are more apt to remember your dreams in winter. You are getting ready to blossom into spring. A winter setting in a dream will indicate a drawing inward of your energies.

SPRING

Yes, Spring has come,
This morning a nameless hill
Is shrouded in mist

Basho

Dreams that occur in the spring have to do with new direction. They will deal with your emotional self, your feelings about self and others. This is when you will most likely have visionary dreams concerning motherhood, teachings and disease. A spring setting in a dream signifies new growth and new beginnings.

SUMMER

The summer moon
Is touched by the line
Of a fishing rod.

Chiyo-ni

The dreams in the summertime have to do with your intellectual self, your thought processes and social concern. Visionary dreams concerning invention and science occur more during this season than the other seasons. Summer appearing in a dream can represent a carefree joy.

AUTUMN

The autumn mountains;
Here and there
Smoke rising

Gyodai

Dreams during the fall or autumn will often have to do with completion. Dreams in this season can concern your physical body. They have to do with sexuality, completion, and creativity. This is the time when you are most likely to get creative inspiration in your dreams. Dreaming about autumn will often relate to harvest and abundance of ideas, beliefs and of material goods.

morning rooster crows,
dreams are ending...
or are they just beginning?

        Denise Linn

ANCIENT CHINESE CLOCK DREAM INTERPRETATION

The veil of fog and mystique that has surrounded Chinese medicine has begun to part in recent years, and western doctors are beginning to give credence to this ancient art. The Chinese were stewards of a sophisticated and practical medical system thousands of years before western doctors even began to bloodlet with leeches. Magnificent finds, such as the circulation of the blood, are mentioned in the *Yellow Emperors's Book of Internal Medicine* written over 4,000 years ago.

In Chinese cosmology the source of all things is the *tao* which is considered the law of the universe. From the *tao* flows the *one* energy. The two opposing yet complementary forces of the universe blending to form the *one* are called yin and yang. Yin represents the female energy - it corresponds to that which is dark, soft, receptive, moist, cool and declining. Yang represents the male energy - it corresponds to that which is light, dry, hot, active and rising. It is the dance, the dynamic interaction between these two forces that create the life force energy of *chi* . *Chi* is the life force that exists in everything, from the most etheric matter such as light, to the most dense such as granite. All matter is imbued with *chi* and chi is divided into different aspects as it is manifested in the universe. These different aspects or elements correspond to the different seasons, the different organs, and the different hours of the day. They are all are manifest within humankind, linking us with the rest of our environment. Each hour of the day corresponds to a different organ and a corresponding emotion.

This system, based on Chinese philosophy, divides the day into different time periods. Each time period relates to a different organ of the body. Just as each organ is thought to have corresponding emotions and characteristics, the dreams that you have during each time period will also be unique to those characteristics. Thus, it is important to note the time of your dream in order to utilize this method and derive the full benefit.

Listed on the next pages is an hourly guide that will help you interpret your dreams based on the hour in which they are dreamed.

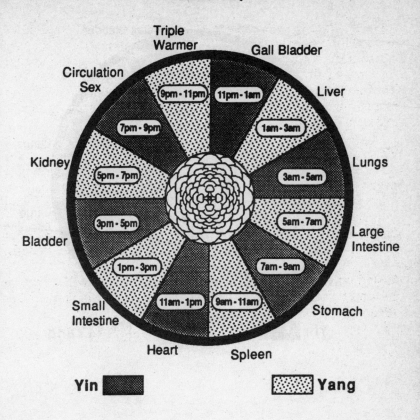

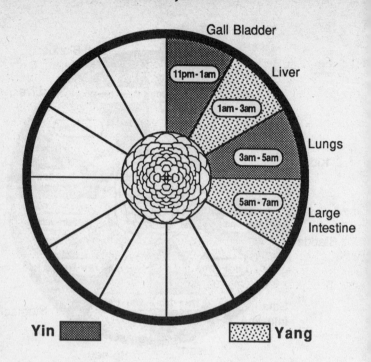

Gall Bladder

11pm-1am

Liver

1am-3am

Lungs

3am-5am

5am-7am

Large
Intestine

Yin

Yang

11 P.M. - 1 A.M.

If you have a dream during the time period from 11:00 p.m. to 1:00 a.m. (the period called gall bladder time by ancient Chinese) your dream will often focus around issues of unresolved anger, especially anger with regard to external circumstances. Any difficulty arising during this time period should be confronted within the dream state. This is also the time of courage. The courage you gain in your dreams will translate to courage in your life.

1 A.M. - 3 A.M.

Dreams occurring from 1:00 to 3:00 a.m., liver time, might concern issues of self-anger, purification and the will to live. Dreams within this time period can reveal areas that need to be cleansed or purified within your life. The liver is the one organ that can regenerate itself. Within this period your dreams will have to do with the future and also with personal regeneration.

3 A.M. - 5 A.M.

Dreams during the hours of 3:00 to 5:00 a.m., lung time, will generally concern issues of spiritual development, inner grief, receiving love, letting go, completion, freedom and expression. It is during this time that you will most likely experience psychic and transformational dreams. This is also the time when you are most likely to receive dreams that are other-dimensional, or dreams from a loved one who has already passed on. This is an excellent time for astral travel and usually is when most astral travel occurs. Ancient Chinese say that this is the beginning of the spiritual day. You will have dreams during this time regarding new beginnings in your spiritual growth.

5 A.M. - 7 A.M.

During the time period of 5:00 to 7:00 a.m., intestine time, you might have dreams concerning things that are cluttering or clogging up your life. This is also a time of outer grief, discernment, caring for others, or self-empowerment. It is a time when you might receive dreams having to do with other people. Also, dreams from the past and even past-life recall tend to occur within this time period. It is a time of discerning the information and the experiences that you have gathered during the day.

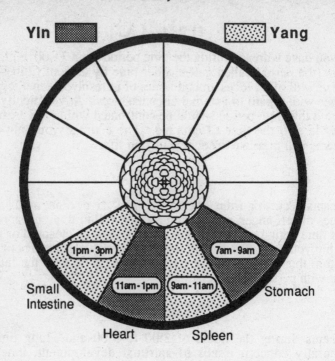

Yin **Yang**

1pm - 3pm

7am - 9am

11am - 1pm

9am - 11am

Small
Intestine

Stomach

Heart

Spleen

7 A.M. - 9 A.M.

Dreams occurring between 7:00 and 9:00 a.m., stomach time, tend to focus on the digestion of new ideas. They may also concern things that you can't "stomach" or assimilate in your outer circumstances. These dreams can also deal with sympathy and empathy for others. It is a good time for the healing of others. This is an excellent time for creative ideas to come through or to receive the answers to problems that have been troubling you.

9 A.M. - 11 A.M.

Dreams from 9:00 a.m. to 11:00 a.m. take place during spleen/pancreas time. This is the time of self-acceptance and these dreams will focus on accepting the goodness of life. This is the time of healing dreams. It is the time of the Mystic Warrior. It is the period for humanely killing all that isn't working in your life. This is a powerful time for physical self-healing.

11 A.M. - 1 P.M.

Dreams during the hours of 11:00 a.m. to 1:00 p.m. occur in heart time. These can be dreams of joy and celebration or dreams revealing the blockages in your life. These can be dreams connecting your spiritual self with your earthly self. This is also another excellent time for astral travel.

1 P.M. - 3 P.M.

Dreams occurring between 1:00 p.m. and 3:00 p.m. are within the small intestine time. Dreams during this time period are for the purpose of absorbing and assimilating that which you have taken in during the day.

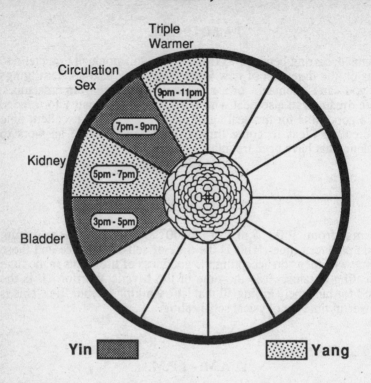

Triple
Warmer

Circulation
Sex

9pm - 11pm

7pm - 9pm

Kidney

5pm - 7pm

3pm - 5pm

Bladder

Yin   **Yang**

3 P.M. - 5 P.M.

Bladder time is 3:00 to 5:00 p.m. Dreams during this time period reveal areas of fear, particularly outward fear. These dreams will assist you in the release of old ideas and relationships that aren't working for you. They will help you let go and let God.

5 P.M. - 7 P.M.

Dreams taking place between 5:00 to 7:00 p.m., kidney time, tend to assist you in letting go of inner fears. These may include the fear of being who you really are. This is the time period wherein you will experience dreams relating to fears from your childhood. These dreams will help you resolve areas of criticism and disappointment. The kidneys are connected with the element of water and water represents transformation. This will be a time of transformation through release of fear. This is also the time of the transition between death and rebirth of ideas, beliefs and attitudes.

7 P.M. - 9 P.M.

Dreams occurring from 7:00 p.m. to 9:00 p.m. are in what is called the circulation/sex time. These will tend to be dreams regarding being at the right place at the right time. They will focus on inner control issues. This is a powerful time for enlightenment dreams. It is interesting to note that within many spiritual communities, the disciples sleep during these hours.

9 P.M. - 11 P.M.

If you dream during the time period from 9:00 to 11:00 p.m. known as triple warmer time, you might find dreams concerning issues of control, not so much dealing with control of yourself, but concerning control of your outer environment. You also may receive dreams relating to the outer movement in your life, the breaking up of old patterns and the re-establishment of new ones. This the time of establishing a balance between too little control in your life and too much control.

Dream of the moon crossing the night sky, eclipsed
as it crosses; feel the ebb and flow of the tides within,
there is a moment of fear in the total eclipse,
let it pass and settle back into the rhythm of the tides.

M. Anne Sweet

THE MOON

She is the giver of visions. She journeys silently into the night, emissary from the land of dreams. She is the silvery white goddess, illuminator of the unconscious, revealer of mysterious forces. All tides are hers. Tides of the great seas...tides of the sky...tides of the inner realms of the night...the secret tides of death and birth...tides of the monthly cycles of women.

She is a celestial goddess of dreams. She carries the moon tides gently to the center of the soul...tides that ebb and flow. All these secrets belong to her.

She rules the great deep where all life began. She is the mistress of the inner tides that never cease. She is ruler of fantasies and intuition. She is queen of the moon-washed night. She brings creativity and vision on the dream tides of the night.

Sleep and darkness are her gentle companions. She returns month after month with renewed strength. She unites opposing elements, transforming darkness into light. She is the source of all physical and spiritual rebirth and illumination. She cascades from the doorways of heaven in waterfalls of light. She is the moon...a powerful spiritual force on our planet and ruler of the dream tides that ebb and flow in the night.

Moon consciousness or moon awareness arises from the deep core of our being; it is inherent within our internal instincts. To primitive people, the moon was a visible and revered symbol of our inner states of dreaming. Today, the moon touches a memory of the forgotten arts, one of which is to recall and understand our dreams. Ancient civilizations honored the moon for it played an important part in their everyday lives. They observed how crops grew seasonally and in tune with the cycles of the moon. A woman's menstrual cycle synchronized with lunar rhythms. The moon was the ultimate symbol of fertility in the universe; her gentle light dew moistened the plants after the heat of the day. The light of the moon invited life to come forth from the seeds during the night. With the same mystical force, it drew plants from the earth, the monthly bleeding from women, and tides to and from the shore. It was the bearer of wisdom in the night through dreams.

The moon was necessary to all of life, and her cycles imperative in all fertility. In past times, an important relationship was acknowledged between one's dreams and one's daily life. Since night, the special dominion of the moon, brought sleep and visions, dreams were revered as messages from the moon to be carefully followed the next day. The moon was believed to be the originator of all creativity.

Early civilizations observed that being in or out of sync with the rhythms of the moon would influence their health and balance. These people measured all life by the lunar cycles. Activities from planting crops to cutting hair to engaging in battle were all acknowledged to be more successful when done in alignment with the moon cycles.

One of the most basic aspects of our existence is our bodily cycles. These internal flows seem to define the very way we experience ourselves and the world around us. The moon is a major regulator of many of these individual rhythms. The moon affects the tides on the surface of the earth, and even slightly distorts the earth in its direction. This cyclical pull dramatically affects our body fluids as well as our dream states. Since the body is 98 percent water, and in view of the fact that our blood has a chemistry very similar to sea water, it is easy to understand how our dream states and body changes synchronize with the ocean tides and phases of the moon.

An intimate knowledge of and exposure to the moon can increase one's inner knowing. A mastery of inner dream states can be acquired by understanding and aligning with moon cycles. All life is cyclical. Developing awareness of moon cycles, as well as our own life cycles, will provide us with greater insight into our dreams. To maximize our understanding and interpretation of our dreams, it is of paramount importance to create our own alignment with the moon and its cycles.

One of the universal principles learned from lunar cycles by ancient peoples was the basic pattern for renewal. Rest, meditation and gestation were treated with the same reverence as productivity. The understanding of equal respect for all parts of the cycle has been most clearly retained in the Oriental concept of yin and yang and its adherence to the cosmic laws of balance.

Each cycle of the moon is divided into four smaller cycles: new moon, waxing moon, full moon and waning moon. Each cycle is about seven days in length. There are no set moments when one cycle ends, and another begins. They simply follow a flow pattern as does our own physical energy.

The new moon is the time of rebirth. During this time, rest, be still; meditate. Dreams occurring during this time reflect the deepest and most internal movements of your inner self. This was a time when ancient American Indian women sought retreat in nature in order to be still and to commune with Great Spirit. In the midst of this stillness, your dreams are preparing the soil of your inner soul for the planting of seeds in the weeks to come.

As the crescent moon appears, be aware as your energy begins to expand. When the moon waxes or enlarges, begin to take action in alignment with the revelations you received in your dreams during the new moon.

The full moon is the culmination of the seed planted in the new moon. During this cycle, release the fullness of your creative forces. Be alive and animated. Participate fully in life and enjoy the dance of celebration. Research indicates this is the cycle when the most vivid dream activity occurs. This is also the time when you are most likely to recall your dreams, and the number of dreams you experience will also increase during the full moon.

The waning moon is a time to assimilate and absorb all you have learned in previous weeks. The dreams during this time will be dreams of reflection and introspection. When you begin to integrate your life movements with the moon's cycles, you will be flowing in harmony with the most primordial and powerful force in nature. Your dream life will become increasingly vivid and viable.

One way to integrate life cycles with those of the moon is to create a moon ritual. In ancient moon rituals, visions, whimsy and intuition were all valued as absolute necessities in the rationale of living. In fact, without these states, it was thought that a balance of life was not possible, and that one's understanding of the universe dwindled. It is essential to our own individual and collective balance to regain an understanding of these states of being. This can be achieved by creating a moon ritual for oneself.

A moon ritual is the channeling of energies of the universe, utilizing the moon as a focal point, in order to usher oneself into more expanded levels of consciousness. All mysteries and powers of the subconscious are symbolized by a moon ritual.

It is that elusive quality with which the moon priestess of old would desire to merge.

A ritual can be used to change one's perceptions of reality. It is a symbolic event. It can either be simple or complex in nature. The ritual attempts to make tangible an event which has occurred on the inner plane. A transformation of personality is implied in every ritual. It is a means to experience connectedness with the entire universe.

Here are some simple modern-day moon rituals that you can use to enhance your dreaming hours:

–Stand at a window or be outdoors during the different phases of the moon.

–Lift your arms to the moon as ancient people have done before you. Feel the energy of the moon surge and fill every cell of your being.

–Take a moon bath and allow the light rays of the moon to bathe and cleanse you, washing over the deepest parts of you like waves of the sea.

–Dance in the light of the moon. Allow yourself to move with wild abandon.

–Leave water out in the light of the moon and just before you go to sleep, drink this water which has been energized from the deepest well-spring of life.

A ritual is a stylized series of actions used to bring about change. It has its origin deep in the psyche of each individual. Therefore, you already possess within you the ingredients from your own unconscious to trigger all the experiences you desire. So, look within and create a moon ritual that speaks to your life and your needs using symbols and artifacts that are representations for you of the inner qualities of dreams.

The dream moon ritual I have created for myself is simple. I lay out a circle with sticks or special stones. The circle represents wholeness and my inner dream world. Without beginning or end, it represents the cycle of the universe, the source and eventual return to the source. I use a circle to represent the moon and my dreams, the source of life and unity. Within this circle, I place things that are special to me and that represent the mystical world of dreams. Among these is the stone, selenite, a name originating from the moon goddess, Selene. This stone is an excellent tool in assisting dream recall and understanding.

To enhance the ceremonial aspect of my own moon circle, I begin by dedicating my energy to the living spirit in all things and to my dreams. I then compose a simple dream song and create a dream dance that will invoke the power of life and my own inner nature. Once I have completed my ritual, I carefully gather the treasured objects I have used in my ritual and place them in a special location until my next moon ritual.

When you first create your own moon ritual and begin to participate in it, it is not unusual for you to experience feelings of foolishness or awkwardness. However, as you persist beyond that point of feeling foolish, you will soon experience the sacred center. At the beginning of the ritual, your true emotions are buried under layers of linear and rational thinking. Yet, as you persist, the right side of your brain, the Isis side, will take over and the inner reality of the acts performed will come through. As a result, you will feel yourself walking in harmony with the inner cycles of nature and in harmony with your dreams and the inner sages of the night.

Blue ocean blends at the horizon into blue sky
expanding into the deep, rich blue of infinite space--
to stand at the ocean's edge, waves lapping
about one's feet, is to touch and be one with the universe.

M. Anne Sweet

COLORS

There is no doubt that color plays an important role in everyone's life. Research indicates that even the blind are affected by color. Colors play a definite role in the theater of the night, providing us with valuable insight into the hue and shade of our life's experiences.

Dreaming in Color

There are several theories concerning whether or not we, in fact, dream in color. Calvin Hall, one dream researcher who has collected records of thousands of dreams, states that two-thirds of all dreams are in black and white. He believes that only one dream in every three is colored or has color in it. Hall relates that few people dream entirely in color, and that some individuals never experience color in their dreams.

This view, however, is not shared by everyone. Gladys Mayer, another dream explorer, says that all dreams are in color. She maintains that just as we all dream, yet perhaps do not remember our dreams, we all dream in color but do not recall the colors.

Aldous Huxley in his book, *Heaven and Hell,* states that to be effective, dream symbols are not required to be in color. He continues, "It is worth remarking that, in most people's experience, the most brightly colored dreams are those of landscapes in which there is no drama, no symbolic reference to conflict, merely the presentation to consciousness of a given non-human fact." He believes that when symbols express psychological conflicts, color is not necessary. Therefore, the color occurs in those areas without conflict. Some dream researchers object to this theory in that all dreams appear to embody some type of conflict. Another objection to this theory is that some people always dream in color regardless of conflict.

One theory concerning the presence of color in dreams is that colors can signify a diseased condition. One hypothesis purports that dreams where there is an excess of green indicate a disorder of the liver. Dreams in which one finds an excess of red warn us of the possibility of hemorrhage or circulation or cardiac problems. I would add that while there may be some credibility to this theory, the shade of green or red is also a factor. A forthcoming diseased condition can be indicated by disturbing shades of colors in dreams. However, a clear spring green in a dream can also signify a major healing force and a clear brilliant red can represent physical strength and sexual potency.

A third theory regarding color in dreams is related to the dreamer's artistic talent. The theory contends that those who dream predominantly in color are far more color conscious than the average individual, and they are also exceptional in the realm of artistic talent. The proponents of this theory suggest that painting lessons will trigger dreams in color.

A knowledge of color significance in dreams is one of the most simple yet most effective tools for understanding our dreams. As we look about us, everything we perceive within our sight reflects color. Where the colors change, where the shadows meet -- this defines the form and shape of everything we see.

Using color to understand dreams has been used successfully for thousands of years in most cultures with esoteric traditions. To understand color is to understand the essence of energy.

We are living in an expansive ocean of energy consisting of vitally-alive vibrations with different speeds and varying degrees of intensity. This is an ocean of energy that is a swirling dance of ever-changing matter. It is energy in the various stages of solid, liquid, and gas, each finding its temporary niche in the universe. Light and color are vibrations in this eternal play of energy. The warm colors of red, orange and yellow have a much lower vibratory rate on the electromagnetic scale while the cooler colors of green, blue and purple have a much faster rate.

Sir Isaac Newton, in 1666, was the first man to break sunlight into its component colors. Using a prism, Newton produced a spectrum dividing the natural sunlight, or white light, into seven bands of color: red, orange, yellow, green, blue, indigo and violet. As light travels at 186,000 miles per second, it vibrates. Light is actually radiant energy traveling in the form of rays or waves. These wavelengths are measured in terms of frequency. The shorter the wavelength, the higher the frequency.

You are also a series of energy fields. Your entire body is constantly vibrating in a field of energy, some subtle and some manifest. You are constantly involved in movement and motion. Your body's energy fields are affected by the constant changing energies in your environment such as sunlight and wind, the energy fields of other people, and the energy of the food you take in. Continuously, your body and very being are affected very deeply by the energy from color.

Even though we might not be consciously aware of it, we do acknowledge the power of color on our life. We use such expressions as: I'm feeling blue today. It was a blue Monday. She's really feeling in the pink. He looks at life through rose-colored glasses. He saw red. She was red with anger...or green with envy...or purple with rage. The list goes on and on. Color plays an important role in every area of our life.

There was a time when color was perceived as being much more significant to humanity than is currently acknowledged. In fact, it was not until relatively recently that color began to be thought of as only decorative or entertaining. In human history as a whole, color was thought to be one of the most important symbols in the world. The profound meaning of each color was something that was an integral part of all ancient civilizations involved in dream exploration. Mesopotamia, Egypt, Greece, China, and Tibet as well as the traditional cultures of native American Indians and even medieval Europeans all used the power of color. Even modern psychologists and scientists are acknowledging the use of color for therapeutic and medicinal purposes.

Dr. Max Luscher, a color scientist, explains, "Today, after hundreds of thousands of color tests given in the United States, Europe, Africa, Japan and Australia, we know that every specific color inspires the same stimulus in every single individual no matter what that person's culture may be. Orange-red has a stimulating effect on everyone. Dark blue has a relaxing effect on everyone. Therein lies the universal validity of color psychology. Just as music inspires feeling, renders mood, and expresses the very subtlest emotions, so do colors. The hue, degree of lightness and intensity arouse the very same specific sensations in every individual."

Of course you will have different shades and different hues of the seven major colors in your dreaming. The clearer the color, the more accurate the description of that symbol. The muddier the color, the more that area is blocked for you.

RED

Red in a dream responds to the first chakra, the area at the base of the spine. Our drive for existence and survival are represented by red. Red stimulates the physical body to respond to and act in an assertive manner. Red stimulates the heart and increases the vibratory rate. It is no accident that restaurants use red in their decor, for its stimulating effect increases the appetite as well. Red is associated with our sexual energy. It relates to sensations of pleasure. The color red brings on reactiveness and physical excitement.

Red can be related to anger. A clear red in a dream symbolizes clear anger. A muddy red represents suppressed anger. It can be pugnacity, aggressiveness, sensation, tenseness, or physical strength. Our perception of time seems longer when exposed to red, therefore it is not an appropriate color for waiting rooms.

Red is a sign of direct action and active employment. It relates to will and power. Strength, courage, steadfastness, health, vigor, sexuality, sexual love and danger are all attributes closely associated with the color of red. Having this color occur in a dream can be extremely vitalizing and stimulating and can assist in overcoming inertia, depression, fear or melancholy. It is a great aid to those who are afraid of life and inclined to feel like escaping. The red ray helps to plant one's feet firmly on the earth. If you are inclined to not feel grounded by dwelling on the future, having red within a dream will help you root in the present. It will help you root in the "now." It supplies the energy and motivation necessary in reaching and accomplishing goals. Red is a "doing" color. It is a "get the job done" color.

ORANGE

Orange in a dream responds to the second chakra. It represents our drive for social acceptance. Orange is a warm, stimulating color but it is lighter and higher in vibration than red, so the energy translates to broader fields in the body. It stimulates less concern with self-survival and more involvment with assisting in group and social functions. Orange is a happy color. It is a funny color used by clowns the world over. This color stimulates optimism, expansiveness and emotional balance. Orange in a dream relates to the herd instinct, ambition, agitation, restlessness, exploration, and business. It can relate to movement of the sexual energies toward the thought processes causing interest in politics and pride.

People who choose orange as their favorite color are generally sensationally ambitious, competitive, expansive, optimistic, warm and hospitable with humanitarian instincts. They seek social contact and acceptance. They are ambitious for their community, for their nation, and for their business. They like big projects of world-wide scope and they love to expand.

Orange in a dream symbolizes optimism, confidence, change, striving, self-motivation, enthusiasm and courage. Orange is a social ray. The tendency to believe too readily without weighing the skepticism or discrimination can be healed by the orange ray. Therefore, if you have a tendency to be suspicious or mistrusting or have selfish pride or are even seeking power, having orange in a dream can assist in creating balance and discrimination. The healing energies of orange in a dream stimulate inner knowing that we indeed are all one. It elevates the consciousness to rise above self. Essentially, orange in a dream is expansive, exploratory and social.

Red is sensual while orange is social. It is the drive to find reality through other people, the drive for fellowship. The red energy is a passion for self-preservation and self-gratification. With orange, the drive and concern is more for social preservation, the preservation of society, family and social gathering. Orange is acceptance of our social love. It is being unafraid to dance and sing and proclaim yourself as a lover of people.

YELLOW

Yellow is intellectual, a response to the third chakra, the solar plexus. It is the last of the warm, extraverted color rays. In a dream, it relates to your intellectual thinking process. The energy of the yellow ray stimulates your logical linear thinking processes and relates to left-brain activities. Yellow stimulates the body to respond with mental discrimination, organization, attention to detail, evaluation, active intelligence, discipline, administration, praise, sincerity and harmony. Thus, yellow gives heightened expression and freedom which translates into the joy within a dream.

Those who choose yellow as their favorite color analyze everything, needing always to know the "what" and "where." They demand a logical framework before they are capable of understanding. They desire originality and change. They are highly creative individuals seeking expression in art, literature and music and talk....talk...talk. They are flexible, expressive, eloquent and intensely self-aware individuals who are efficient in planning and organization. The spontaneous reaction to stimuli or events unique to both red and orange energy are not experienced by stimulation of the yellow ray. Instead, there exists a more detached understanding of how the events originated, i.e. where they took place, when they will be brought to focus, etc. Yellow understands the larger scope of life. It stimulates our need to live in an orderly world while at the same time expressing our individuality and our need to understand.

The healing power of the yellow ray in a dream works on fear. Often, when one is fearful, his stomach feels as if it is going to turn over. Through various incarnations, a tremendous amount of fear may have been locked away in the solar plexus region. Frequently, an individual cannot understand the cause of his fears. Yellow in your dreams will gradually release the tension from the fearful experience centered in the the solar plexus. Yellow is very healing for judgmental, critical, verbally-aggressive individuals. It is a color that stimulates flexibility and adaptability to change. When we tune in with the yellow ray, no problem will remain unsolved under the scrutiny of our intellects. We also learn it is better to work to change ourselves rather than others. The need for balance between our head and our heart remains clear.

GREEN

Green in a dream responds to security. It responds to the heart chakra, the fourth energy point of our body's energy field. Green is the balance between the warm extraverted spectrum of red, orange and yellow and the cool introverted colors of blue, indigo and violet. Thus, green stimulates feelings of love, balance, harmony, peace, brotherhood, hope, growth and healing. I find often with my clients that as they are moving through healing they will tend to have green in their dreams during this period. People who choose green as their favorite color are generally generous, vital, open-hearted, and nurturing by nature. In order to establish an inner security, green stimulates our need to feel secure, certain, assertive, powerful and to love and be loved.

Green within a dream is very beneficial for any deep brooding feelings of regret. Green in the dream is also helpful in overcoming any limiting attachments. Many anxieties are created in the heart through various attachments. While it is valuable to enjoy whatever one has in the moment, it also facilitates peace of mind to develop the art of being unattached to having.

Green is found everywhere in nature symbolizing the abundant, replenishing forces of the universe. There will always be enough. You may notice that the American dollar is green and has been strong for many years. New Zealand's money used to be green and when the color of their money changed, there was a decline in the worth of the New Zealand dollar. Green energy is very healing for doubt and insecurity as well. Through meditation on the purity of green, we can call on our true expansive, compassionate, open-hearted nature. When the heart is open and we feel the love of the universe streaming through our being, we feel the greatest security and self-confidence. We learn to live without attachments and with fewer possessions. Green is a very healing color to have in your dreams.

BLUE

Blue is conceptual. It is the color associated with the throat chakra. Blue is the first of the cool spectrum colors. It stimulates you to seek inner truth. When you have blue in a dream, it helps you to attain inner peace, mental security and to live out your ideals. Blue is stimulating to our spiritual security and desire for inner understanding.

People who choose blue as their favorite color are apt to be idealistic, patient and enduring souls. They tend to be nostalgic, committed, devotional, peaceful and loyal in nature. These highly sensitive individuals live in a mental world of their own commitment to idealistic ideas and feelings. They seek contentment and peace of mind and are not prone to change.

Blue in a dream stimulates inspiration, creativity, spiritual understanding, faith and devotion. The concept of time flows quickly in blue, and memories of the past are stimulated by this color. It is an ideal color for waiting rooms and places of study. If there is a lot of blue in your dream, this allows for gentleness, contentment, patience and composure. Therefore, blue is beneficial for someone who acts compulsively without stopping to think. It is also extremely liberating for those who have become rigid and resistant to change. The blue ray gives the power of synthesizing and combines separate elements into a complex whole. The true blue of sincerity manifests in all relationships in life. When we are sincere with ourselves, we can be sincere with others.

PURPLE

Purple relates to the brow chakra, intuition, and is the color most deeply associated with dreams. Listen carefully to dreams containing the color of purple or indigo or violet. This color in our dream stimulates our need to feel at one with the universe, to have conflict-free relationships, and to be out in front in the realm of human development. As with the color blue, its effects are calming, soothing, and comforting. Very often, when one has purple in a dream, it will be indicative of psychic awareness and intuition. Listen carefully to these dreams!

As we move through the color levels, it becomes interesting to note what happens to our vision of time. The closer we are to our senses, for example, the more time seems to flow forward, the closer we are to our imagination, the more time seems to flow backward. When we view the color red with our senses, we receive a vision of the immediate now like the cat eyeing a mouse. When we view the present with our intellect, (yellow), we get a vision of logic like the flow of traffic on a freeway. When we perceive with our feelings (blue), we receive a vision of history like rings on a tree. When we view reality with our intuition (purple), we get a vision of the future like an eagle soaring high above the plains and looking down. From that vantage point one can see what is near but also what is beyond. Therefore, when you see purple in a dream, you are seeing beyond. These tend to be dreams of prophecy, the dreams of a visionary. When a person chooses purple as a favorite color, he usually is abstract, inspired, trusting in the future, and able to tune in to the inner world of others. Purple stimulates our spiritual perspective and intuition.

WHITE

White within a dream relates to imagination and the crown chakra. Its vibrations are the fastest and the most frequent of the color spectrum. Its effects on our being are divine realization, humility and creative imagination. It can be purifying like white snow in the wintertime. White is the color that encompasses all colors. These are also dreams to observe and watch. It is the energy and the power to transform the focus of the imagination. It is a useful color for those who tend to be daydreamers or have trouble manifesting. The white and violet rays are the creative imagination leading us toward higher spiritual attunement and divine love through our dreams. People who are attached or attracted to this color have a deep sense of wonder, bliss and self-surrender. This can be a great healing color for a person with a negative self-image, for it holds within its energy the power of transformation.

RED

Inspires: Freedom, determination, honor, will, power, strength, activity, alertness, independence, motivation, initiative, leadership.

Releases: Anger, frustration, confusion, violence, destruction, revenge, rebellion, impulsiveness, impatience.

ORANGE

Inspires: Optimism, courage, victory, confidence, enthusiasm, encouragement, attraction, plenty, kindness, expansion.

Releases: Superiority, mistrust, power-seeking pride, superficiality.

YELLOW

Inspires: Joy, expression, ability, mental discrimination, organization, attention to detail, evaluation, active intelligence, discipline, administration.

Releases: Criticism, stubborn constriction, contempt, sorrow, selfish judgment, bitterness, cynicism.

GREEN

Inspires: Encouragement, generosity, vitality, power, security, open-heartedness, nurturance, self-assertion, compassion, expansion, sharing, harmony, balance.

Releases: Self-doubt, possessiveness, jealousy, selfish attachment, envy, insecurity, mistrust.

BLUE

Inspires: Love, wisdom, gentleness, trust, understanding, detachment, kindness, compassion, patience, forgiveness, sensitivity, contemplation.

Releases: Self-pity, fear, self-rejection, separateness, isolation, worry, depression, passivity, anxiety, coldness, detachment.

PURPLE

Inspires: Inspiration, vision, farsightedness, trust in the future, tuning in to the inner worlds of others, supersensitivity.

Releases: Inability to live in the now, spacing out, forgetfulness, lack of discipline, resentment, separateness, arrogance, pride, contempt.

WHITE

Inspires: Mystical instinct, creativity, spirit-inspiration, meditation, reflection, deep inner wisdom, grace, delight, spiritual unity.

Releases: Obsessiveness, martyrdom, restriction, intolerance, day-dreaminess, criticalness, feeling of negativity.

I wake surrounded in shimmering light,
an ether taproot grounds me to the
center of the earth,
ahead, handrails wrought of gold,
seven steps... beckon me to climb.

           M. Anne Sweet

NUMBERS

Numbers play an important part in dreams. Each number has a spiritual power and significance. Through increased understanding of numbers, we can gain new insight into ourselves. Essentially, numbers are only symbols. They alone will not cause any change; however, they do give insight into our inherent potential and the energy that surrounds us. You will know a number or series of numbers is significant if it clearly appears in your dream, for example a number on a house such as "723." In addition, notice the number of similar objects as they appear in your dreams.

Pythagoras, the Greek philosopher, metaphysician and mathematician, took the art of divination through numbers to new heights. It was Pythagoras who first experimented with the essence of numbers, creating numbers as a science in 540 B.C. Fortunately, his teachings were not lost in the great fire which destroyed most of his library. Century by century, the secrets of Pythagoras were passed from master to student. As the student became a master, he would teach the mysteries to a new initiate and this lineage has continued. Below are some of the metaphysical perceptions regarding numbers.

ONE

Independence. New beginnings. Oneness with life. Unity with life. Self-development. Individuality. Progress. Creativity.

TWO

Being a couple. A balance of male/female energies. A balance of the yin and yang energies of the universe. Needing people. Self-surrender. Putting others before yourself.

THREE

Fun. Self-expression. To give outwardly. The Trinity: mind, body, spirit. Harmony. Openness.

FOUR

Self-discipline through work and service. Productivity. Organization. Wholeness and unity.

FIVE

Feeling free. Self-emancipating. Active. Physical. Impulsive Energetic. Changing. Adventuresome. Resourceful. Well-traveled. Curious. Free soul.

SIX

Self-harmony, particularly through service by meeting responsibilities. This is the number of balance.

SEVEN

The inner life; inner wisdom. A mystical number symbolizing wisdom. Seven chakras. The seven heavens of the Hawaiian kahunas. Symbol of birth and rebirth. Religious strength. Sacred vows. Tendency toward ritual, particularly spiritual ritual. The path of solitude.

EIGHT

Material wealth. Self-power. Abundance. Infinity; cosmic consciousness.

NINE

The humanitarian number. Selflessness; dedicating your life to others. This is a number of completion and of endings.

TEN

Wholeness. Perfection.

ELEVEN

Self-illumination. Intuition. A higher expression of the energy of two.

TWELVE

Power within wholeness: twelve disciples, twelve planets, twelve months.

TWENTY-TWO

Self-mastery. All things are possible.

THIRTY-THREE

The inner sanctuary; the spiritual teacher. One of the master numbers of the universe.

If there are any numbers appearing in your dream that are not outlined above, here are some guidelines which may assist you. Look at the individual numbers. For example, with the number 43, look at the meaning of 4, and then check the meaning of 3. Or in accordance with numerology philosophy, add the numbers together thus creating the new number 7. Now look for the meaning of number 7.

In the example of the three numbers in a dream like the house number, you add the three together. If the number was 249, add the 2, 4 and 9 for a total of 15. You then add the 1 and 5 together, equaling 6. Then look up the significance of the number 6.

Another context in which to analyze numbers that appear in dreams is to explore the possibility they point to some significant age or date in your life. The dream number may also symbolize a specific item such as the number of children that you now have or will have, or the number of years it will take to reach a goal. Ask your dream guide for clarification in regard to the numbers appearing in your dreams.

Stately grizzly bear emerges from the fog,
jowls clamped around a struggling salmon;
Grandfather emerges from the study,
jaw set on determining the family destiny.

M. Anne Sweet

ANIMALS

Throughout history, animals have played an important role in the evolution of mankind. To the American Indian, they were guardian spirits or power animals. In Australia, the aborigines referred to them as assistant totems. It was virtually impossible in most tribes to be a medicine woman or a medicine man without seeking help from the animal kingdom. Each animal represented a particular human ability or strength, and having an animal appear in dreams signified that the qualities of that animal spirit were being bestowed upon the dreamer.

A Coyote, traditionally, is the wise prankster and represents mischievousness. The Owl is a symbol for transformation and wisdom, and the Bear is a symbol for healing and strength. Thus, to dream of one of these animals is to embrace those qualities in your life. Children or people close to nature tend to dream of animals considerably more than most adults. When an individual begins to align with the cycles of nature, animals will play a more predominant role in his dreams, and he will discover himself assimilating those associated qualities. In traditional shamanistic methodology, when one dreams of an animal three times, this signifies that it is one of his power animals. A shaman can have many power animals (totems), but more often than not, he will have one main totem. An animal appearing in your dreams may be your totem or it may also represent the qualities associated with that animal.

CALLING ANIMALS

As you begin to enter the animal kingdom through your dreams, you will also begin to find a deeper connection with the animal kingdom in your waking life.

The American Indian's heritage was closely interwoven with the animal kingdom. Indians developed the skill of "calling animals" as necessary for their survival. They learned to speak with the elk, deer and buffalo spirits in asking for guidance in regard to the hunt. There was an absolute dedication involved in the taking of life. It was believed that the spirit of the animal evolved through sacrificing itself in providing sustenance for the tribe.

The ability to call animals is a doorway leading to a deepening of your connection with the earth's cycles. I have discovered that even those individuals who are certain they cannot master the calling technique are able to do so once they connect with the animal kingdom in their dreams. It has definitely been a worthwhile vehicle for me in reaffirming my own connection to Mother Earth.

To illustrate, I recall an incident in Mexico. It was 4:00 a.m. and I was resting quietly on a dark beach in the small fishing village north of Puerto Vallarta. I hugged my knees close to my chest and felt the deep rhythm of the gentle ocean. As I watched the dark form of a lone seagull silhouetted against the velvet morning sky, I found myself wondering about life's purpose. Ordinarily, I don't believe in a random universe, yet in that early morning solitude, I was wrestling with many questions about God and the meaning of my life. Each wave seemed to echo my hollow thoughts.

226

As night receded and the soft, black blanket of darkness melted into vivid blue and violet, I walked slowly back to the bungalow I shared with my family. I was greeted by my husband, David, who was on his way fishing with a local fisherman. I have never before fished in the ocean, but this particular morning, it seemed like it would be a salve for my questioning heart.

As we swiftly glided through the calm waters, I allowed my consciousness to penetrate deeply into the azure ocean, hoping to connect with the Spirit of the Sea. For many years, I have had the ability to "call" animals due, perhaps, to a carry-over from my American Indian heritage. I generally bond with the spirit of one particular species of animal or plant at any one time. However, this morning, I simply wanted to relax into the Spirit of the Sea. Although my earlier mood had left me doubting my ability to connect with any spirit at all, I nevertheless requested to visually experience some wonders of the sea. I noticed I did not have any one particular species in mind.

Suddenly, with the explosive power of a charging locomotive, 40 feet of raw energy shot up from the sea like a giant missile, leaving a shimmering geyser of spun-crystal ocean spray. Again and again, one whale after another surged through space, leaving a fountain of spray and foam.

Then, just as suddenly as it had begun, there was silence...the deep calm silence of rocking gently in a 14-foot boat on a still sea. The majesty of those moments of power and grace held us stunned. Then, piercing the veil of silence, within feet of our small boat, a younger whale arched out of the depths and hung in the air. Rivulets of sparkling water streamed from its sides back into the churning ocean foam. Just as serenely as it had appeared, it was gone. Silence...stillness...awe.

The old fisherman was overwhelmed. Although he had been out on the water nearly every day during the last six fishing seasons, he had never seen anything like that morning's display. We three sat quietly, pondering what we had witnessed.

"Shark," David urgently whispered under his breath, shattering our mood of awe. I had requested gifts from the sea, but I wasn't sure I was ready for sharks!

As our eyes followed the ominous black fins, there was an unexpected burst of joy dancing skyward from the sea as dolphins playfully dipped in and out of the water near us. The fins had belonged to dolphins, not sharks!

There were at least 50 dolphins dancing in the water near the boat, so near that I could reach out with my hand to within inches of some of their arched backs. The fisherman, unnerved by so many of them near his boat, turned the engine up to high speed to try to elude them. No matter how fast the little boat traveled, the dolphins adjusted their speed to stay with us. Finally, as the dolphin pod began to trail off, two of them remained nearby to keep us company. As we slowed our speed, the pod kept its distance. We watched the sun dance in crystal reflection off their backs until they blended into the blue of the distance. Our very confused guide could only mumble something under his breath about "...mating season."

This unforgettable connection with the animal kingdom had reaffirmed how much I was a part of all things.

To Call Animals

First Step: Embrace the reality that you <u>can indeed</u> connect deeply with plant and animal spirits.

Second Step: Begin to program your dreams to connect with the animal kingdom.

Third Step: Reach out in your imagination to the spirit of a particular animal or plant. If you are trout fishing, you might imagine what the trout spirit would be like. Then, converse with that spirit just as you would a friend.

"Greetings, Trout Spirit! I come to you in dedication and love of the Trout Kingdom. I ask that you send forth one of your members in dedication. We know there is no death...only transformation...and as one of your species comes forth, we accept the gift as a great service and you will be honored." Usually about that time there is a tug on your line.

Fourth Step: Each animal and plant has its own sound or vibration. Imagine what the sound is and attempt to duplicate it vocally. Otherwise, imagine that you either hear the sound in your mind, or imagine that you are making the sound. This is the "call." Remember not to doubt yourself and your ability to do this. Doubt is the greatest barrier to the technique working for you.

You can also practice the "call" just before sleep. Call for a particular animal to come forth in your dreams, and then listen carefully to the message given in each dream.

Sometimes, my "calling" has backfired! A humorous episode occurred when I had noticed a swarm of bees in the neighborhood and impulsively decided it would be wonderful if the bees could hive in our back yard so that my daughter could observe them through our window. I had never attempted to call anything in the insect world, but I couldn't imagine it being that different from calling a plant or an animal.

First, I tried to find the vibration, or the tone or resonating quality of the vibrations of the bee kingdom. Once I had a sense of that tone, I repeated it mentally. I sent out the "call" and waited. Nothing happened.

About an hour later, I heard my daughter screaming and urgently ran outside to be greeted by a huge swarm of wasps! They were settling in to make our back yard their new home.

Below are some of the more common meanings for animals as they appear in dreams.

ALLIGATOR	•Hidden, formidable strength and power.
	•Trouble below the surface.
	•Misuse of communication.
ANT	•Industrious; productive.
	•Community or social cooperation.
ANTEATER	•Wish to be more productive or focused.
APE	•Primitive power.
	•Mischief maker.
	•Something or someone is copying or being copied or imitated.
BABOON	•Oafishness.
	•Community-minded; social.
BADGER	•Baiting or teasing.
BAT	•Fear of the unknown.
	•An old harridan.
	•"Batting" around an idea.

BEAR
- Represents Mother Earth.
- The protective mothering female aspect.
- Force and power.
- The Indian totem for healing.
- Cuddly; lovable.

BEAVER
- Busy; industrious. Prosperity through your own efforts.

BEDBUG
- Something unpleasant that is covered up. A small nuisance.

BEE
- Busy; industrious.
- Social cooperation.
- The possibility of hidden sweetness.
- You are feeling "stung" by some circumstance or remark.

BEETLES
- Can be a sign of good luck.
- Represented eternal life to the ancient Egyptian.
- May foretell hostility among associates.

BIRD
- Soaring to new heights; soaring above your problems.
- A fortunate dream omen.
- If singing, may be the harbinger of good news.

BIRD'S EGGS
- In a nest, signify money.
- New beginnings.

BOAR
- A swinish personality.
- Someone or something is boring.

BUFFALO
- Represents abundance, harvest and plenty.
- Sacred to the American Indian.

BUG
- Small annoyance.
- Inconvenience.

BULL
- Great strength; force; power.
- Optimistic sign.

BULLDOG
- Tenacity; holding power.
- Defiance.
- Seize the opportunity and don't let go.

BUTTERFLY
- Romance. Social success.
- New beginning on a higher plane.
- Gentle enjoyment.

BUZZARD
- Feeling picked on or preyed upon; preying on others.
- Contemptible; rapacious.

CALF
- A happy symbol of carefree youth in healthy surroundings.
- Notice the dream. May refer to the calf of the leg.

CAMEL
- The ship of the desert; a way to get through a difficulty.
- Endurance.

CANARY
- Music; harmony.
- May indicate tattling or telling of secrets.

CAT
- Your intuitive self.
- Your feminine essence or the female part of yourself. The goddess within.

CATERPILLAR
- Unharnessed potential of which you are unaware.

CHAMELEON
- Adaptability; flexibility.
- Whimsy.
- Capricious and changing.
- Not showing one's "true colors."

CHICKEN
- Cowardice. Timidity.
- Counting on something prematurely.

CLAM
- Someone is not talking. Lack of communication.
- Concern over something that must be kept secret.

COBRA
- The power of the kundalini energy.

COCK
- Strutting; proud; egotistical.
- Masculine energy.
- About to erupt or go off as when a gun is cocked.

COCKATOO
- Showy.
- Talking without thinking.

CRICKET
- A joyful dream symbol.
- Domestic joy; peace in home.
- Long life.

CROCODILE	•Dishonesty. A show of false feeling as in "crocodile tears."
	•Hypocrisy; it's a "crock."
	•Trouble beneath the surface.
DOG	•Faithfulness; loyalty.
	•Protection. Rescue.
	•Friendship.
	•May indicate the feet.
DOLPHIN	•Unharnessed joy; playfulness; spontaneity.
	•Intelligence.
	•Spiritual enlightenment.
	•A significant dream symbol.
DONKEY	•Patience.
	•Stubbornness.
	•Domestic servitude.
DOVE	•Peace; freedom.
	•There may be someone or something with which you wish to make peace.
DRAGON	•A powerful dream symbol.
	•Represents life force and great potency.
	•Dragon fire is very purifying.
	•Slaying the dragon is confronting and overcoming fear.
DUCK	•Get out of the way of something.

EAGLE
- Very significant to the American Indian.
- National power.
- Your spiritual, soaring self.
- Ability or need to be far-seeing.

ELEPHANT
- Something that needs to be remembered.
- Something you are willing to forgive and forget.
- Thick-skinned.
- Ponderous; powerful.
- May have connotations of excess in use of alcohol.

ELK
- A sexual symbol. It is a reassuring dream sign.
- Power; beauty; dignity.

FISH
- Spiritual food.
- A symbol of Christianity.
- May be a desire for acknowledgment or compliments.
- Misrepresentation; something seems "fishy."

FOX
- Slyness; sneakiness. Manipulation.
- Can concern physical attraction.

FROG
- The beauty behind the surface ugliness.
- Inconsistency; hopping from one thing to another.

•May reflect a desire to find "the prince" among a group.

GIRAFFE
•Stretching for what you want.

•Someone above the crowd.

•Stiff-necked or unbending.

GOAT
•Lecherous; old and cranky.

•Someone or something is taxing your patience.

•Feeling blamed or made the scapegoat for something you haven't done.

GOOSE
•A prod in the rear. You want someone or something to get going.

GRASSHOPPER
•Feeling that time could be better spent.

GREYHOUND
•Speed; swiftness.

HARE
•Overconfidence that can lead to trouble.

•Look before you leap.

HEN
•Domestic, nesting instinct.

•Plump; satisfied.

HIPPOPOTAMUS
•Weighty; ponderous.

HOG
•Overindulgence.

•Feeling that you are not getting your share or not giving your share.

•Selfishness.

HORSE
•Expanded sense of self.

•Freedom; movement.

•Questioning of another's motives: "Don't look a gift horse in the mouth."

HYENA

•Foolish.

•Noisy; merriment out of proportion or not appropriate to the situation.

JACKAL

•An evil influence.

•Going along with something you don't feel good about; helping in something that you don't really approve of.

•A warning symbol.

JELLYFISH

•Floating; drifting along.

•No backbone.

KANGAROO

•Restless energy.

•Mobility.

•Mock justice.

LADYBUG

•A symbol of good luck.

•Easily solved personal matters.

LAMB

•Sacrifice; martyrdom

•Easily led.

LEECH

•Blood sucker; you may feel something is taking your strength or property, or that you are taking advantage of someone else.

LEOPARD

•Prowess; cunning; stealth.

•Possible "spots" in your life need attention.

LICE

•Petty annoyances.

LION
- King of the jungle; majesty; power; bravery; leadership.
- A test of courage. For some African tribes, part of the rite of manhood concerned pitting one's strength against the lion's.

LIZARD
- A wonderful dream symbol.
- Earthy; primordial; steady.
- Considered guardians of the inner worlds by the aborigines.

LYNX
- Quick-witted.

MERMAID
- Unobtainable lover.
- Temptation.

MINK
- Material value.

MOLE
- Burrowing.
- Something beneath the surface. Something not willing to be seen.

MOTH
- Happiness at night.
- Perseverance beyond reason.
- Something is being eaten away without your attention.

MOUSE
- Feeling of insignificance.
- Temerity; fear.
- A need for quiet or a concern about being quiet.

MULE
- Stubbornness.

OCTOPUS
- A powerful symbol of transformation.
- Tenacious; grasping.
- Wise.
- Shy and retiring.

OSTRICH
- Avoidance of looking at something in life.

OTTER
- Capricious; playful. Fun-loving.

OWL
- A significant dream symbol.
- A powerful symbol of transformation.
- Ability to see clearly where things may seem dark.
- Wisdom.
- May signify a coming transformation.

OYSTER
- Guarded energy.
- Hidden beauty; beauty developing unseen.

PANDA
- Tranquility.
- Lovable; cuddly.

PARROT
- Insincerity; speaking another's words without thinking.
- Copying; imitating.

PEACOCK
- Pride; vanity.
- Confidence to the extreme.

PEGASUS
- Winged inspiration.
- Soaring strength.

PENGUIN
- Whimsical; comical.
- All dressed up with nowhere to go.

PHEASANT
- The better life.
- Pleasant.

PIG
- Overindulgence: grasping.
- Selfish.

POLAR BEAR
- Cut off from your strength.

PORCUPINE
- Something prickly. There is a prickly situation.
- There is something you want to stay away from.

PYTHON
- A significant dream symbol.
- Symbolizes kundalini energy or that potent life force within you.

QUAIL
- Fear; to recoil in dread. To wither or decline.
- Go back into your dream and turn the quail into the eagle, the symbol of courage, and then soar!

RABBIT
- Can signify prosperity.
- Temerity, fear.
- Fertility; children.
- Gentleness, softness.
- Going fast with no organization; hopping from one thing to another.

240

RAM
- •Masculine strength.
- •Pioneering spirit. The ram is the symbol of initiation or that initiating energy. It is a new beginning.

RAT
- •Betrayer; wrongdoer.
- •Letting things gnaw at you.
- •Judging yourself through others.
- •A rat's nest.

RAVEN
- •The unknown. Death.
- •Flying into unknown parts of yourself.
- •Fear of the unknown.
- •Messenger from the other side.

RHINOCEROS
- •Sexual symbol.
- •Powerful; forceful. Charging ahead at full steam without stopping.

ROBIN
- •A most fortunate omen.
- •Harbinger of good tidings.
- •New beginnings.

SALMON
- •The sacred fish of the celts.
- •Moving ahead against all odds.

SEAL
- •Seal of approval.

SHARK
- •Omen of danger.
- •Hidden fear.
- •Cruel misuse of power.

SHEEP	•Following without using your own judgment.
	•Non-thinking trust.
	•Being taken advantage of monetarily; being "fleeced."
SKUNK	•Social disapproval.
	•Something is faked or "smells."
SNAIL	•Things are moving slowly. Something is going at a snail's pace.
	•Break out of your shell. Get going!"
SNAKE	•A very significant dream symbol. It is not to be feared.
	•Healing; life potency; the power within. The kundalini power or that energy at the base of the spine in connection with spirit.
	•Spiritual awakening; spiritual healing.
	•Feeling tempted or wanting to tempt someone.
	•"Snake in the grass."
SPIDER	•Industry.
	•The eight legs of the spider are material wealth. Wealth through industry.
	•Trap; entrapment. Getting caught in our own web.
	•Manipulation; controlling others or being controlled.

SQUIRREL
•Frugality; comfort through patience.

•Not quite honest; "squirrelly."

STAG
•Sexual vigor.

•Powerful; potent.

STORK
•New beginnings.

•Conception; birth of a new idea.

•Can be an omen of domestic happiness and contentment.

SWAN
•The sign of the white goddess.

•Beauty. Strength. Gliding to new heights. Freedom.

•A black swan can mean the inner mysteries of life. Intuition.

TIGER
•Cunning; prowess.

•Power; energy.

TOAD
•The philosopher's stone.

TURTLE
•A powerful symbol.

•Slow but steady progress toward reaching the goal.

•Completion through diligence.

•May signify a wish to withdraw from a problem or a need to withdraw and go inward to gather forces.

UNICORN
•Traditionally the symbol of Christ. Spiritual unfoldment. Purity, virginity.

•A powerful dream symbol.

VULTURE
•Feeling there is something or someone waiting for you to make an error.

•A need to clean away something that you may consider complete or "dead."

WASP

•Feeling threatened.

•Stinging thoughts. Stinging words.

WEASEL

•Treachery; betrayal.

•A feeling someone is pushing you out of the way or "weaseling in on your territory."

WHALE

•Perception; intuition.

•Tremendous power and strength.

•May concern the size of something; a "whale" of a job.

•Womb of Mother Nature.

•May be a cry for help as in "wail."

•A significant dream symbol.

WOLF

•Community, social feeling; family support.

•May indicate a need for more affection or emotional support as in "wolfing down" one's food.

•Fear, especially concerning being pressed for something without the resources to meet the need; "wolf" at the door.

•Inappropriate flirtatious behavior.

WORM

- Earth's energy; earth's mysteries.
- Hidden preparation or work beneath the surface.
- Low life; someone with no backbone.
- Being intruded upon; someone "worming" his way in.

STONES

Oneirocritica, or "ancient dream books" were written in the second century A.D. These were books designed to assist individuals in the deciphering of the symbols in their dreams. One of the most popular books of this period was based on the work of a man named Artemidorus. It is interesting to note the significance given to stones which appeared in dreams. Artemidorus believed that if an unmarried woman saw a ring of precious stones in her dream, she would soon be wed. If a married woman observed the same she was to conceive a child. If a dream had sparkling jewels, it portended the acquisition of great wealth. Artemidorus believed that red stones in a dream signified good fortune and great joy. He stated that if the stones were light green (the color of new leaf buds in the spring), this foretold that the recipient of that dream would gain a great honor in the world. He also added that this light green color in stones also reflected a strong faith and a sincere religious devotion to God.

According to Artemidorus, the following stones represent:

Agates---------------------------A journey
Amber---------------------------A voyage
Amethysts----------------------Freedom from harm
Aquamarines-------------------New friends
Beryls --------------------------Happiness in store
Bloodstone--------------------- Distressing news
Carbuncles--------------------- Acquirement of wisdom
Chalcedony-------------------- Friends rejoined
Crystal --------------------------Freedom
Diamonds ----------------------Victory
Emeralds----------------------- Future good fortune
Jasper--------------------------- Love returned
Lapis-lazuli-------------------- Faithful love
Onyx --------------------------- Happy marriage or
partnerships
Opals----------------------------Great possessions
Rubies-------------------------- Unexpected guests
Turquoise-----------------------Prosperity

Similar to a Freudian client who will tend to have Freudian-type symbols appearing in his dreams, a Jungian client will tend to have Jungian symbols in his dreams. The stones which appear in your dreams will be appropriate for your belief at the time and the reigning collective consciousness concerning those stones. Since you have read the above dream symbols associated with their respective stones, these meanings are now in your consciousness. It is a self-fulfilling prophesy. Whatever you believe in will create a reality that will support that belief. Therefore, if you believe that turquoise suggests prosperity, don't be surprised if shortly after dreaming about turquoise, abundance in some area of your life comes your way.

Massive shoulders draw energy up through the spine
from ancient fires deep in the earth, thrusting
the spirit like mighty Atlas beneath the heavens -
deep breath of eternity fills the lungs of the soul.

M. Anne Sweet

PARTS OF THE BODY

It is not accidental that we use the parts of the body as a way to communicate our   feelings and emotions. People throughout the world share this tendency and it has been evident in the writings that have been passed down through history. It is interesting to note that the specific parts of the body associated with a particular emotion seem to be common throughout the world.

An expression such as, "She broke my heart," with all the associations of pain and loss that one can feel when disappointed by another, is very descriptive. "He makes me sick" or "I can't stomach that fellow" are two other easily-understood symbolic expressions for describing a reaction to someone.

When part of the body appears in a dream, there is usually a corresponding emotion or feeling associated with that body part. Listed below are some of the more common symbologies for various parts of the body.

ACHILLE'S TENDON
- Traditionally thought to be a place of vulnerability.

ADRENALS
- Anxiety; an adrenal rush.

ANKLE
- Mobility.

ARMS
- Reaching out.

ASS
- The meaning is obvious. A pain in the ass.
- Get moving.

BACK
- Get off my back.
- He's a pain in the back.

BLADDER
- Fear of letting go; holding on to old beliefs and old attitudes.

COLON
- Elimination of things from the past.

EARS
- Being willing to hear the truth.

EYES
- Being willing to see; clarity.
- The apple of my eye.

FEET
- Putting a best foot forward. Understanding. Feet are your connection with the earth; feet are grounding.
- Being afraid or unwilling to step forward.
- Having the courage to step forward. Movement.

FINGERS
- The details of life.
- Pointing a finger at.

GALL
BLADDER •Anger; he had a lot of gall.

GENITALS •Potency; power; sexuality.

•Impotence.

•He was a real dick; acting like a prick.

HAND •Negative: can't get a handle on it; can't
handle it; can't get a grasp of it.

•Left-handed compliment.

•Positive: I can handle it.

•Your name, your handle.

HEAD •Getting ahead; headway; thinking;
analyzing.

HEART •Love; bliss.

HEEL •He was a real heel; she was a real heel.

•To heel or being commanded to walk a
certain way.

HIPS •Positive: support; power; throwing your hip
into it.

•Hip, hip hooray!

•Negative: Fear of moving forward.

JAW •Talking; gossip.

KIDNEYS •Fear.

•Disappointment.

•Criticism.

KNEE
- Fear.
- Inflexibility; not wanting to give in.
- Being in awe of or worshipping as in kneeling.

LARGE
INTESTINE
- Release of toxic matter; release of that which you do not use or do not need.
- Freedom of movement.
- Assimilation.
- Courage; having the guts to go forward.

LEG
- Feeling that you do not have a leg to stand on.

LITTLE
FINGER
- Manipulation; being wrapped or wrapping around the little finger.

LIVER
- Anger.

LUNGS
- Grief.
- Taking in life; the breath of life; taking charge of your life.
- Needing breathing space.

MIDDLE
FINGER
- Sexuality.
- Anger.

NECK
- Positive: Represents flexibility; being willing to see both sides of a circumstance.
- Negative: a pain in the neck.
- Being stiff-necked or immovable.

NOSE
- Nosey.
- Self-recognition.

RING
FINGER
- Union; marriage.

SHOULDER
- Shouldering your responsibilities; shoulder to the wheel.

SOLE/SOUL
- The heart of a matter.

STOMACH
- Just can't stomach it.
- Stomach holds nourishment; helps you digest attitudes, ideas, feelings.
- Can be inability to assimilate that which is new; fear of the new.

TEETH
- Chewing; preparing for digestion.
- Biting into a problem.
- Chewing the fat; talking; discussing.
- If teeth are falling out, it can mean talking too much; scattering your energy. Not understanding a problem or situation.
- Loss of teeth can reflect a loss of face; a spoiling of the appearance in some way. A loss of power. Keeping your mouth shut because you are talking too much, according to Edgar Cayce, meant careless speech. False teeth signified falsehood.
- An infected tooth signified foul language.
- Teeth stand for decisiveness. Loss of teeth symbolizes loss of the power of decisive action.

TEETH (cont.) •The loss of teeth can symbolize growing up; moving to a new stage of development, a new stage of life as baby teeth are replaced by permanent teeth.

•Sometimes a dream of loss of teeth can indicate dental problems. Check with your dentist.

THROAT •Positive: Being willing to speak your own truth.

•Negative: feeling strangled.

•Can't swallow it.

THUMB •Will.

•Thumbs up, go ahead. Thumbs down, forget it!

UPPER LIP •Carrying on in spite of difficulties; keeping a stiff upper lip.

Difficulties that we have in waking life in these different parts of our body can also be indicative of the emotions that are usually associated with the body parts.

It is a valuable exercise to listen to the expressions that you hear and/or use in regard to the body. For example, people who say frequently, "I can't stand it," inevitably suffer back pain. We actually announce our ailments by the expressions we use habitually.

Someone who continually says, "It 'pisses' me off," may have bladder or kidney problems.

Habitually saying, "I can't stomach this," may cause indigestion or difficulty in terms of digesting food.

If we say, "I could have died," or "I am sick to death of it," we may subconsciously be expressing a death wish.

The expression, "It makes me irritable when..." can go in conjunction with skin irritation."

'It is the dreamer himself who should tell us what his dream means.'

Sigmund Freud

DREAM SYMBOLS

A dream dictionary can install a false sense of security in the interpreter and stop any further search for understanding. For example, Freud's way of describing cylindrical objects as phallic symbols may direct the dreamer into one particular frame of mind. It is interesting that people who are seeing a Freudian therapist tend to have Freudian dreams while those working with a Jungian therapist tend to have Jungian dreams. Those seeing a humanistic psychologist will have a predominance of humanistic-type dreams. People who are involved with psychic phenomena tend to have psychic dreams. Our belief systems seem to program the content of our dreams.

Even dream authorities don't agree on what dream symbols mean. The use of a dream dictionary is, at best, a vehicle for you to use to find your <u>own</u> interpretation. Since even those who are authorities in the field cannot agree on definitions, it is wise to remember only the dreamer can know the true meaning of a dream.

To give an example, a dream that contains green apples could be interpreted many ways. One dream dictionary interprets green apples as indicating a loss through one's own foolishness. Another might suggest an upset stomach. Another might be concerned about the significance of the apple in the Garden of Eden and point out the aspect of temptation. However, the associations <u>you</u> have with green apples may have to do with your visits to your grandfather's orchards when the apples were ripening. Perhaps your grandfather took you along as he walked among the trees and you were able to share his pride and pleasure as he saw the results of his hard work maturing. Your memories may include a variety of rich feelings, from the love you felt for your grandfather, to the anxiety associated with the hard work necessary to bring forth the harvest. Your dream may be sharing these feelings with you.

Sometimes your dreams will play delightful little tricks and you will notice that the symbol is a metaphor. The pine tree in your dream that kept appearing in the strangest places may have to do with something you are longing for or "pining" for. The panting dog that seems to be so "hot" may leave your with a passionate craving for a ballpark frank (a hot dog).

Remember, only the dreamer, and not the interpreter or a "list of meanings," can know the true meaning of a dream. So, use the suggestions you find in this book as a place to start when you are interpreting your dream. Some of these dream meanings are literal, some are common symbolic interpretations, some are metaphors or puns, and some are just plain intuition.

After you have had a dream, read over the dream meanings for your dream symbols and see if any seem to fit. See what meanings <u>you</u> assign to that symbol. The meanings listed are to stimulate your <u>own</u> inner knowingness.

ABANDONED

•Feeling left out or not included.

•Denotes leaving behind people, circumstances or characteristics that aren't necessary anymore.

•Need for self-acceptance.

ABDOMEN

•Often represents the second chakra which is called the hara or tanden. This energy center which is located in the area beneath the navel, is associated with emotions.

•Vulnerability.

•See chapter on "PARTS OF THE BODY."

ABDUCTION

•Feeling out of control or that you have no control in a situation.

ABORIGINE

•The very primordial part of you; your instinctive self.

•A part of your basic nature that perhaps is still foreign to you.

ABORTION

•Fear of loss of new birth within yourself.

•Miscarriage of justice.

ABOVE

•Can denote inspiration or the higher self.

•Things looming above you; fears that seem bigger than you are.

ABYSS

•Bringing to consciousness a fear that has been buried for a long time.

ACCIDENT

•Going too fast in life. A need to slow down and integrate.

ACE	•Hidden talents; an ace up your sleeve.
	•Excelling at something.
ACORN	•Great self-potential.
ACTOR	•The roles we play in life are only illusions.
	•Deception or false appearance.
ACTRESS	•See "ACTOR."
ADDICT	•Giving power away to someone or something.
ADOLESCENT	•Great change.
	•Gathering power for new beginning.
ADULTERY	•Conflict between duties and desires.
	•Being drawn to quality in another that you don't experience within yourself.
AIRPLANE	•High ideals.
	•Soaring to new heights.
ALCOHOL	•Dulling the senses; not feeling.
	•Can symbolize camaraderie; wine, women and song."
	•Can symbolize transformation. Jesus said, "This is my blood," in regard to the Last Supper.
ALIEN	•A part of ourself we aren't acknowledging.
	•Going home.
	•Can symbolize higher wisdom.

AMPUTATION

•Giving up that part of yourself associated with the limb in the dream. An amputated leg may mean you feel you don't have a leg to stand on. A hand may signify inability to grasp the situation.

•Releasing parts of ourselves that we may have identified as being a part of who we really are, but that aren't actually a part of our true being.

ANCHOR

•Strength and groundedness.

•Attachment to a person or place.

ANGEL

•A messenger from God. Represents our most spiritual ideals. Many visions of prophets are based on the appearance of an angel in a dream.

•These dream messengers are very special. Listen to what is being said!

ANIMALS

•See chapter on "ANIMALS."

ANKH

•The ancient Egyptian symbol of spiritual wisdom.

ANTENNA

•Transmitting and receiving ideas and energy.

•Awareness of the world around you; tuning in.

ANTIQUE

•A connection with the past.

•An old pattern or belief system that is no longer useful.

ANTLERS
- An omen of happiness.
- Protection of the divine masculine part of yourself.

APPLAUSE
- Self-acknowledgment or needing acknowledgment.

APPLE
- Wisdom.
- Healing potential.
- Wholeness.

ARCHERY
- Specific direction; clarity; single-mindedness.
- Pointing to one thing.

ARGUMENT
- There are parts of yourself that are in conflict.

ARK
- Balance.
- Safety and protection in the midst of the waters of emotion.

ARMY
- Major obstacles to be overcome.
- Opposition.

ARROW
- Clear direction; a goal; a straight course.

ART
- Creative expression in life.
- Potential ability.

ARTIST
- See "ART."

ASHES
- Spiritual purification.
- The essence.

ASTHMA
- Not being able to get enough oxygen can be suppressed grief.
- A feeling of going too fast; not being able to catch your breath.
- Indicates stress and not feeling connected with life

ASTRONOMER
- Looking ahead.
- Highest ambition.

ATOMIC BOMB
- Incredible energy potential; however, there is a need to harness that power.
- Can be a tuning in to the collective consciousness fear for planetary and personal safety.
- An indication of kundalini fire awakening within; great potential for spiritual expansion.

ATTIC
- High ideals. The top floor represents upper chakras.

AUDIENCE
- Congratulations!
- If the audience is responding positively, this is an acknowledgment of self-acceptance.
- If they are not responding positively, you need to work on self-acceptance.

AUNT
- Can represent the industrious part of self.
- The spinster or that part of youself that feels cut off from happiness.

AURA
- A bright, clear aura indicates clarity and good health.
- An aura that is dim and close to the body indicates a lack of clarity and health disturbances.

AWAKE
- If you experience being awake and aware during a dream, this is most probably a lucid dream.
- See chapter on "LUCID DREAMING."

AXE
- Fear of loss.
- Wielding power with certainty.
- Cutting away that which is not needed.

BABY
- This is a new birth within yourself.
- A positive outcome for the future.
- Birth of a new idea.

BAGGAGE
- Things or thoughts that you carry around that aren't necessary.

BALL
- The spherical shape suggests completion, wholeness or unity.
- The planet.
- A social occasion; suggests joy.
- Can have sexual connotations.

BALLOON
- Unrestrained joy.
- Soaring to new personal heights.
- If the balloon breaks, an illusion is shattered.

BASEMENT
- The base or root of a problem.
- Your physical energy. Very often a house will represent our body with the attic associated with upper chakras and the basement with our lower chakras.
- Can be the subconscious.

BATHING
- Purification.
- Washing one's hands of a situation.
- Baptism or rebirth.

BATTLEFIELD
- Deep inner conflict. The antagonists are either those you have hostility toward in waking life or they are symbolic of inner conflict. Remember, a person in your dream is most often an aspect of yourself.

BEACH
- The border between the subconscious, emotional part of you that is represented by water, and the earthly physical side of you.
- Balance.
- Beaches are purifying and rejuvenating.

BED
- An obvious symbol that can regard sexuality and intimacy.
- Comfort; security; eternal womb.
- Rejuvenation. Nurturing.

BELL
- If the sound is clear, then a resonance within the wellspring of life.
- A warning.
- Joyous developments.

BILL   •Karmic payment.

BIRTHDAY   •New beginning.

BLIZZARD   •Emotional upheaval.

                        •A "snow job" on someone or on you.

BLOOD   •Life force; nourishment; power; energy.

                        •Psychic energy.

                        •If you were bleeding, it was an energy drain for you.

BOAT   •Traveling through emotional times. The water is your emotions and the boat represents you and how you are handling your emotions.

BOIL   •A situation about to erupt.

                        •Suppressed anger.

BOTTLE   •Feeling bottled up.

                        •Notice the size and color of the bottle and whether the cap is on or off. A clear bottle can signify more clarity in your life than a cloudy one. A bottle with the cap off is more open than one with the top securely fastened down.

                        •A message in a bottle can be an answer from an unexpected source.

BREAD   •Communion with others.

                        •Abundance.

BRIDE
- The peak of the feminine force within us.
- New beginning.

BRIDEGROOM
- See "BRIDE."

BROTHER
- The religious male aspect of self.
- Common tie; brotherhood.

BURIAL
- Death of old patterns and thought forms.
- Denial of a situation.

BUTTERFLY
- Rebirth; inner beauty; transformation.
- Romance and joy.
- Success.

CABIN
- If in the woods, connotes peace and contentment.
- If on a boat, see "BOAT."

CACTUS
- A prickly situation.
- Something or someone that can't be touched.

CAGE
- Self-imprisonment through fear.
- Feeling trapped.

CAMERA
- Keeping a distance between yourself and life.
- Preserving the past; preserving fond memories.

CANAL
- Related to childbirth and delivery.
- A directed and narrow emotional path.

CANCER   •Something is eating away at you emotionally.

CANDLE   •The spiritual life force within you; your true inner light.

CAR   •Most often represents our physical body or self.

•Notice where the car is going and the condition of the car. Who is in the car?

•See chapters on "NUMBERS" and "COLORS."

CARDS   •The game of life. Your destiny.

CARNATION   •Death and rebirth. Reincarnation.

CARPENTER   •Making repairs in your life. Rebuilding physically, emotionally and spiritually.

•Jesus was a carpenter.

CAVE   •A powerful dream symbol.

•Our great spiritual wealth. Our unconscious self.

•Consolidating your energy.

CEMETERY   •Rest; peace.

•Fear of death.

CHAIN   •Many together creating strength.

•Feeling "chained" to a situation.

CHAIR

•Your position or attitude. Where you "sit" in regard to the matter.

•Rocking in a rocking chair can indicate an out-of-body experience or a building of psychic energy.

CHILDREN

•The child within you. Those inner aspects of yourself such as playfulness, joy, openness.

•Very often it is the child part that isn't being acknowledged.

CHRIST

•The God force within you.

•Love.

•Sacrifice.

CHURCH

•Faith, hope and love.

•The temple of the soul..

•Sanctuary; haven; safety.

CIRCLE

•A very powerful dream symbol.

•Signifies harmony, beauty, balance.

•Completeness.

CLIMBING

•Going upward; a personal ascension in regard to business or a personal goal. Reaching the top of the ladder in your profession.

•May have sexual connotations in terms of sexual excitement.

•In Jacob's dream, he climbed upward to heaven.

•Climbing down can be the opposite of ascending. It can also be the exploration of your subconscious.

CLOTHES
- Your outer persona.
- The roles that you play in life.

CLOUDS
- Clear clouds denote spiritual uplifting. A positive, healthy sign. Inner peace.
- Storm clouds may indicate spiritual questioning. A personal storm is brewing.

COLORS
- See chapter on "COLORS."

COMET
- Heralds tremendous personal and spiritual expansion.
- A powerful dream symbol.

COOK
- Nourishment.
- Material comfort.

COOKING
- Synthesizing the different ingredients in your life.
- See "COOK."

CROWD
- Anonymity; secrecy.
- Strangers or something strange.
- The perceived opinion that the crowd has of you is the subconscious opinion that you have of yourself.
- Feeling a part of something larger than yourself.

CRYING
- Emotional release in the dream state of something still in the subconscious level in waking reality.
- Tears of joy from resolving a difficulty or release of an attitude that was not serving you.

CRYSTAL
- Spiritual transmitter and magnifier.
- A powerful dream symbol signifying clarity, spiritual energy. It is the symbol of the mystic. Listen carefully to this dream.
- See chapter on "STONES."

CUTTING
- Depending on the context, can mean the cutting away of undesired opinions, habits, attitudes and beliefs.
- If you are cut and bleeding, you are losing your vital force.

DAM
- Pent-up emotions about to release.

DANCING
- Joy. The dance of life.
- Sexual enthusiasm and whole-heartedness.

DARK
- The unknown; your subconscious.
- Your fears.

DAUGHTER
- The feminine child part of us.
- May be your own daughter.
- Eternal youth.

DAWN
- A new awakening.

DEATH/DYING
- Not a bad omen.
- Symbolizes transformation, the death of old patterns, and programs, and the making way for rebirth.
- Very rarely indicates the death of one that you see as dead in the dream.

271

•Usually the death of an old belief system of yours that was represented by the dying person.

DEMON   •See "DEVIL."

DESERT   •Jesus went to the desert for spiritual rejuvenation.

               •Desolation. Forsaken; barren; no growth.

DEVIL   •The internal struggle between the part of you that you have labeled as "good" and that part you have labeled "bad."

               •It is important to face this entity, either in your dream or using imagery once you have awakened, as a way to integrate these separate parts of yourself.

DIRT   •Grounding. Connection with Mother Earth.

               •Something in your life that needs to be cleaned up.

DISEASE   •Disharmony. "Dis-ease."

               •After determining which part of the body is affected by the disease, see chapter on "PARTS OF THE BODY."

DOOR   •Great opportunity for new adventure and self-discovery. An open door means that you are ready and a closed door that it is not quite time.

               •Significant dream symbol.

DREAM
- If you dream you are having a dream, you are most likely lucid dreaming.
- See chapter on "LUCID DREAMING."

DROWNING
- You are feeling overwhelmed by emotions.

EARTH
- Mother Earth.
- The female receptive, rejuvinating principle of the universe. Womb. Sensuality.

EARTHQUAKE
- Great change approaching.
- Fear of the change you are undergoing.

EGG
- Wholeness.
- New life; new potential.
- A powerful dream symbol.

ELECTRICITY
- You have bio-electrical systems that surge through you. This can represent the life force.

ELEVATOR
- See "CLIMBING."

ELF
- See "FAIRY."

ESCALATOR
- See "CLIMBING."

EXPLOSION
- Personal crisis, particularly in regard to a relationship.

FACES
- An unknown face or faces can represent those parts of yourself that you aren't currently experiencing.

FAIRY
- A spirit of nature.
- Bringing to manifestation your inner desires.

FALLING
- Loss of control, feeling out of control.
- In the process of learning to walk, we often fall. If you are on unsure ground in a situation or you are in a personal growth spurt and unsure of yourself, there will be dreams of falling.

FAT
- Suppression of emotions and feelings.
- Abundance.

FATHER
- The Divine Father; God.
- Protector; provider.
- Can be your own father or father image.

FEAR
- If anything is fearful in your dreams, face it. It is most likely an unacknowledged part of yourself. Imagine going back into your dream and facing your fear.

FEMALE
- The feminine energy; the female within.
- The receptive energy; yin.

FIGHTING
- Suppressed emotions. Be willing to have and enjoy all of your emotions. They are a part of life.

FIRE
- Kundalini life force within you. Potency; psychic energy.
- Opening to spiritual communication and energy.

•Initiation.

•Sexual passion.

•Purification by fire.

FLAME
•Your own eternal bright flame.

•The light of spirit.

•See "FIRE."

FLOATING
•You are in harmony with your intuition and your emotions. There is great spiritual alignment and you are moving toward feeling at one with all things.

FLOOD
•Overwhelming emotions.

FLOOR
•Foundation or your support.

FLOWERS
•A happy omen of beauty and unfoldment.

FLYING
•If you are flying through the air, you are most likely astral projecting. See chapter on "ASTRAL PROJECTION."

•You are moving beyond the bounds of physical limitation.

•A very significant dream.

FOG
•An obstacle.

•An area of your life that you can't quite see.

FOOD
•Nourishment, can be spiritual, mental, physical or emotional.

FOREST
- •Abundance. Growth. Strength.
- •Protection.
- •Feeling overwhelmed. You can't see the "forest" for the trees.

FORK
- •A fork in the road means you are confronting a choice, and will have to make a decision.

FOUNTAIN
- •Spiritual rejuvenation. Excellent symbol of intuition.
- •Spiritual wellspring.
- •Listen to what you are being told in this dream.

FROZEN
- •Emotionally closed off.

FRUIT
- •Reaping the rewards of your labor.
- •A fruitful harvest. Bearing fruit.

GALAXY
- •Unlimited possibilities.

GARBAGE
- •Things you no longer need in your life.
- •Things you need to release.

GARDEN
- •Creative activity.
- •Peace.
- •If the garden is well tended, harvesting the results of your labor.
- •If it has weeds, there are things in your life you need to weed out.

GHOST

•Some part of your feelings about a particular person have not solidified.

•May be undelivered communication with someone who has died.

GIFT

•Accept the gift. It is to acknowledge you and the growth you have made.

GLACIER

•Frozen emotions.

GLIDER

•Usually, if you are soaring in a glider, you are having an out-of-body experience. See chapter on "ASTRALTRAVEL."

•Riding on the winds of change in life. Going with the flow.

GOD/GODDESS

•Incredible unity and oneness. Universal love. Total self-acceptance in that moment.

•Power to create and manifest.

•Without question, the most powerful symbol in the dream states.

GOLD

•Great inner treasure.

•The golden light of inner peace.

•Heart of gold.

GRANDFATHER

•To the Amerian Indian, it was Grandfather Sun.

•The wise old man. That mature aspect of self; the part of you that knows.

•Can refer to your own grandfather.

GRANDMOTHER
- Grandmother Earth.
- The wise old woman.
- The mature aspect of self.
- Can refer to your own grandmother.

GRAVE
- Serious.
- Self-imposed limitations. Making your own grave.

GURU
- Giving you guidance; the guru within.
- Listen to this dream.

HAIR
- If brushing your hair, you are getting the tangles out of a situation.
- Cutting your hair signifies new beginnings.
- Braiding your hair indicates forging new links.
- Putting gel or brilliantine on your hair is smoothing a situation.
- Hair falling out means that you are worried.
- Thick, luxurious hair is good health.
- Energy streams out of the crown chakra in the top of the head. Thick hair can symbolize great spiritual power flowing out of this energy center, a chakra that connects you to spirit.

HALO
- A halo around something signifies a blessing.

HATRED

•This can sometimes be very emotionally healing. It can be an emotion that you aren't allowing yourself to experience in waking life because it is inconsistent with your self-opinion. By having hatred in your dreams, you can begin to release that emotion so it doesn't physically and emotionally damage you.

•Very often, hatred in dreams is not directed toward the person or object seemingly hated. Most often it is self-anger and the person or thing represents that part of yourself with which you are angry.

HEAT

•Passion; intensity.

•Desires can be the kundalini fire being stimulated.

•Anger.

HEAVEN

•Enlightenment. Bliss. Oneness. Peace.

HELL

•Personal difficulties you are going through.

HOLE

•Something that you are not acknowledging or facing.

•A hole in your argument.

HOME/HOUSE

•Approximately one-third of all dreams take place inside a building, including a house or home. The most common association for a house is one's physical self, spiritual self, or both.

•Whatever is happening to the house is what you are experiencing happening to you. For example, if the plumbing is clogged, it may be that your emotions (symbolized by the water in the pipes) are blocked.

•The different rooms in the house symbolize different aspects of oneself.

•The kitchen represents nourishment, sustenance, creativity as in "cooking" up ideas.

•The hallway is a transition area.

•A bathroom would be elimination of the old.

•The basement, our subconscious and the attic our superconscious.

•Waking in a dark room is about exploring unknown parts of ourselves.

•Clutter in a house represents areas of our lives we need to clean up or things that need to be discarded. (Note the room where the clutter is located.)

HOSPITAL •Center of healing.

ICE •Frozen emotions.

•On thin ice means a dubious circumstance.

•Slipping on ice is being in a circumstance where you don't feel on stable ground or where you are unsure of yourself.

ICEBERG •Tip of the iceberg signifies that your blocked emotions are beginning to surface.

•Drifting without emotional direction.

ICICLES •Whatever emotions have been blocked
are beginning to release. There will be
much more flow in your life.

ILLNESS •Very often a dream of being ill will
indicate an area of your body that needs
attention.

•The thought form, "You make me sick,"
can precede a dream about being ill.

IMPOTENCE •Insecurity. Fear.

INCEST •Integrating parts of yourself;
integrating the adult part of you with the
child part of you, or the male part of
you with the female part of you.
Remember, most often the different
people in a dream are different aspects
of yourself.

INDIAN •A deep, primordial connection to nature.

•A part of your basic nature that is still
foreign to you.

•Higher self-guidance.

INITIATION •Awakening to a new level of
consciousness.

INJURY •See "ILLNESS."

INSECT •Something is bugging you.

•Depends on the insect.
Maggots can represent decay.
Butterflies are transformational.
Flies are small annoyances.
Ants are industrious.

IRON
- Pressing out problems.
- Too many irons in the fire.

ISLAND
- Self-contained.
- No man is an island.
- Refuge.

IVORY
- Favorable sign for all concerns. Represents purity and strength.

IVY
- Stability. Wealth.

JACK
- Diversification. Jack of all trades.
- An automobile jack can be the relief of a heavy burden. It ensures an easier trip. Jacking up one's spirits. Jacked-up.

JAIL
- Feeling confined or feeling at the effect of your life rather than at its cause.

JAM
- The "sweetness" of life.
- May be symbolic of feeling you are in a "jam."
- Traffic jams or log jams signify delays and confusion, and frustration. Feeling stuck with no way to turn.
- Take time to be still and reassess your life's situations.

JAR
- See "BOTTLE."
- A "jarring" experience.

JAW

- Communication. To "jaw" or talk with friends comfortably.
- If tightly closed, there is a need for more open communication.
- Scolding. Boring. Longwinded.
- A square jaw connotes strength, toughness.

JEALOUSY

- Not feeling included; feeling left out.
- Work on knowing that you are complete and whole exactly the way you are now. Your presence is enough.

There is nothing more that you need to be, do or have in order to be whole.

JELLY

- See "JAM."

JESUS

- See "CHRIST."

JEWEL

- Note whether it is worn on the body or is by itself.
- See chapters on "STONES" and "PARTS OF THE BODY."
- She's a real "jewel."
- Can symbolize abundance and brilliance.

JOG

- A reminder; a "jogging" of the memory.
- Connotes movement and self-betterment.
- Can be jogging in place without getting anywhere.

JOURNEY   •Self-exploration and growth.

JUDAS   •A betrayal. Usually self-betrayal. Not being true to yourself.

JUDGE   •Self-judgment.

•It may be directed at another but look at what it is that you have judged to see if it is something you have judged within yourself. An important thing to remember is that everything that you have done to others was necessary for you to do to get to where you are now. It was necessary for your growth. Holding this viewpoint helps you release judgment and guilt.

•Can be guidance or your higher self giving you information.

JUGGLER   •Trying to juggle many things at once.

•If the juggler is doing a good job, so are you.

•If the juggler is a little out of control, consider eliminating some things from your life or taking some time to assess what is really important in your life.

JUICE   •The essence. Virile strength and vigor.

•"Juice up" or give life and energy to.

•Piquant or racy.

•Drunk.

JUMP   •Leaping to a new venture. Getting ahead.

•Look before you leap.

JUNK
- That which is no longer needed by you like ideas, feelings, habits, relationships, etc.

- To get rid of "junk" in your emotions, get rid of junk in your life. The symbolic act of cleaning closets and drawers and getting rid of things that you don't use or don't love will contribute to getting rid of those emotional states that aren't contributing to who you really are. It works!

JURY
- Self-criticism. Note the judgments that you feel the jury is making. Most often, these will be judgments you have made about yourself. Know that what you have done and who you have been was necessary for you to be who you are today. It was necessary for you to get where you are going. Your life is unfolding perfectly for your evolution.

KEY
- A powerful dream symbol connoting opening doors for yourself both on the spiritual and the physical plane.

KEYHOLE
- Being close to a solution or close to a new direction in life, but not quite there. Go back into your dream and imagine that you are taking a key and opening the door. This will assist your waking life.

KIDNAPPING
- Self-sabotage. Feeling out of control in a situation or at the effect of a situation. Feeling the victim of a situation.

- If a child is kidnapped, it is a taking away of your childlikeness.

KILLING

- If you dreamed of killing someone, you are releasing parts of yourself that aren't necessary in your present evolution. You are killing off beliefs or behaviors that are no longer needed by you.

- If you are killing a child, most likely you are killing off your own inappropriate childish behaviors.

- Killing a parent may indicate getting rid of the way you have related to your parents or with your own parenting.

- Do not feel guilty if you have a killing dream. It usually signifies the beginning of a great spurt of self-growth.

- It is a positive dream symbol.

- If you dream you are being killed, you are most likely needing to take control in your life so that you feel empowered rather than powerless. As the Senoi did, go back into your dream and do battle with your antagonist and WIN! This will help you in waking life. (See chapter on MALAYSIAN DREAMERS.")

KING

- Signifies power and majesty; God.

- Self-responsibility; taking charge of your own life.

KISS

- Deep communion with self.

- Warmth. Affection. Love.

- Aligning the masculine and feminine aspects within ourselves.

- The "kiss" of death.

KITE
- Incredible spiritual soaring, yet grounded and anchored.
- Childlike freedom.

KNIFE
- Can be a powerful symbol both creatively or destructively.
- It can be the cutting away of that which isn't needed anymore, as in cutting the thorns from a rose. The cutting away of old patterns of thinking and being.
- If someone is chasing you with a knife or knifing you, perhaps it is a fear of being penetrated emotionally, physically or sexually.

KNITTING
- Tying ideas and life themes together. Unifying.
- Domestic peace.
- Mending; repairing. The broken bone was "knitting."

KNOCK
- An awareness trying to make itself known to you.
- Opportunity knocking.

KNOT
- Tension; tied up in "knots." A stomach in "knots."
- Making a commitment; tying the "knot."
- Untying a knot signifies finding a solution or relaxation in a certain area of your life.

LABORATORY
- Finding solutions through experimentation.

LABYRINTH
•Winding through intricate passageways in a dream can signify feeling that there is no way out. The solution to being in a labyrinth is to stop and still your mind. Let your intuition come through and the way out of your difficulty will become clear.

LAKE
•Notice the nature of the lake. A still, clear lake connotes intuition and deep inner wisdom.

•Choppy water can indicate emotional turmoil.

•A cloudy lake can signify stagnant emotions.

LAMENESS
•See chapter on "PARTS OF THE BODY."

LAMP/LANTERN
•Inner light.

•See "LIGHT."

LAND
•This is your solid grounding; your foundation.

LASER
•Pinpointed consciousness. Intense focus and concentration.

LAUGHTER
•Laughter is a great healer. Don't take life so seriously.

LAUNCHING
•Beginning a new venture.

LAUNDRY
•Personal cleansing.

•Cleaning up your "act."

•Airing dirty laundry.

LAVA •Something that has been suppressed for a long time, usually anger.

LAWN •Nurturing. Grounding.

LEAPING •See "JUMPING."

LEATHER •Strength. Tough as "leather."

LEAVES •Green leaves are showing abundance and growth; life.

•Yellowing leaves or leaves on the ground have to do with completion, letting go and releasing.

LEMON •Poorly constructed.

•Cleansing and purifying.

•See chapter on "COLORS."

LEPROSY •Wasting away; deteriorating.

•See what part of the body is affected.

•See chapter on "PARTS OF THE BODY."

LETTER •Information or news.

•Indirect communication.

LIBRARY •Knowledge. Inner knowing.

•A powerful dream symbol.

LIFEGUARD •This is often a dream guardian or your higher self leading you through an emotional crisis.

LIGHT
- The spiritual light within.
- The quality of the light signifies that of which we are conscious. What we are aware of in life.

LIGHTNING
- A potent dream symbol that connotes great power and a breakthrough ahead.
- Speed. Strength.
- Awakening of the kundalini life force.

LILY
- Rebirth. Life, death and rebirth. Transformation.

LOCKING
- Locking up something indicates a need for feeling more self-acceptance in your life. There is an element of locking something up within yourself that you find undesirable.
- Being in a house or structure and locking others out is shutting yourself away from the realities of the world or locking out other people.

MACHINERY
- Feeling out of touch with the organic process of life.
- Utilization of natural forces for power and strength.

MAGICIAN
- Illusion; not real.
- The tarot meaning for magician is realizing aspirations by reaching inner resources. The magician is the transformer and the manifestor.
- Magic comes from the ancient word "magh" meaning power. The magician symbolizes channeling power from the inner realms to the outer realms.

MAGNET   •Irresistible attraction.

MALE   •Someone who is male in a dream traditionally represents the male part of self, the yang energy, that masculine energy within. The projecting energy.

MAN/MALE   •This is the male part of yourself. Usually represents that linear, rational, practical part of yourself. Focused consciousness as opposed to diffuse awareness.

MANDALA   •A circle. Any time a circle or a mandala appears in a dream, this signifies harmony, beauty, balance.

•This is a very, very powerful dream symbol. It is often used as a visual aid in meditation and religious worship.

MANSION   •See "HOME/HOUSE."

MAP   •Planning your journeys - inner and outer.

MARRIAGE   •Uniting the male and female sides of yourself. Integrating aspects of self.

•A uniting or coming together of ideas or people.

MARS   •The Roman god of war. Can represent small disharmonies.

MARSH   •Emotionally stagnating. Unsure of yourself emotionally.

MARTYR
- A lack of personal power. Feeling that you are a victim of life's circumstances.
- It also has to do with giving to others and feeling resentful when you do not get appreciation.
- Work with self-acceptance. Accept responsibility for the circumstances in your life.

MASK
- Different aspects of yourself.
- Dishonesty.

MASSAGE
- Personal integration.

MATCH
- Unlit, a match is potential yet unrevealed.
- A lit match is your inner light beginning to shine forth.

MAZE
See "LABYRINTH."

MEADOW
- A place of spiritual harmony and balance.
- Rejuvenation and nurturing.

MEAT
- The essence. The heart or "meat" of the matter.

MEDICINE
- Healing.
- Getting some of your own "medicine."

MELONS
- Wholeness.
- Something full of opportunity.

MELTING
- New dimensional understanding.

MENSTRUATION
- Releasing the old. New beginning.
- If blood is evident, feeling loss of life energy.

MERCURY
- Messengers of the gods; the bearer of messages.
- God of trade, commerce, gain, luck, travel and good gifts.
- Eloquence.
- Rapid changing of moods.

MERMAID
- Your intuitive emotional self.

MERRY-GO-ROUND
- Feeling like you are going around and around without making any progress.

METAL
- Strength. Hardness.
- Immobility.

MICROSCOPE
- Intense self-examination.

MILK
- Mother's milk. Nurturance; sustenance.
- "Milk" of human kindness.

MINE
- Inner treasures undiscovered.

MIRROR
- A step apart from reality. Seeing a reflection of what is.

MISCARRIAGE
- A miscarriage of justice.
- Plans aborted or not fulfilled.
- See "ABORTION."

MISSING THE
BOAT/PLANE/
TRAIN

- Feeling a lack of progress in your life. Feeling left out because of the circumstances in life.

- Lost opportunity.

- Not making enough of an effort. Take time to reassess your goals.

MONASTERY

- Inward spiritual retreat.

- Can mean a withdrawal from the world.

MONEY

- If coins, can signify a change coming in your life.

- Can connote wealth of experiences or finances, etc.

MONSTER

- Some unacknowledged part of yourself that you fear. Your hidden fears in manifest form.

- Really examine your monster(s). The greatest fear is of that which is unknown. Become familiar with your dream monster. Ask yourself what parts of yourself it represents. You might even ask the monster what it represents.

- If you are confronting a threatening monster, instead of being victimized, go back and fight it. Do this by going back into your dream in your imagination and doing battle. Emerge victorious and as the Senoi would do, ask this monster for a gift that is either valuable or beautiful.

- See chapter on "MALAYSIAN DREAMERS."

MOON

- The feminine aspect of yourself.
- Inner emotional peace.
- The phases of the moon indicate different states. A full moon represents wholeness and creativity from an intuitive base. A new moon or a crescent moon show a time of feeling at one with our internal spiritual self. It is a time for deep inner reflection.

MOTHER

- Can reflect that part of yourself that your own mother represents.
- Nurturance. "Mother Earth." That wiser part of the female part of yourself.
- Divine Mother.

MOUNTAIN

- An attainable goal or opportunity. Going up the mountain means you are progressing toward that goal. Going down the mountain means you are moving away from the goal.
- Can be a spiritual uplifting experience. Monasteries and lamaseries are in the mountains because the mountain is a place of spiritual retreat.
- "Don't make a mountain out of a molehill."
- Can be viewed as an obstacle or an opportunity.

MOURNING

- Releasing parts of yourself such as habits, attitudes, relationships that no longer serve you in order to make way for more appropriate ways of being.
- A releasing dream.

MOUTH
•Communication; expressing yourself.

MOVIES
•Observing life.

•Becoming bound up in the drama of life.

•These are your different roles in life.

MUD
•Feeling stuck; not moving or growing.

•Things seem "muddy" in your life, not clear.

•"Mud, mud, glorious mud" that a child enjoys; childlike joy.

MURDER
•See "KILLING.

MUSEUM
•See "HOME/HOUSE."

•Knowledge. Bringing wisdom from the past and assimilating it into the present.

MUSIC
•Beautiful, harmonious music signifies the uplifting spiritual alignment; inner harmony.

•Music out of tune signifies feeling out of tune with your life.

MUSICAL INSTRUMENTS
•Depends on the instrument in the dream. A piano might be the keys of life. A flute connotes nature or freedom or the child within. Drums can indicate primitive nature or primordial instincts. Staying with the beat. Marching to a different drum. A harp might suggest celestial alignment; angels. A harmonica is the wandering minstrel. A time with friends, enjoyment and

contentment.   Bagpipes are a cultural
fellowship. Violin or strings connote
dedication. The sitar is Eastern culture;
mysticism; internal peace.

NAIL

•Depends on its use. A carpenter's nail
can represent support for larger
structures or a binding together.

•Getting to the essence of the problem or
"hitting the nail on the head."

•Getting "nailed" or getting caught.

•Chewing fingernails represent anxiety.
Remember that your life is divinely
guided and there are no accidents in
life.

NAKEDNESS

•Total freedom.

•Vulnerability. Feeling exposed.

•Exposing a situation; baring your soul.

•Sensuality.

NARROW

•Restriction.

•Focused attention and discipline to
reach your goal.

NAUSEA

•Something is making you sick to your
stomach.

•Getting rid of what isn't wanted.

NAVEL

•See chapter on "PARTS OF THE
BODY."

•Symbolic of silver cord that connects
your astral body to your physical body.

•In the Orient, the navel is thought to
symbolize the center of the universe.

NEST
- •Incubating ideas or projects.
- •Nesting. Home and family life; domestic life.
- •Pulling inward for rejuvenation.

NET
- •Can connote feeling caught in a web or net of your own perception of what reality really is. Take time to still your mind and allow for the myriad of other realities to be made available to you so you can choose one that is more in alignment with who you truly are.
- •A fishing net or butterfly net may also help catch things that are needed in life.
- •A safety net to catch you if you are feeling out of balance.

NIGHT
- •Obstacles or delays or not seeing things clearly. Not being in touch with your inner knowing.
- •If it is a clear night with visible stars or moonlight, then it is a symbol of your intuition and your inner realms.

NIGHTMARE
- •Nightmares should be looked on as positive experiences. They allow us to deal with unresolved issues in our waking life that we are not allowing into our consciousness. These unresolved issues are affecting every aspect of our life including our health and relationships. The nightmare is our subconscious way of healing these unresolved issues. Celebrate your nightmares!
- • Imagine you are going back into your nightmare and play it through in your

mind a few times. Change the circumstances so that there is a positive outcome from your dream. This will assist healing the unresolved area of your life that was the source of the nightmare in the first place.

NUDITY •See "NAKEDNESS."

NUMB •Most often there is some external physical cause such as sleeping in an awkward position. If this isn't the cause, it may be that you are cut off from your feelings or you are suppressing something that is fearful to you.

NUMBERS •See the chapter on "NUMBERS."

NUN •Pulling your energies inward.
•Celibacy and spiritual attunement.

NURSE •Healing; caring; nurturing.

NUTS •New life; potential yet to unfold.
•Abundance; gathering nuts for the winter.
•"A hard nut to crack."

NYMPH •Minor divinity of nature in mythology. Mystical maiden that dwells in the mountains, waters and trees.
•Joyous sexuality.
•Immature insects. Incomplete development or incomplete metamorphosis.

OAK
•Powerful strength. Solidarity. Steady progress.

OAR
•A boat without an oar may signify you are feeling adrift within an emotional dilemma.

•Oars can mean feeling in control in the midst of emotional imbalance.

OASIS
•Refuge. Place of rejuvenation.

OBITUARY
•Release of old ideas, thought forms and beliefs.

OBSERVATORY
•Getting the bigger picture. Seeing the deeper meaning in life.

OCEAN
•The meaning varies according to the condition of the water.

•A calm ocean connotes great inner power and emotional and spiritual balance.

•A rough or choppy ocean indicates the need for courage to allow you to move to calmer waters amid emotional upheaval.

•Sea of life. Tremendous intuitive power.

OFFICE
•Production.

•Linear thought process; organization.

OFFICER
•Authority.

•Can connote protection or guidance.

•Conscience. Punishment. Self-righteousness.

•Can sometimes indicate guilt and that the dreamer wants to be punished or kept out of trouble.

•Can be an affirmation for accepting authority for your own life.

OIL

•Lubrication; smoothing difficulties. "Pouring oil on troubled waters."

•Anointing with oil is a blessing.

•A greasy or oily personality.

OLIVE

•Peace. "The olive branch of peace."

ONION

•Potential sadness.

OPERATION

•Note where on the body the operation occurred then see chapter on "PARTS OF THE BODY."

ORCHARD

•See "GARDEN."

ORCHESTRA

•Synthesis. Harmony. Synergy.

ORGASM

•Depends on the feelings associated with orgasm and whether you physically reached the orgasm or not.

•It can be a powerful alignment with your inner male and female energies and a connection to your kundalini energy, or creative energy, that coils at the base of your spine.

•For a male to reach orgasm in sleep may indicate a need to strengthen the prostate gland.

•See chapters on "DREAM LOVER" and "DREAMS FOR SEX AND LOVE."

ORGY

•Your creative force may be being dissipated. Focus on your life goals.

ORPHAN

•See "ABANDONED."

OVEN

•An idea or project is incubating.

PACING

•A dream where you are pacing back and forth means you have uncertainty as to your life's direction. Take time to be still. Thinking about the situation isn't always the best solution. As you take time to quiet your mind, the correct solution will gently bubble to the surface.

PACK

•If you are carrying a pack, there is something or someone or an idea that you are carrying around with you that it not necessary. You can let it go.

•If you are packing, it symbolizes preparation for a change in your life.

PACKAGE

•If you are sending the package, you are letting go of something.

•If you are receiving a package, you are acknowledging an unrecognized part of yourself.

PAIN

•See chapter on "PARTS OF THE BODY."

PAINT

•Note the color and see the chapter on "COLORS."

•Redoing. Making new.

PALACE
- See "HOME/HOUSE."
- Your sense of your true magnificence.

PAN
- Greek god of shepherds and hunters who originated panpipes. Symbolizes the joy in nature.
- Panning as with a movie camera can mean getting the bigger picture.
- Panning for gold can be looking for the true essence.
- Pan or cooking pot can be incubating an idea.

PARACHUTE
- You can soar. You are protected.

PARADE
- Being willing to be recognized particularly for your community efforts.
- Each of the participants in the parade is an aspect of yourself.

PARENTS
- Note: (Although, fortunately, family members' roles are changing dramatically, yet our soul memory holds stereotypical images of parents.)
- Fathers represent authority and the linear, rational thought processes. A projecting force. The yang energy.
- Mothers stereotypically represent the yin principle of nurture and the inner realms of intuition and magic.
- Your dream could pertain to your own experience of your parents or your parenting skills.
- Could pertain to the mother/father energy that dwells within you.

PARTY •Celebration.

PASSENGER •If you are the passenger, you are "along for the ride." You are not deciding the direction; someone else is.

PASSPORT •This is your ticket for change and for creating what you want in your life.

PATH •Notice the width and direction and the straightness of the path.

•A straight and narrow path going upward means you are making progress. You are in alignment with your life's goals and purpose. You are staying on the path.

•A crooked path means that you are wandering off course or that you are not quite sure which direction to go.

PATTERN •A sewing or an embroidery pattern can connote your usual reality system or the one in which you are comfortable.

•Changing patterns can mean breaking out of old patterns.

PAVEMENT •New pavement is new direction.

•To pave is to make your way easier or smoother.

PEACH •Uplifting; "peachy keen."

PEDESTAL •Putting someone or yourself in a position of elevation or seeing that one as "above you." This detracts from your inner power because when you experience yourself within all things nothing becomes higher or lower.

PEGASUS	•Freedom. Inner magic.
PEN	•Expressing yourself fluidly; communication.
	•All "penned" up; feeling restricted.
PENCIL	•Ability to express yourself. Less restrictive than a pen.
PENDULUM	•Uncertainty. Weighing several choices.
	•Needing to find a balance in your life.
PENIS	•Yang. Projecting energy; the male principle. Power. Potency.
PENNY	•See "MONEY."
PEPPER	•Spicy emotions.
	•Stimulating.
PERFUME	•If you can actually smell perfume in your dreams, it represents sensuality.
PERISCOPE	•Subconscious observation of conscious reality.
	•Objective observation.
	•If the periscope is in water, it is observing your conscious reality from your emotional intuitive self.
PETAL	•Petals falling from the flower signify sadness.
	•Pulling petals off a flower; "he loves me, he loves me not."
PHONE	•See "TELEPHONE."

PHOTOGRAPHY
- Objective observation of a situation.
- Memories from the past.

PIANO
- See "MUSICAL INSTRUMENTS."
- If the piano is out of tune, you are not in tune with yourself.

PICTURE
- See "PHOTOGRAPH."

PIE
- An opportunity; "getting a piece of the pie."
- The roundness of pie suggests wholeness combined with nourishment.
- A positive dream symbol.
- A whole with the possibility of being divided into shares.

PILL
- Something unpleasant or repugnant that must be endured.
- Someone disagreeable or tiresome; a real "pill."
- Can represent healing.

PILLAR
- Strength.

PILLOW
- Intuitive; inner realms.
- Relaxation; letting go.

PIN
- Solid material that fastens separate articles together or a support that allows one article to be suspended from another.
- A petty annoyance.
- Getting "pinned down" or held fast or immobile.

PINE
- •Excellent cleanser and purifier. Pine creates negative ions that are a healing electrical charge in the air.
- •To pine away for someone or something.

PIONEER
- •Entering new areas within yourself and within your waking life.

PIPE
- •As a musical instrument, it connotes joy and freedom.
- •As a solid structure that conducts liquids or gases it depicts the flow of energy within yourself and the universe.
- •The peace pipe of the Native American was an object of holiness and reverence. It symbolized unity with Spirit.

PIRATE
- •Unauthorized use of another's product, conception or creativity. You need to feel your own authority in life.

PIT
- •See "ABYSS."

PLANETS
- •Heavenly bodies; illumination.
- •The rhythm of the universe.
Earth is associated with grounding, nurturance.
Jupiter can mean expansiveness, vastness. A huge, imposing connotation.
Mars means aggressiveness, passion. A warlike connotation.
Mercury was a Greek messenger of the gods. Signifies communication and speed. Swift change of mood.

Neptune was the god of the sea.
Connotes psychic awareness,
mysticism.
Pluto may be small, concentrated. Can
be a spiritual unfolding. Also can be
seen as capricious joy as found in the
Walt Disney character of that name.
Saturn can be sardonic and slow to act.
A feeling of coldness.
Uranus denotes hidden abilities.
Changes.
Venus calls forth images of beauty,
harmony, femininity, gentleness.

PLASTIC
- Flexibility; capacity to be molded or
  shaped, pliable.

- Artificial; bogus.

PLATFORM
- Taking a stand.

- Stating your beliefs; a declaration of
  your principles.

PLAY
- Children at play connote joy and
  spontaneity.

- "All the world's a stage...." Your life is
  your script and you can choose to
  become involved in the drama or not.
  You can choose the script. It's all your
  play.

POCKET
- A place of safekeeping.

- A cavity containing something of value;
  a receptacle or container.

POISON
- Something destructive or harmful.
  Most often, it is pointing to an attitude
  about self. A fear or a judgment.

POKER   •You are gambling with something.

POLICE   •See "OFFICER."

POND   •As with any area of water, a pond represents emotions and intuition. A calm and clear pond suggests calm, clear emotions as troubled water suggests a problem or problems.

•The boundaries of a pond are smaller than those of an ocean or lake indicating less of an emotional concern.

POOL   •A pool is more suggestive of intuition and the deep inner realms of self than are other bodies of water.

POPCORN   •Popping indicates lots of creativity and new ideas that are moving into manifestation. The kernels (ideas) are expanding.

•Stale popcorn indicates an unsatisfactory ending.

POPLAR   •Popular. Enjoyment. Contentment.

PORRIDGE   •An added-on part of yourself; an extension of yourself.

•That which is not a part of your basic nature, yet something you consider in relation to yourself.

PORT   •See "HOME."

•Safety

•Depending on the nature of the water nearby, can concern emotions. Was the seawater rough, clear, cloudy?

•Good wine. Enjoyment with friends.

PORTRAIT
- Relates to how you see yourself or how you think others see you.
- Not necessarily your true nature.

POSTMAN
- Messages or news coming to you.
- Information from an outside source. Guidance.

POT
- Something you are cooking; can be nurturing.
- Something you are creating.
- Someone who is "potted."
- Marijuana; a different level of consciousness. Dependent on outer stimulation rather than inner resources.

POTTERY
- Concerns molding your life, your attitudes, your beliefs.

PRAISE
- Congratulations! You have done well!
- You have earned something.

PREGNANCY
- There is something you are about to give birth to as an idea, a feeling, an emotion.
- New creative project. Going in a new direction.
- Can signify a desire to be pregnant.
- This is a powerful dream symbol.

PREMONITION
- Note: Dreams that seem to be premonitions where the happenings seem literal, not symbolic, are usually pointing to aspects of the growth of your inner self.

•As upsetting as dreaming of the death of a child may be, it can signify the "death" or putting away of "childish things" in your life. Seen in this light, the dream may be something other than a premonition.

•It takes practice to recognize a premonition dream from a symbolic, self-growth dream, but there are some things found in <u>premonition dreams</u> you can look for:

•Usually, the colors are quite a bit brighter in a premonition dream.

•Very often, there is a rounded or round object. The round shape symbolizes the energy of prophecy, of premonition.

•In a premonition dream, the symbol will repeat itself three times.

•If you are not sure, interpret the dream both literally an symbolically, as I do, until the meaning becomes clear. Or, you can ask for clarification in another dream.

•The more comfortable you become with having premonitions in your dreams, the easier it will be for you to access this part of yourself.

PRESIDENT

•You are your own authority.

•Control. Leadership.

•Priest; spiritual authority.

•Guidance; showing the way.

PRINCE
- The most divine masculine part of yourself.
- The masculine force in the universe. Yang.

PRINCESS
- The most divine feminine part of yourself.
- The feminine force in the universe. Yin.

PRINTING SHOP
- Communication.
- A solution to the current problem.
- Repeating the situation over and over again.

PRISON
- Self-imposed bars; self-imposed confinement. You always have the key to let yourself out. The only person who can imprison you is you.

PRISONER
- Limiting your own potential. Self-confinement.
- Experiencing fear.

PROFANITY
- Sometimes profanity can express unexperienced emotions within normal waking life.

PROP
- Something that is supporting you temporarily until you step into your own wisdom, your own judgement, or your own strength.

PROPHET
- This is an important dream.
- Guidance, teaching, and divine direction.
- The mystic, the visionary, the master.

•Listen to what the Prophet has to say to you.

•A powerful symbol of guidance.

PROSTITUTE
•Prostituting yourself; using your energy inappropriately. Misusing your creativity.

•Latent draining of sexual energy.

•Revealing sensuality.

PRUNE
•Shriveled. Dried up.

•Old. An older person.

PUDDLE
•Nuisance. Some small emotional difficulty that is bothering you.

PUMP
•Getting those life-affirming energies going. The awakening of the kundalini energy that resides at the base of the spine.

•Sexuality. Power. Strength. Potency.

•Water, free-flowing from a pump indicates easy, free-flowing emotion. To pump without result indicates emotional constriction or restriction. Priming the pump connotes opportunity ahead.

PUMPKIN
•A happy, comfortable home life.

PUPPET
•Manipulation. Feeling manipulated or that you are manipulating others.

•Giving away your power; not remembering that you are in control.

PURSE

- Tied to another's purse strings.
- See "POCKET."

PUZZLE

- Not seeing the whole picture of something.
- Each part of your life is a different part of the puzzle. A completed puzzle indicates unification.
- Can indicate feeling puzzled, unsure; lacking clarity.
- Take time to concentrate or focus your energy. The answer will be forthcoming.

PYRAMID

- A powerful symbol of inner unification and alignment.
- This is a symbol of initiation. You have moved to a new level of awareness, a new level of understanding within yourself.
- You are open to guidance from those higher energies around you and from your higher self.

QUAKER

- Members of this sect are generally very balanced. They represent balance and a peaceful life.
- Family unity and harmony.

QUARANTINE

- Feeling isolated or in a state of isolation.
- Feeling separate from your true nature.

QUARREL

•Different aspects of yourself are at war. You might visualize the two quarrelling parties in your dream discussing each person's position with an attitude of understanding or of peace. This will allow you to put at rest the parts of yourself that are quarrelling.

QUARTZ

•Transmitter. Energy conductor.

•Spirituality.

•Clarity.

QUEEN

•That powerful female energy within you. It has more strength and more power than "princess."

•It is the wisdom of womanliness rather than the purity of girlhood.

•The goddess within.

QUEST

•Usually signifies a spiritual journey.

•Spiritual yearning. Remember the answers are within you. Make your quest within.

QUICKSAND

•Fear. Feeling like you are being pulled under. The way to deal with quicksand in your life is to be still. Expand your horizon; expand your perspective. There is a way out of the difficulty in which you are involved. Become one with the quicksand so that there is nothing that is not you. Become one so that all possibilities are open to you.

QUILT
- Domestic happiness.
- Its cover is protection.
- A patchwork quilt represents different parts of yourself coming together to make a whole.

RABBI
- Guidance; showing the way.
- Teacher.

RACE
- The only person with whom you are competing is yourself. Slow down; enjoy the run; smell the flowers.

RADAR
- Being able to see beneath the surface.
- Attunement. Intuition.

RADIO
- Communication. Guidance from another source.

RAGE
- Allow the anger that has been held in for so long to be expressed. Rage expressed in a dream will allow you to release that rage that is being suppressed in waking life.

RAGS
- A feeling of poverty of spirit.

RAILINGS
- Feeling your boundaries; being aware of your boundaries.
- Holding on to railings for support.

RAIN
- Cleansing, purifying, emotionally refreshing.
- Rain means that perhaps you are going through an emotional time and a cleansing process.

RAINBOW

•A very powerful dream symbol signifying joy, celebration, completion. You have made it through the emotional difficulty and there is a completion.

RAPE

•You are accepting someone else's reality as your own.

•You are feeling penetrated.

•A loss of power and self-esteem. Feeling "ripped off."

RAZOR

•Cutting through.

•Can be separation; release.

•Depends on the type of razor or blade and how the razor is being used.

•Safety razor denotes mental clarity.

RECIPE

•Combining the ingredients of your life in such a way that there is unity.

RECORD

•Feeling like you are going around and around. Stuck in a rut or a groove. Same old attitudes; same old feelings. It is time to step off the treadmill.

RED CROSS

•The sign of healing. Self-healing.

REDWOOD TREE

•Symbol of strength, wisdom, grounding, yet with spiritual aspirations.

REFRIGERATOR

•Emotionally feeling closed off. Freezing the emotions. A lack of warmth.

REPAIR •If you are repairing something in a dream, there is something in your life that you feel needs mending or needs to be repaired. You might continue within your waking time and repair whatever it was that you were trying to repair in the dream. As you do this symbolically, it will allow that which needs to be repaired in your life to repair itself.

RESCUE •You are needing to be rescued. You are not feeling in control of your life. You are feeling there are others who are in control. It is coming from the point of victim. Remember, there are no victims. There are only volunteers. Begin to move to a place of responsibility for your life and your environment.

•If you are rescuing others, there is someone that you feel needs help.

RESTAURANT •Sustenance. Nourishment.

•Fellowship.

REVOLUTION •There are different aspects of yourself at war. Usually a dream of this kind suggests a coming time of change. Within your awake state, move to resolution of the rebellion or the revolt.

REVOLVING DOOR •Opportunities that are being missed or passed.

•Feeling like you are moving around and around with old attitudes, old ideas.

RICE
- •Domestic happiness. Wedding. Joy. Celebration.
- •Good harvest.

RIDING
- •If you are riding an animal, it is a feeling of alignment with nature. Mastery. Conquest.
- •If you are in a vehicle and someone else is driving, perhaps you feel that you are not in charge of your life. Someone else is guiding you.
- •You are being taken for a ride; being deceived.

RING
- •A long friendship. Marriage. Engagement.
- •A ring of truth. Promise.
- •Eternal love.

RIVER
- •The river of life. The flowing waters of life.
- •The expression, "Don't push the river, it flows by itself."
- •Trying to swim upstream. Allow the river to carry you. Don't fight the current.
- •You are trying to get across the river and you can't find the way. The river usually represents an emotional barrier you are having trouble crossing. In your waking state, imagine a bridge across the river and walk to the other side. Make yourself a new route in order to resolve the situation.

ROAD
•The road is your direction in life. Look carefully at the road. Is it rocky? Crooked? Straight? Does it go uphill? Downhill? Is it clear? This represents your destiny, your direction in life. Look for forks in the road, forks representing major decisions to be made.

•The condition of the road suggests the way that your life is running at this moment.

ROBBER
•Tremendous fear and insecurity.

•Feeling a victim of life. Feeling at the effect of life. Remember that the other side of what is so is so what! There are no victims. Begin to take responsibility for your life. Accept responsibility for your life.

•Go back into your dream and defeat the robber. Become the hero or heroine of your own dream and you will move toward greater strength and greater security within yourself.

ROBOT
•Mechanical feelings.

•Feeling of being shut off from your feelings; unfeeling.

ROCK
•Grounding. Strength. Personal power.

•The rock of Gibraltar.

ROCKET
•Soaring to spiritual heights. Unlimited potential and power.

ROOF
- •This is your protection. This associates with your crown chakra.
- •The condition of your roof suggests the condition of your spiritual connection.
- •See "HOME/HOUSE."

ROOM
- •Room is an aspect of yourself.
- •See "HOME/HOUSE."

ROPE
- •An attachment to a person or place or thing.
- •It can be your kundalini power.
- •The lifeline.
- •A rope that is neatly coiled represents organization, inner twining and balancing of mind, body and soul.
- •A rope that is frayed or knotted represents disassociation.
- •Feeling tied up. Feeling in knots. Feeling restricted.

ROSE
- •Love. Beauty. Innocence.

ROW
- •A fight. Having an argument.
- •Can represent organization, soldiers in a row.

ROWING
- •Rowing across water can represent moving through an emotional situation.

ROYALTY

•Depending upon whether it is male or female, having to do with the divine aspects of self. The divine feminine, the divine masculine.

•Feeling a sense of your own royalty, your own divinity.

RUNNING

•Stop! Turn around. Face the truth.

•Running from a situation is running from something you are not ready for. You are unsure of yourself. You are afraid of a situation or experience you are not willing to acknowledge. Turn around and face the antagonist, whether you are within your dream state or your waking state, and as you face that from which you are running, you will begin to dissolve that barrier within your waking life.

•Running in slow motion means the time is coming soon when you will have to face that difficulty.

•If you are running toward something, you are in a time of great acceleration within your spiritual life. Celebrate.

RUST

•Talents or abilities not being used.

•You are a bit rusty in your skills. Polish up those talents and abilities.

SACK

•Future events yet to be revealed.

•Can suggest hiding or self-concealment.

•Getting "sacked." Losing your power.

SACRIFICE
•If you dream of someone or something being sacrificed in a dream, there is an area of your life where you feel that you are making a sacrifice. This is martyrdom.

•Feeling at the effect of life rather than at its cause. You are in control of your destiny. Affirm to yourself: "I choose my life and I choose it completely. I am in control of my life. I have chosen my life's circumstances."

SADDLE
•Feeling bound. Feeling saddled to a situation that you wish to be free of.

SAFARI
•Exploring unknown parts of yourself.

•See the chapter on "ANIMALS" for the specific animal.

SAILBOAT
•Navigating through emotional change.

•If moving quickly and easily, you are soaring through emotional change with ease.

SAINT
•This is usually your guardian angel or protector, your higher self in a manifested form within your dreams. Listen very carefully to the messages and notice the symbols that occur within this particular dream.

SALAD
•Healing. Nature. Simplicity. Health.

SALT
•The salt of the earth.

•The element earth.

SAND
- The sands of time. Nothing is permanent. Everything is an illusion.
- A house built on sand. Not a permanent foundation.
- Changes. Things changing.
- Irritations. Small annoyances. Not lasting.

SAW
- Cutting one down to size. Construction. Building. Creating. Making. Doing.
- Pruning.
- An emotional wound from the past that is healing but is still not forgotten. Check the other symbols, people and situations to help identify the emotional scarring that still needs to be healed.

SCARECROW
- Not real; false. Being afraid; scared.
- Like in the WIZARD OF OZ, little intellectual ability.
- Scaring people off with a false front or false appearance.

SCHOOL
- The school of life. Those lessons that you have chosen for yourself within this lifetime.
- Listen to the echoes; you don't have to hear the screams.
- Allowing the environment, allowing life to be your teacher. Let each circumstance that you are in, each person whom you are with be your teacher. Let these show you the way. When you leave the body every night, you are learning lessons of higher

truths. Each level of consciousness is teaching you something about yourself and your destiny and the nature of who you are.

SCIENTIST
•Left-brained; analytical; thinking; rational; intelligent. Let the heart rule as well as the head.

SCISSORS
•Cutting away, releasing that which is unnecessary in your life.

•Feeling cut off from others, from yourself.

SEA
•See "OCEAN."

SEAM
•Coming apart at the seams.

•That which binds things together.

SEASONS
•See the chapter on "SEASONS."

SEEDS
•Great things grow from small beginnings provided they have all the right ingredients.

•A new beginning.

•As you sow, so shall you reap.

SEESAW
•Feeling as though you are going up and down but not getting anywhere.

SEMEN
•Power; potency; strength. The creative potential.

SEX
•See chapter on "DREAMS FOR SEX AND LOVE."

SHADOW
- This is the latent potential of an individual.
- It is fear. It is the illusion.
- It is the unknown part of yourself.

SHAPES
- If there are undefined shapes in a dream, in your waking state say, "What does that shape remind me of? What feeling do I have about this shape?"
- Allow the shape to take form. It can be something unformed or not quite solidified within your life. If you allow the shape to take form within your imagination, soon that project, idea or feeling will begin to take shape in your life.

SHAVE
- A close shave; a close call.
- Grooming. Bolstering self-opinion.

SHELL
- Emptiness; an empty shell.
- Pulling into your shell. Closing off from the outer world. Nonactivity. Nongrowth.

SHEPHERD
- The guardian of the spirit. The guardian of the inner way.

SHIELD
- Your protection allowing you to stay balanced and centered amid change.
- It can be a defense mechanism.

SHIP
- This is yourself, your whole self when life is uncertain, particularly in regard to emotions.
- See "BOAT."

SHOES
- •Steps to be taken in life.
- •Grounding. Connecting you to the earth.
- •Don't judge another until you walk in his shoes.
- •Filling too many shoes; filling too many roles.

SHOOTING
- •Shooting at a target. Focusing energy for a particular goal.
- •Shooting someone else can mean killing off an aspect of self.
- •Being shot denotes feeling penetrated, the victim.

SHOPPING
- •Decisions; choosing.

SHOULDER
- •Strength.
- •Accepting responsibility. To shoulder; push through.

SHOWER
- •Emotional cleansing. Cleaning up your act.

SILK
- •Luxuries; riches; wealth.
- •Excellent conductor of bio-electrical energy.
- •Sensuality. Ability to flow.

SILVER
- •Second best.
- •Can be the silver cord. Spiritual connection.
- •Inner light.

SINGING
- Celebration; joy; uplifting of spirit. Spiritual light.
- Troubles are over; harmony.

SISTER
- Female aspect of self.
- Religious aspect. Nun.
- Relatedness; sisterhood.

SKELETON
- Things unacknowledged. A skeleton in the closet.
- Doesn't necessarily mean physical death. It can mean emptiness. Devoid of content.

SKI
- If you are going too fast, perhaps it's a sign that you are going too fast in life. Feeling out of control.
- Can be spiritual alignment.

SKY
- Heavens. No limitation to success. The sky is the limit.
- Freedom; expansion.

SLAVE
- Being a slave to old habits, old ideas, old beliefs.
- A slave to other people, other situations.

SLEEPING
- Dreaming that you are sleeping may mean that perhaps you are astral traveling and observing your body from out of the body.
- It can be that you are unwilling to change. Stagnation.
- Not moving. Not changing.

SLIDE
- Feeling out of control.

SKI
- •If you are going too fast, perhaps it's a sign that you are going too fast in life. Feeling out of control.

- •Can be spiritual alignment.

SKY
- •Heavens. No limitation to success. The sky is the limit.

- •Freedom; expansion.

SLAVE
- •Being a slave to old habits, old ideas, old beliefs.

- •A slave to other people, other situations.

SMOKE
- •Where there is smoke, there is fire. This can be a warning of danger.

- •It can be a lack of clarity. Things are confused.

- •A warning.

SNEEZE
- •The cleansing of emotions.

SNOW
- •Cleansing.

- •Purity. Untouched virgin. A fresh start; a new look at the world; a new beginning.

SOAP
- •Cleansing; purification.

SOLDIERS
- •War within and without.

- •Can represent organization and discipline.

SOLVE
- •A binding together; integration of ideas, feelings, different aspects of a project.

SPEEDOMETER
- Going too fast; going too slow.
- Look at the numbers on the dial and then see the chapter on "NUMBERS."

SPERM
- See "SEMEN."

SPHINX
- Spiritual understanding.
- Perhaps past life recognition from Egypt.

SPIRAL
- The image of evolution.
- It represents that intricate component of all of life, DNA and RNA helix.
- This is a very powerful transformational symbol.

SPIRIT
- This can be a ghost from the past. A haunting memory from the past.

SPONGE
- Soaking up everything; learning indiscriminately.
- Sponging off other people. Feeling others are sponging off you.

SPOON
- Born with a silver spoon in one's mouth.
- Energy; "spoon full of sugar helps the medicine go down."
- Kissing or making out; spooning; hugging.

SPRING
- See chapter on "SEASONS."

SPY
- Not feeling safe.
- Being intruded upon or intruding upon others.

•Involved with another person rather than involved with one's own development.

SQUARE
•Stability.

•Old-fashioned; not in touch with the times; out of step.

•Boxed in; controlled.

STAGE
•The stage of life.

•The role that you play in life.

•How you feel you appear to others or are seen by others.

STAIRS
•Note the direction the stairs are going-
Ascending indicates a rise in status; success.
Descending can mean loss of recognition; loss of confidence.

STAR
•A birth.

•This is a significant symbol representing light, guidance, insight.

•You are your own star. You are your own light.

STATUE
•Frozen feelings and emotions.

•Feeling immobile. You can't move.

•Lifeless.

•Not coming from your own strength and your own energy.

•Needing to work on self-confidence.

STEEL	•Strength. Immobility; inflexibility. •Determination.
STONES	•Leave no stone unturned.
STORK	•New arrival. New birth.
STRAW	•"This is the last straw." •Suffocation. Feeling suffocated in life. Feeling that you can't express your own creativity. •This can also be a health warning.
SUCKER	•Being suckered into something.
SUCKING	•Nursing. Nurturing. •If you are suckling a baby, you are nurturing new ideas, a new way of being. •If you are being suckled, you are being given sustenance, nurturing. •New beginning.
SUICIDE	•Self-guilt. Self-persecution. •Killing off aspects of yourself. •Giving up. •This is a warning. Don't give up. Know that you are never given anything in life that you can't handle, that you can't do or accomplish. You can do it.
SUMMER	•See the chapter on "SEASONS."

SUN
- •God. Great Spirit. Christ. The god within.
- •The source from which all flows.
- •Power, strength, clarity.
- •Your inner light.

SUNFLOWER
- •Joy.
- •Embracing life.

SWAMP
- •Feeling completely bogged down with absolutely no clarity. No way to get out. Feeling overwhelmed or swamped with work.

SWASTIKA
- •Ancient symbol of power.

SWEETS
- •The sweetness of life.
- •Lovers
- •Honoring oneself.

SWIMMING
- •Don't swim against the current.
- •Stay afloat amid emotional changes.

SWORD
- •Defense.
- •Attack.
- •Power. Truth. Honor.

SYRUP
- •Overly sentimental. Overly emotional to the point of insincerity.
- •Stickiness.

TABLE
- •Putting off making a decision; tabling a decision or emotion. Those beliefs that are clearly seen by others.
- •Putting your cards on the table.

TAPE	•Playing the same problems over and over again. Stuck in the same pattern.
	•Taping things together can also represent unity or unification.
TAPESTRY	•The tapestry of life. Each part of the tapestry represents a different part of you.
TAPPING	•If you hear a tap in your dream, it means you have made contact.
TARGET	•This is your direction. This is your goal.
	•Self-focus and self-discipline is needed.
TAX	•Burden.
	•Being taxed to your limit. The taxing of your strength.
	•Needing to rebuild or reassess.
TEA	•Friendships.
TEACHER	•The guru within.
	•Self-reliance.
	•Each person in our life is our teacher. Each aspect within our dream is our teacher teaching us during the night.
TEARS	•Release; cleansing; balancing.
	•A healthy aspect of dreaming.
TEETH	•See "TEETH" in chapter on "BODY PARTS."

TELEGRAM •Staying in touch with the world around you.

TELEPHONE •Listening to others.

•Can be some guide who is trying to get your attention. Listen carefully to the message that is being given you. Telephone dreams are important. Listen carefully.

TELESCOPE •Farseeing, but not all is revealed.

TELEVISION •This is you. These are aspects of your life. Note how you deal with situations.

•This is also you talking to yourself.

TEMPLE •Private retreat. Inner sanctuary.

TENT •Impermanence. Temporary.

•The image of self is not solidified.

THREAD •Karma. Fate.

•A thread of truth.

THUNDER •Release of suppressed emotions and feelings.

•The warning voice of the gods.

•Can indicate anger, hostility, rage. The aftermath of a powerful emotional psychic release.

TIDAL WAVE •A huge emotional upheaval.

TIDE •The ebbing and flowing of your emotions.

TIGHTROPE

- •Feeling tense.
- •Feeling as if you had to walk a tightrope. Great pressure. Stress.

TIRES

- •Mobility. Movement.
- •A flat tire means you are not balanced.

TOILET

- •Elimination of that which isn't needed in your life.

TOMB

- •Mobilizing one's creativity.
- •Restriction.

TOWER

- •Can represent isolation. Being locked in an ivory tower. Cut off from different aspects of yourself.
- •Can represent spiritual point of clarity.
- •Spiritual vision.

TOY

- •Joy. Life is a play.
- •Feeling like you are being toyed with.

TRAIN

- •The collective and individual journey through stages and events of your life.
- •Power.

TRASH

- •Junk. Emotional junk that you are carrying around with you. Letting go of it; eliminating it; releasing it.

TREADMILL

- •Feeling like you are getting nowhere. You are stuck with the same beliefs, the same attitudes, the same thought forms.

TREASURE
•Original ideas. Personal wealth.

•Inner wealth. Gifts from spirit.

TREES
•Family matters. A family tree.

•A symbol of life's development.

•Feeling rooted and grounded within the earth plane yet soaring to spiritual heights.

•Each tree has its own properties.

•An old gnarled tree can represent wisdom, strength.

•A slender willow tree can mean being able to bend with circumstances.

•An aspen can represent fear; quaking with fear.

•An oak - strength.

•A pine - spiritual clarity; purification.

•A cedar - clarity; spirituality.

•An apple tree - See "APPLE."

•A fruit tree can mean bearing fruit in life.

•A palm tree - warmth; freedom

•The meaning can depend on whether the tree is just beginning to leaf, is in full leaf, is losing its leaves or has no leaves. See the chapter on "SEASONS."

•Is the tree straight or crooked. As the tree bends, so it grows.

TRIANGLE
•Trinity. Protection. Body, mind and spirit.

•Integration.

TUNNEL
- A light at the end of the tunnel.
- The inner passageway to self.
- Tunnel vision; closemindedness.
- This can be a sign that you are having an out-of-body experience. Very often you will have a dream of moving through a tunnel.
- This can be a near-death experience. Changing realities. Changing levels of consciousness.

UFO
- The quest. The search for the Holy Grail.
- Personal integration. Psychic potential.

UMBRELLA
- Protection. Being sheltered from life's storms.

UNCLE
- Cry "uncle," or give up.
- Feeling foolish. Being a "monkey's uncle."

UNDERGROUND
- Your unconscious. Your subconscious.

UNDERTAKER
- Undertaking an unpleasant situation or experience.

UNDRESSED
- Feeling exposed.
- Personal secrets revealed. Being open.

UNIFORM
- Rigidity; inflexibility.
- Authority.

UNIVERSITY
- Center of learning.

URINE
- Relief after tension.
- Emotional release. Cleansing.
- A need to relieve yourself.

URN
- Ashes to ashes; dust to dust.
- Reincarnation.

VACATION
- Enjoyment. Relaxation.
- Letting go; release.
- Take a new look at your ideas and your goals.

VACCINATION
- Emotional protection.

VACUUM
- A feeling that you are living in a vacuum. Feeling isolated, not creative.
- To vacuum is to clean or remove that which isn't needed. Eliminate the negativity in your life.

VAGINA
- Openness; acceptance; receptivity.
- Womanliness.
- The inner valley.

VALLEY
- The low point in life. The mountains and valleys in our life.
- Pulling in.

VAMPIRE
- Exhaustion and draining of vitality by others.
- Feeling exhausted. Each person is responsible for his own energy level. In truth, no one can drain anyone else.

VEGETABLES •Basic necessities of life.

VELVET •Sensuality. Look to see what is beneath the surface.

VENTRILOQUIST •What you hear might be the wrong source of of information or not an accurate source of information.

VETERINARIAN •Healing our animal nature.

VINE •A spiritual connection.

VINEYARD •Harvesting the fruits of our experiences.

VIRGIN •Purity; wholeness.

•Mother Mary. The female aspect of God.

•The myth of the virgin as being the most desirable partner in marriage is a damaging one. It is from maturity and understanding that there is unity within relationships.

VOLCANO •Explosion of suppressed emotions.

VOMIT •Getting rid of that which you don't need. Getting rid of old ideas, old attitudes, old beliefs.

•Needing to express and communicate that which you are holding back or that which is making you sick.

•Getting things out in the open.

WAITER •Being of service to others or of service to yourself.

•The male part of yourself that serves.

WAITRESS   •See "WAITER."

WALKING   •Your goals will be met through a slow but sure pace.

WALL   •An obstacle; a blockage.

                    •Feeling walled off from others.

WALLET   •The masculine aspect of a woman's purse.

                    •The personal beliefs and thoughts that you hold privately. Personal.

WAND   •Spirituality.

                    •You can change things instantly. Transformation.

WAR   •Conflict and inner aggression.

WAREHOUSE   •This is your potential. All that you ever need is within.

WASHING   •Releasing the past. Forgiving.

                    •Celebration.

WATCH   •The passage of time. Time is passing.

WATER   •Your emotional energy. Your intuition.

                    •Check and see the form of the water whether it is clear or murky.

                    •Spiritual alignment and attunement. This is your unconscious self. The waters of life.

WATERFALL
- •Complete healing; emotional release.
- •Complete emotional recharging.

WAVE
- •Waving at someone or someone waving at you. Love. Connection. Acknowledgment.
- •An ocean wave suggests surging forward; great strength and power.
- •Using your emotions creatively.
- •Watching waves means recharging your inner batteries.

WAX
- •Easily molded. The situation can be changed.
- •Cleaning. Making a surface shiny. Making like new.

WEATHER
- •Weather can signify your emotional state. It can also signify your health.
- •Clear weather indicates excellent health.
- •Stormy weather may perhaps suggest some area in your body needs alignment.

WEAVING
- •This is the pattern of your life woven in and out. The tapestry of your life.
- •Putting things together; creating wholeness.

WEB
- •Feeling caught; feeling entangled.
- •Beware of a trap.

WEDDING
- •A union of your conscious and unconscious, of your body and spirit.

WELL
•Inner riches. Wisdom accumulated from past experiences.

WHEEL
•The wheel of life.

•The wheel of fortune.

•The wheel of karma; sewing and reaping; endings and beginnings. Completion.

WHISPER
•Feeling held back.

•Not willing or not being able to communicate and say what is in your heart and mind.

WHISTLE
•Warning. Something is trying to get your attention.

WILLOW
•Sadness.

•Being able to bend and move within the situation.

WIND
•The winds of change.

•The element of air representing thought, intellect.

WINDOW
•Interdimensional viewing; being able to see into different levels of consciousness.

•Seeing the future or the past.

WINE
•Prosperity; abundance.

•Celebration.

•Relaxation.

•Spiritual attunement with wine representing the blood of Christ or that spiritual energy within. God.

WINGS

•Freedom. Soaring.

WITCH

•The current implication of being fearsome or ugly.

•In the past, "witch" came from the word "wica" meaning wise woman. It can represent that wise female energy within you.

WOMB

•Nourishment. Safety. Protection.

•Pulling in and regrouping your energies before the next endeavor.

X-RAY

•Unseen forces.

•Seeing what is within with more clarity, with more understanding.

•Going to inner depth, inner understanding.

XYLOPHONE

•Being in tune with life.

YAWN

•Boredom. Needing another outlet for creativity.

•Can be an emotional release.

YEAST

•Through nature, expansion and growth.

YO-YO

•Feeling like you are going up and down, repeating the same patterns.

ZIPPER

•Things opening and closing.

•Note whether the zipper is open or closed.

I reach out into the night without fear,
Silent dream companions tread softly beside me.

Denise Linn

STARTING A DREAM GROUP

A very powerful way to connect more deeply with your own dreams is to be part of a dream support group, perhaps even form your own. A dream group is a group of individuals who gather together periodically for the purpose of sharing and discussing their dreams. It is definitely a means to receive encouragement and support in your own dream journey.

Purpose

If you form your own dream group, first determine the purpose in gathering together. Perhaps your function is to develop individual psychic abilities. Or, it could be to process daytime difficulties through examining your own theater of the night. Write down your intentions in very clear, concise language. Carefully define all your intentions so that each group member can consciously choose to be in alignment with the group purpose. This first step is imperative, and will enhance the synergy in future meetings. Decide on a mutually-agreed time (perhaps once a week), when you can gather to share your dreams.

Certainly, each dream group will have its own dynamics, however, here is a simple format that you might consider using. For the first meeting, you may want to sit in a circle, as this is one of the major symbols for dreaming. Then go clockwise around the circle (in the northern hemisphere) and counter-clockwise (in the southern hemisphere), with each person sharing briefly about herself, or himself. Have each include information that is of value such as personal goals, purpose in life, etc. Let the first meeting be a time for clarification of purpose and intent, as well as for developing the beginnings of synergy among all members of the group.

Grounding

Each time you gather, begin the session by devoting a few moments to centering and relaxing. (You may wish to have a leader for this particular process.) Sit in a circle with spine straight, feeling very relaxed. Form a grounding cord by imaging a silver light moving up through the earth, up through the soles of your feet and the base of your spine and moving on up and out the top of your head, cascading down around you as a waterfall. After you have completed this, begin breathing in the essence of each individual within the circle, again moving in a clockwise or a counter-clockwise direction (depending upon your location). Take a deep breath, breathing each person into your own being, then slowly releasing that person. As you do this allow yourself to experience each person as strong, healthy, well and balanced. In doing so, you are weaving a deep spiritual connection between yourself and each of the other dreamers in the group. Once you have completed this, breathe in the essence of your own being three times. Now imagine a brilliant silver-white light spinning around and around the group, creating a whirlpool of energy and light. When you've completed this meditation, take just a few moments of silence before proceeding with the dream sharing.

Dream Sharing

It is necessary, in sharing around the circle, that each person be given adequate time to share dreams. If an individual feels that the events of the week are connected to the dream in some way, sharing these events may be valuable. It is important to keep in mind, however, that it is very easy to wander from the point so that others may be denied a chance to share. Also, before selecting a specific dream to work with, make sure everyone has had a chance to share. Not being able to share a dream simply because you have run out of time can be very disappointing. Since every dream is a composite of multitudes of complex imagery spanning several dimensions, it would be easy to invest several sessions on only one dream. Keep in mind the value of doing some work with each dream represented by those in the group.

When each individual has the opportunity to communicate dreams, this begins to build a deep connection with others in the room. As a result of the synergy experienced in the group, you will no doubt witness a heightened sense of telepathy occurring among individuals in the room and even a similarity of dream symbols.

When you are sharing your dream, always utilize the present tense rather than the past - "I am running" rather than "I was running." This enables you to be far more present in the moment with the dream as you communicate it to others. Also, in speaking in the first person, i.e. "I," "me," "my," it will usually be easier to discover some new insight about yourself. If an individual begins to share her dreams using the present tense and then slips back into past tense, this generally indicates a point in the dream where there are difficult emotions for the dreamer. It is valuable to point this out to the dreamer. Occasionally this will enable that person to experience a new revelation or an "Aha!"

Listen very carefully to the specific type of words a person uses in describing her experience. Also, closely observe body language; how is each body expressing the dream.

Maintain the attitude that each dreamer in the group is a different reflection of yourself. As a dream's secrets unfold to the others, it will also be generating a new awakening within you. Listen carefully to the manner in which each person discusses the dream. Every dream will have a special significance for you. Each person's dream is also about you. You have all been drawn together because of like energies. It is no accident that all the others in the dream group are present with you.

For each session, have a leader who can monitor the group in staying on purpose. One means of doing this is to have a revolving leadership with a different individual volunteering at each new meeting.

Dream Meaning

When a dream is selected to be explored more closely by the entire group, it is valuable for the person sharing the dream to receive new insights from the group. However, it is crucial that the dreamer accept only what "feels right" regarding the others' interpretations. Each individual can easily incorporate what is significant to her in interpreting another's dream. So, Dreamer, accept only the advice that is in alignment with your own inner guidance.

If your group is an especially expressive one, you might have occasional "Theme Weeks." One week you may all decide to incubate for prophetic dreams concerning happenings for the coming year. Or, another week you may focus on emotional cleansing regarding blockages formed during childhood..."Childhood-Cleansing Week." Or, if you are feeling especially whimsical, you may even have "Telepathic-Communication-with-Aliens Week," or more practically, perhaps the theme of the week may be to determine the actions of the stock market. You also may request dreams that will increase your ability for healing, night healing, day healing or healing of self... "Healing Week."

Be creative in your dream groups. In one session you could all dance your dreams, while in another, come equipped with crayons and paper to draw your dream. You might choose to select dream partners and dream for each other during the week, setting aside one specific evening for this purpose. I've discovered this last exercise to be especially powerful for me in gaining new insights into myself. Often what is a blind spot for one dreamer is easily perceived by another dreamer. Even those with relatively little experience in dream work have been able to successfully dream for another, unwrapping dream symbols extremely significant for that other person.

Bring your dream journals to each session, sharing them freely with one another. You can also choose to set apart a section in your journal where you note some of the insights given by others in the group. Other creative ways to explore your dreams are to construct a dream mask or dream shield. Also, the group as a whole could take a particularly significant dream and act it out as a play with each member taking a different role in the dream script. Have fun!!

It is wise to set a specific starting time as well as closing time so the group can operate out of knowing the amount of time they have and when they can count on the session being over. Following this plan facilitates a sense of completion for each one in the group.

A dream group is like a rose in slow bloom, with each person representing a different petal of the fragrant delicate blossom.

THE ENDING

Row Row Row Your Boat
Gently down the Stream
Merrily, Merrily, Merrily, Merrily
Life is but a Dream.

A MESSAGE FROM THE PUBLISHER

After reading this fascinating book you will probably want to hear and meet Denise Linn in person. Denise regularly conducts seminars on dreams in almost every english speaking country in the world.

For information about any of her seminars in the Southern Hemisphere write to:

Nacson Promotions International Pty. Ltd.,
Suite 204, 720 George Street,
Sydney, Australia,
telephone 61-2-2812075.

For information in the Northern Hemisphere write to:

Denise Linn Seminars,
P.O. Box 58644,
Tukwila, Washington,
U.S.A. 98138-1644

Denise Linn is currently researching her second book and would be pleased to hear from any reader about their experiences with dreams. Letters should be addressed to either of the above addresses.

Cover design and concept by Leon Nacson,
Chris Willis, Max Laye and Jenny Davis.

Place

Kings   Doctor Karen Pra;
             Jane Macdoo

             Ms Penny Sewell
             Dept French
             Birkbeck

Queen Mary + Westfield
College. Head Dept

This book was written, edited, proofed and printed using a desktop publishing system.

Writing and editing was done on Apple Macintosh 128K, 512K and Plus computers, using MacWrite and Microsoft WORD.

Proofing was done using an Apple Imagewriter II printer. Final printing was done using an Apple Macintosh SE computer and an Apple Laserwriter II printer.

Body type is Times 12pt
Headers are ITC Zaph Chancery 10pt.

Formatting, graphics, final proofing, final printing and computer consulting was provided by Karl Bettinger of:

ZENO AMERICA SERVICES
Post Office Box 23228
Seattle, Washington 98102
USA
tel (206) 328-6244